GREEN FIRE

2ND EDITION

IAN COHEN

This edition published by
Cilento Publishing
55 White Street
Lilyfield NSW 2040
Copyright © Ian Cohen 2017
ISBN:978-0-6482398-6-4

Design and typeset by Green Avenue Design

First Published by
Angus & Robertson
An imprint of HarperCollinsPublishers, Australia
First published in Australia in 1996
by HarperCollinsPublishers Pty Limited ACN 009 913 517
A member of the HarperCollinsPublishers (Australia) Pty Limited Group
Copyright © Ian Cohen 1997

This book is copyright.
Apart from any fair dealing for the purposes of private study, research, criticism or review, as permitted under the Copyright Act, no part may be reproduced by any process without written permission. Inquiries should be addressed to the publishers.

National Library of Australia cataloguing-ix:-publication data: Cohen, Ian.

Green Fire
ISBN (First Edition) 0 207 18633 2.

1. Environmental protection – Australia – Citizen participation. 2. Environmental policy – Australia – Citizen participation. 3. Green movement – Australia.
4. Radicalism – Australia. I Title.
363.70570994

'Rip Rip Woodchip' is the title of a John Williamson song Copyright © Emusic Pty.

Paperback available on recycled paper.
www.iancohen.com.au

DEDICATION TO CEDAR

A young man once named Cedar,
Tall and beautiful as a young tree,
Next generation, Earth warrior,
Feral and free.

At ancient Washpool from the police we hid.
The dozer pushed,
Tree, simply in the way,
Cedar scampered up that huge rainforest fig;
As the blade stabbed,
The tree trembled and swayed.
An old forest giant was set to fall,
Nature's ladder, strangler fig, gave Cedar hold.
High above the dozer's roar,
A plea, an invocation he called.

The driver looked up from his controls,
At a man waving frantically.
Stop! The demand was desperate yet bold.
Motor cut, shaken,
Away the driver walked.

Against that massive dozer,
Successful was Cedar's play.
The rainforest that he struggled for
Stands alive and well today.
Yet his own beauty he could not see,
Nor the forest of his life
Which could set him free.

Estranged from society that made no sense,
He simply couldn't cope.
In despair one day he climbed another tree,
A rope around his throat.

Through Cedar I wish to acknowledge that many of us live on the edge of despair, but for those of us who dance along the boundaries of life and death, failure and success, struggle and hopelessness, there is a way. By sharing our fears and finding ways of liberating our anxieties, together we can access our dreams. All is possible.

Seeds of the tree that Cedar saved are among many being planted today. North Washpool in northern New South Wales is one site in a series of rainforest regeneration locations in eastern Australia. Under the guidance of Emeritus Professor Len Webb, rainforest on that disputed site is being replanted and monitored as part of an innovative biological study. Both the Forestry Commission and environmentalists are cooperating on the project which, it is anticipated, will continue for generations. Thousands of students in the future will study the effects of Cedar's stand.

CONTENTS

Acknowledgments	7
Author's Foreword – Second Edition	8
Introduction By Bob Brown	10
Preface – Radicals' Revenge	13
1. Terania Rainforest	17
2. Green Dawning	26
3. Middle Head	32
4. Nightcap	41
5. Franklin	59
6. Daintree	88
7. Errinundra	102
8. Roxby Downs	111
9. Buga Up	123
10. Warships	141
11. Elections	164
12. South-East Forests	184
13. Chaelundi	201
14. Killie Kranke	221
15. Ducks And Bats	227
16. Ocean Outfalls	235
17. Parliament To Pacific	247
Appendix 1	258
Appendix 2	263

ACKNOWLEDGMENTS

For those who expected and deserved to appear in this book and have been omitted I am truly sorry. Similarly to those who have been mentioned and are not resultantly ecstatic, I equally apologise. To the many helpers on the task of writing this book I am deeply grateful. As usual I have found myself in the position of taking the public credit. Despite my constant struggle with the publishers biographical bent (whom, I am confident has my best interests in mind) this book is a product of many minds and hearts. The inspiration is that of a movement of which I am but one small part.

I have included the names of people in this book, to acknowledge the 'who dunnits' where appropriate. There are those who do not appear on these pages to whom I am greatly indebted. Tom Thompson who accepted my manuscript, perhaps his parting gesture to HarperCollins, Paul White, whose late night philosophical raves gave direction to the introduction, Kevin Childs, who was a frequent inspiration when I was flat as a page in this book. Thanks also to Marianne Loyd Smith, Elsebeth Nielsen, Natalie Falla, Clover Wade, Sue Wilke, James Langley, Gerard Keenan, Steven Taylor, Wendy Faulkner, Cindy Cox, Jim Elkin, Bill Sokolitch and Clive Evatt.

Also most appreciated were the local Nimbin musicians whose songs front many chapters and whose music, freely given, fed our spirits from one end of the continent to the other. They included Mook Hanley Brenda Liddiard, Paul Josephs, Shanto Oliver, Lisa Yeates and Frog.

The most inspirational support came from Jan 'B' Barham, whose sense of the important and editing skills were combined with a drive to keep me working to completion for the duration of this project. Green Fire would surely have been relegated to a cardboard box going the way of all cellulose based products in the rainforest

Content to support in the background Jan was launched by others into a political career serving on Byron Shire Council as a green councillor and then as the first popularly elected female mayor until 2011. Jan was the first popularly elected green mayor in Australia and we believe, the world at that time. Following her terms on council she successfully ran for NSW Parliament serving for six years in a total of 18 years of public service.

AUTHOR'S FOREWORD
SECOND EDITION

It has been two decades since the publication of Green Fire. A Parliamentary career engulfed me for the sixteen years that followed. Now in 'retirement' I can give adequate attention to other matters including a more effective distribution of this second edition.

Known at the height of my career as the Guide who 'always got lost' (see Franklin River Chapter). I invite you to walk a path where we leave the comforts of civilisation behind and extend ourselves in what is considered by many to be a harsh and alien environment. On the way, lost and somewhat nervous another feeling seeps in. Then you can have a true Wilderness experience.

Combine this new found feeling with the sense that it may all end under the bulldozer blade and the shriek of the chainsaw, backed up by the power of the state. This is a heady mix for empowerment growing out of the depths of loss and despair. It is a worthy cause to protect our environmental heritage for future generations and recognise the intrinsic value of the planet and its creatures. The greatest intensity emerges when we are moved to act against the destruction, to stand up for that which resonates with our sense of a deeper belonging, a spark deeply imbedded in us from our evolutionary past.

So, as my past grows longer and future shortens the thought of the stories dissolving in the mists of time relating to actions in the 80's and 90's would be an historical loss. Many of the stories are so ridiculous that people would not believe them to be true unless further rendered to the printed medium.

Before I commence in earnest on my next book I feel the need to set Green Fire up as originally intended, an enduring statement from the various front lines of the Australian environmental protest movement. It is more relevant today than three decades ago.

Given the increasing awareness of global environmental and social issues it is an appropriate task to continue the work of past generations of activists. If this book were to encourage even a small number of young people to carry on the work of Earth guardianship in its many forms, the effort to republish will be extremely satisfying.

Big beautiful planet, there is only so much that individuals can do against the onslaught but our collective efforts in recent decades have achieved so much. May this book be a small continuing contribution to current and future generations in opposing the forces of destruction.

Ian Cohen 2017

INTRODUCTION
by Bob Brown

Green Fire is a rollicking history of spectacular efforts to stop the impending destruction of some of Australia's most beautiful, spiritual and wildlife-rich places. It tells how loggers, miners and polluters have found themselves face-to-face with courageous Australians, young and old, who rate this nation's natural and Aboriginal heritage ahead of dollars and macho imagery.

Ian Cohen doesn't hold back. With compelling honesty about himself, his fellow campaigners and their opponents, from locals to premiers and prime ministers, he takes us into the thick of battles which re-shaped the map of Australia as much as the nation's mindset.

From being locked-on to bulldozers deep in the rainforests, to riding the bow-wave of ships built for unthinkable nuclear war, to being elected as the first Greens member of the New South Wales parliament, Cohen's defiance of stifling conventional norms provides us with a journal of impudence in the service of our one and only life-giving planet.

Some readers may find the rebellious behaviour of Cohen or, more likely, some of his fellow protesters, as dangerous, counter-productive or self-indulgent. Questions which follow for all of us include: 'what have you done for life on Earth and how come this planet is now in greater crisis than ever?' And: 'is being blotto in a derelict car blocking the destruction of a valley of wildlife-filled forest a worse social indiscretion than being blotto at a stock exchange dinner or a football party?'.

Does our herd of eight billion mammals consuming Earth's finite living resources at 150 percent of their replacement rate not justify some sort of insurrection?

Necessarily, Green Fire is much about the interreaction of police and protesters. But what, in this Twenty-first Century, is the state of policing of environmental vandalism? And what of the business leaders who cajole weak-spined politicians into making that vandalism legal?

Bafflingly, most Australians vote for politicians who pass laws which require the police, often against their own wishes and more often still against public opinion, to aid and abet the destruction of our natural commons.

I am opposed to violence. But aren't we too ready to see interference with lethal-to-wildlife machinery as more deplorable than the habitat destruction which is the chief factor in an accelerating extinction rate of Earth's creatures now approaching ten thousand times that of natural attrition? And what of the vocal critics: aren't Rupert Murdoch's opinion writers more out of touch with human-induced biospheric disintegration than the average seven-years-old Australian schoolchild?

I was in the thick of the Franklin River campaign and remember being mightily glad when Ian Cohen and the Nightcap Action Group arrived to set up and sustain the blockade of bulldozers in the remote riverside wilderness. I was also mightily glad of the volunteer bookkeepers, office workers, media and political strategists working for years back in town, without whom the river would be dammed. That said, Green Fire gives us a gripping and true view of the up-river campaign which proved equally vital to the river's rescue.

Australia in 2017 has Amazonian rates of woodlands destruction, a disgustingly long lists of impending extinctions, a shameful disregard for Aboriginal culture and heritage, and a huge coal export industry in the face of harrowing global warming and acidification. The unnecessary rape of natural forests continues and even Tasmania's Tarkine, with the largest temperate rainforest in the nation, remains on the drawing board of destruction. The obscene Adani coalmine proposal in Queensland is a latest test as to whether Australians rate world wonders like the jobs-rich Great Barrier Reef as high as a foreign-owned corporation's profit margin.

Ian Cohen's philosophy is deep green. He has acted on his convictions. While a remarkably good history, Green Fire challenges Australians who lack green convictions, lack fire and couldn't care less about the ecosystem which cradled them into existence. It is, above all, a recipe and stirring call to action for those of us who aspire to save the life of this glorious planet Earth.

Bob Brown

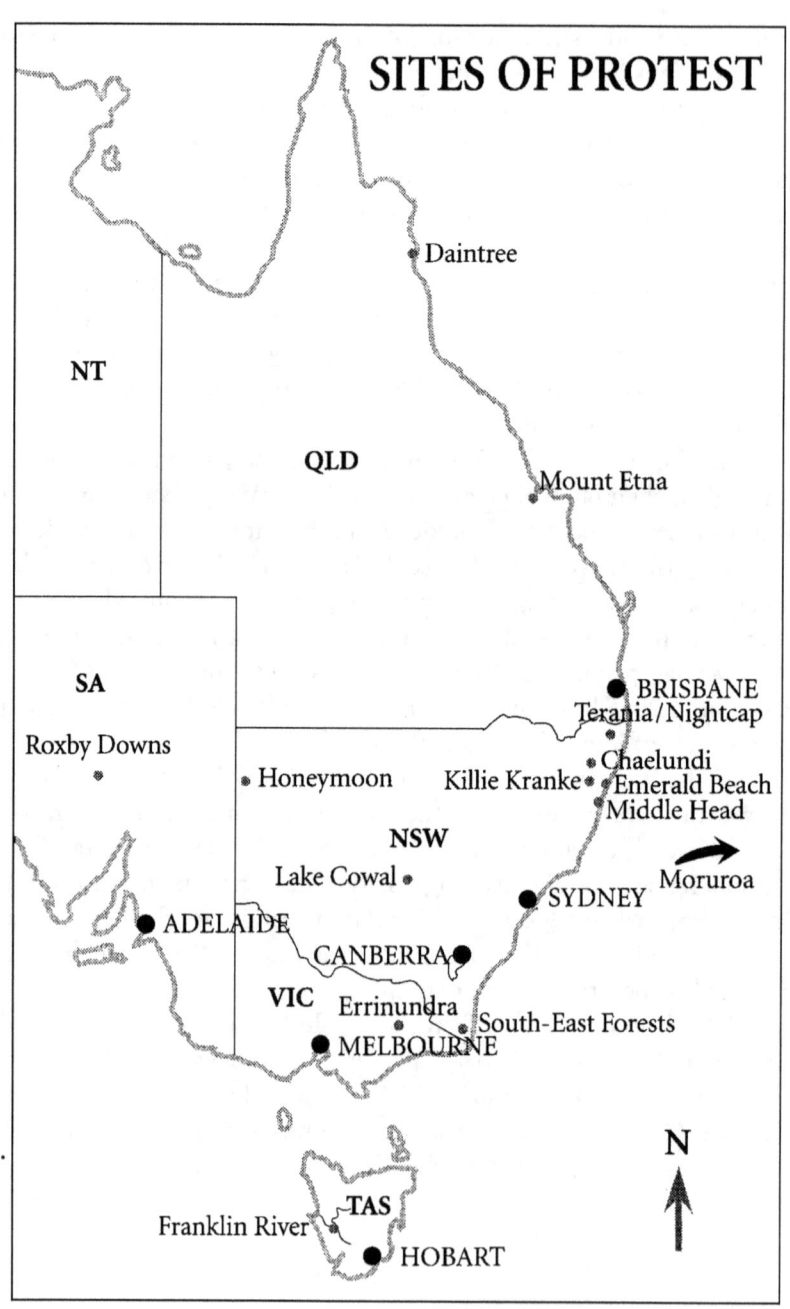

PREFACE
Radicals' Revenge

A decade after the Franklin River blockade, the summer of 1992 in Tasmania witnessed another influx of conservationists from the mainland. For some years a plot had been brewing, the brainchild of a coterie of incorrigible activists. David Rainbow, stocky and rough around the edges, was no newcomer to controversy. Born and bred in a Tasmanian logging town, during the Franklin campaign he had dressed as a woman and driven his three-ton truck in high heels onto the Melbourne-to-Tasmania ferry using a borrowed pension card. Upon arriving at the river, his intransigence proved such that he was unable to disengage from the back of the Cape Martin, which towed a heavy equipment barge, carrying the first dozer upriver. He was last seen waving and laughing as he sailed straight into police hands, incapable of letting go for the sheer joy of being a ratbag.

Thrown out of innumerable alternative communities for transgressions, he categories himself as an anarchist individualist. Another conspirator, John (Jonno) Williams, whose near-death exploits pepper the following pages, was the green movement's on-the-ground action man. Highly skilled in the technical side of radio communications, he was central to the success of countless campaigns. Jonno wielded a chainsaw with such alacrity and drank so hard that he came to be known as a 'greenneck'. Benny Zable was also on site. As a green true – believer he was a tireless pioneer of art and living theatre, giving his life to the radical conservation movement. He created and directed the visual backdrop for action.

The audacious aim was to hold up a logging train to highlight the destruction of Tasmania's Old Growth forests. The summer Forest Festival, an annual music event, was the starting point. Here, a train driver who had been made redundant told them of the best spot to stage the hold-up – a straight stretch with a half kilometre clear view. They needed two hundred metres to stop the train, which was predicted to be travelling at thirty kilometres per hour. To avoid suspicion they timed their arrival just prior to its approach.

Safety gear was assembled. Red flags were to be held further up the track. Banners were designed to maximise safety. "When we stopped our cars we could hear the train coming," Jonno said. As the train rounded the bend (they did not even make it to the designated straight section) three jumped onto the tracks and waved it down. No time to run up and warn the driver. No time to fly the red flags signalling danger. The train ground to a halt.

Had they stopped the wrong train? Not a log to be seen. The front carriages were containers. Someone ran up the track; the train was so long it went around the bend. Misplaced, mistimed, miscalculated, but they stopped it. The runner reported back, that in the distance, logs were present. The front carriages contained chemicals. With the latest information there were congratulatory nods all round.

One member of the group, Sofie, locked herself onto one of the carriages. A number of helmeted Ned Kellys stood in front of her, their banner declaring, (BUSHRANGERS NEED BUSH) A tripod was erected with its legs between the carriages, and another member scampered to the top. The media and the State police arrived shortly afterwards. The police asked the protesters to leave. The latter refused; the offence they had committed was a federal one, beyond state police jurisdiction. With only six federal cops in Tasmania, the protesters maintained their blockade for three hours. No one was arrested. After comprehensive media coverage the group dismantled the blockade and allowed the train to go on its way.

It was discovered that explosives were on board, but this information was a mere firecracker compared to the media explosion that occurred in the following weeks. David Rainbow did it again: he casually reported the protest as an Earth First action and, despite the fact that it was nonviolent, the media equated it with terrorist activity – a hardline terrorist organisation had hijacked a train. It was front page. Debate centred on the acceptability of the action. The Wilderness Society slammed them, and the timber industry called on Green politicians to denounce the group. They refused.

Such tactics, such audacity. It was the authorities' nightmare.

Horror for every decent greenie working industriously in offices around the country attempting to lobby, pressure, convince and save the precious little we have left of our tortured environment. When so many inroads had been made toward acceptability, respectability and political acumen, these scruffy individuals, without consultation, concocted an action and carried it out with disastrous consequences in the national media. They inadvertently branded the whole movement extremist. Cooperation with politicians and industry was laid to waste like the forests the green movement was trying to save. All those peaceful constructive actions, the rapport built up in the community. Where did we all go wrong? Was this the end product of a decade of hard work?

Green Fire offers an insight into the rise of radical environmentalism in the eighties. Is the out-of-control passionate struggle for the earth the only way? Will future generations perceive this period of history as barbaric in its utilitarian onslaught against the environment and recognise green extremists as pioneers? Or is their role an integral part of a dynamic movement without which less radical groups would be ignored as paper tigers by those in power?

The events and participants matured over the years. A core group of people attended these sequential events, passed on information, developed strategy and facilitated action.

History is coloured by the people who record. Often it is those with expertise in communication far removed from the events who tell the story. Many front-line activists are too busy or lack the skills to tell the story of recent events. The pages which follow view the phenomena of action in defence of an ideal. These events have flashed across media channels for over a decade.

This book paints another picture. It portrays a series of stories and the ensuing debate as seen from the 'front line'. In every action, methodology has been questionable, actions thrilling and sometimes downright objectionable. The controversy generated has and continues to be argued with passion throughout the movement and the wider community.

There is little doubt that the pages to follow will add fire to this ongoing debate.

A pioneering American ecologist and one-time hunter, Aldo Leopold, saw a wolf in the forest. He was a young man then and in those days a wolf you saw was a wolf you shot. Leopold and his men hurriedly pulled their 30-30s from the holsters on their horses and began to blast away. The wolf dropped, a pup dragged a shattered leg into the rocks, and Leopold rode down to finish the job on its mother.

He later wrote:

> *We reached the old wolf in time to watch a fierce green fire dying in her eyes. I realised then, and have known ever since, that there was something new to me in those eyes – something known only to her and to the mountain. I was young then and full of trigger itch; I thought that because fewer wolves meant more deer that no wolves would mean hunter's paradise. But after seeing the green fire die, I sensed that neither the wolf nor the mountain agreed with such a view.*
>
> *Green fire. We need it in the eyes of the wolf. We need it in the land and we need it in our own eyes.*

Quoted from Dave Forman's *Confessions of an EcoWarrior*.

CHAPTER 1
TERANIA RAINFOREST
Action Birth

BEHIND ENEMY LINES

© Brenda Liddiard 1979

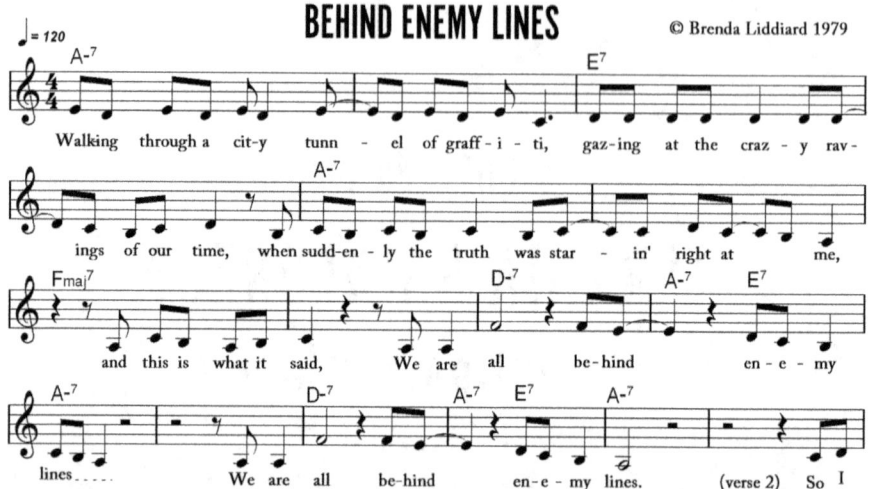

So I went back to the country looking for some peace, and what do you think I did find?
A battle had begun to save Terania, our rainforest home,
And I was still behind enemy lines. I was still behind enemy lines.

So I learned to be a peaceful rainbow trooper, using my guitar and voice to get inside
The castle walls of a hundred policemen, and this is what I sang,
We are all behind enemy lines. We are all behind enemy lines.
                                              CHORUS : Behind enemy lines . . .

For this is not a war of guns and bullets. This is not a war of bombs and napalm.
This is a war of smiles and singing, and this is how we'll win,
We will dance behind enemy lines, and we will sing behind enemy lines.

LAST CHORUS :

Behind enemy lines. Behind enemy lines. The dollar man is the enemy of mankind.
Behind enemy lines. Behind enemy lines. We must all get together to save our world in time.

Transcribed by Bruce McNicol

Terania, like a lightning flash in the night sky, was nature's herald of a new ecologically based movement for social change.

Like 'refugees' from the cities, new settlers had moved to Terania valley, a rainforest nestled in the lowlands of a sinewy range of mountains, located in the Nightcap Range in northern New South Wales. Living at the end of a road they presumed the surrounding rainforest would remain intact. A chance meeting with foresters taught them the error of their expectations. The plan for the Terania forest, they learnt, was clear-felling. The terrain of the valley was difficult, and it contained little in the way of good timber.

For the timber industry's purposes rainforest was seen to be growing too slowly so it was to be burnt and replaced with eucalypts to create a 'useful forest'.

Terania's overawing beauty inspired something new, an irresistible drive to protect. People were shaken out of their apathy. Equipped only with a nonviolent philosophy, they gathered in their forest and proclaimed a new way. They took on the power of the State. The politics of the environment caught the government unawares.

New beliefs were put to the test. The society was split. Local farmers who had previously supported them saw the action as anarchistic. At first, conservationists in Sydney were reluctant to offer their support, fearing extremism more than forest destruction. The local conservationists were discouraged but stood their ground.

The Terania basin was of insignificant size. There were numerous Wilderness conservation areas and issues in need of attention in the northern region of New South Wales. Nevertheless, the locals felt they had little choice – they had to win Terania.

Their determination was formidable. A tentative alliance was created between radical new settlers and the city-based conservation groups, and between them they stumbled upon a formula for success. Terania initiated a new phase in Australian environmental politics and began an era of direct action blockades. The people who had come to this Wilderness to escape society were compelled to re-enter the world they had left. They did so with considerable expertise and energy. Their skills, along with the city/country alliance, gave the activists a powerful front against the forestry industry.

Terania has been synonymous in the environmental movement with the birth of radical action in defense of the forest. It has echoed down the years at succeeding forest actions. The spirit of Terania lives on. People move across the face of the earth spreading the message of that birthplace of Australian eco-activism. So overpowering was the draw of those trees that people risked their lives. A spirit of transformation emanated from the forest. It was an event which inspired many who were pioneering a new way in their lives.

The year was 1979, and Terania had lit a green fire.

The new settlers formed the Terania Native Forest Action Group (TNFAG). The group had researched their subject for years and with each find their resolve grew. Scientifically and historically there was a strong argument for conservation. When significant Aboriginal sites were found, the debate in the media hotted up against the logging interests. One conservationist, Bren Claridge, formerly in advertising, produced what was believed to be the first television advertisement by a conservation group. It depicted a potential collision between a logging truck and a mother with a child. The tag line was, 'If Standard Sawmills is allowed to use Terania Creek Road, will there be room for Cathy and the kids?' Standard Sawmills complained that their name was used in the advertisement. It became a news item which ran many times over. Free of charge, of course.

Five years of intensive work had preceded the first confrontation in the forest. TNFAG represented the massing of varied expertise for a common goal, and the group used every political trick in the book to achieve success. Its actions reached into the Labor Party machine and the media in a way which was unashamedly premeditated.

The devastation of the forest was like a war zone. The tactics of the adversaries changed every few days. The confrontation between blockaders and loggers was superb fodder for the media, who had in their hands the potent images of rainforest as a revolutionary tool in the Australian context.

The first police contingent expected a few local protesters. A CB radio network and the fortuitous timing of the local Channon market had enabled organisers to rally over 200 people for the first day's action. The front line of defence consisted of a blockade of twenty cars jacked up, some with their wheels taken off. Police and private tow truck operators moved in. Cars were rolled off the road and many of them left on their sides. Those with tyres had them punctured. When the cars had been removed, protesters lay in the path of a bulldozer. Seventeen arrests resulted.

The following day the police came in force. They were prepared, in a fashion. Aware of the media presence they wore dress uniforms, which seemed like a good idea until fifty protesters came careering down the track at the bulldozer and veered off into lantana bushes at the last minute.

Pushing through lantana on a hot day in dress uniform frustrated the police contingent.

The protesters were organised. Each participant wore a coloured armband denoting a function, which included front line, healing, transport, media or catering. This focused newcomers and maintained camp cohesion. It was a rainbow alliance.

By the end of the first week the bulldozer had moved a third of the way along an old logging track known as Lantana Lane. The police withdrew at week's end, so the camp celebrated. The group was not wholly united. The bulldozer was twice sabotaged. Others repaired it, fearing bad media. They felt the dozer was a setup: the loggers had brought in their oldest machine, clapped out and ready for sacrifice, a pawn to the loggers' advantage.

The following Wednesday the police returned, parking their cars on the property of Hugh and Nan Nicholson. While police are generally quick to give out parking tickets for illegal parking, the situation was not the same when the Nicholsons asked them to remove police cars parked illegally on their property. The officers in charge interrogated Hugh and asked for his title deeds. After further requests to park elsewhere, the police said they would consider it, but still the vehicles stayed there. Hugh tried pouring a line of paint to delineate his boundary. This wasn't visible enough, so he grabbed a jerrycan and ran a line of petrol around his boundary. At this, the police got anxious. They appeared from everywhere, peering over the bonnets of their vehicles. The call went out; keys quickly arrived from the forest and the vehicles were removed.

With loggers now having entered the forest, it was time for a new brand of action. Men and women took to climbing trees, first to stop the advance of the dozer and later to hamper the cutters. In the path of the advancing machine, protesters followed the lead of Michel Fanton and scaled the trees. (Michel, a local new resident and Frenchman of expressive emotions, and his wife, Jude, have gone on as pioneers to develop the Seed Saver Network, an international organisation for the collection and distribution of seeds worldwide. Based in Byron Bay, they are a wonderful example of the continuum of the 'Terania energy'.

Slender and agile, Michel was the quintessential tree climber who knew his species and loved his trees with a passion. He recalls the events which followed: "I climbed one tall tree directly in the path, quite high, perhaps twenty metres. The dozer had a rocky outcrop on one side, which it was unable to dislodge, and a gully beyond, so it started to scratch the roots of my tree in an attempt to get enough width. The whole tree shook at every pass of the blade. People below screamed, "There's someone up there!" The driver stopped. Following this success, people took to the trees at night with hammocks and set up camps high in the canopy."

Chainsaws were wielded, first in threat, then loggers began cutting the trees with people in close proximity. Only the fear of media exposure kept loggers and police acting relatively safely. Protesters in trees equipped themselves with cameras. Functioning or not, they made loggers and police below stop and think. As the action progressed the position of opposing sides became increasingly extreme. It had been a month of unrelenting pressure. Michel related: "Three of us were in one tree, twenty metres up.

We knew they were cutting towards us. It was late in the protest and tempers were frayed. We coo-eed when they were felling but they ignored us. We could hear them cutting the wedge in preparation; they were 150 metres away."

"The first tree fell a short distance from us. We were afraid we could cop the next tree on us, so we started to climb down. The woman above us in the tree top couldn't hold on with her legs and slithered down onto us. The three of us slid down the trunk. I slowed the fall. It could have been fatal. I felt my balls and screamed, "My god! What have I done?" They'd started swelling and were enormous. I couldn't walk. My companions had to drag me along. We yelled out 'Wait!' because we could hear the cutters preparing a second log. It started to crack. Others near the loggers screamed to them to stop. They were ignored. We moved towards an outcrop of rocks for safety but couldn't reach it in time, so we huddled behind the buttress root of a rainforest tree as the felled tree cracked.

Masses of leaves and branches crashed like a huge storm on either side of us. The others dragged me off. We were terrified: it could have been murder. We knew they would keep dropping trees, so we staggered back, with me putting my bum in the creek whenever I could. I was in agony. I was driven to hospital. Since then I've had more children, so my family jewels are still intact." Like Michel, many protesters ran the gauntlet of police, loggers and the rugged terrain in the cutting area, attempting to prevent further felling until the police flushed them out. Loggers and police continually turned a blind eye to people in the felling area. They joked with each other, wondering if anyone had been hit as people flitted through the forest in the fall line of the trees in a brave attempt to slow the destruction. The loggers cut rapidly to dishearten the activists. Legally, unrestricted access was allowed in the forest. It was a potentially fatal recipe.

Protesters were driven to try new tactics. Trees were wired together with steel cable so that the entire section of canopy in the cable web could collapse if logging continued. Despite the danger, the loggers kept cutting. These tactics slowed but did not stop the work.

Others lobbied in Sydney. Opposition was still strong in Cabinet, and Premier Neville Wran was not wholly convinced of significant public support. TNFAG lobbied all parliamentarians but received little positive feedback. Wran would not talk to the Terania 'hippy lobbyists'. There was a

significant battle in Cabinet on the issue. Two powerful groups emerged. The pro-logging faction included Don Days the Member for Casino, who had wrested a seat from the National Party on the strength of his personality and commitment to his electorate. Other members of this faction included Lin Gordon, the Minister for Forests, and Pat Hills, the former leader defeated by Wran in a leadership battle by one vote. This old guard had powerful support in the Timber Workers Union and the New South Wales Trades and Labour Council. Opposing them were Wran, Environment Minister Paul Landa, Attorney General Frank Walker and Jack Ferguson, the Deputy Premier.

Once the Terania story hit the front pages, Wran announced, "My door is always open to you guys." His request was that protesters get out of the forest and talk to the government; danger lurked both physically and politically in the forest of Terania. Michael Murphy was a new settler to the Terania Creek valley and one of the main organisers still living close to the logging site; he was an architect, a refugee from the city choosing a quiter lifestyle – until Terania. Michael's reply was: "The people at the camp are now planting lettuce in expectation of a long stay." The media image of tired police being massaged by protesters was difficult for Wran to bear.

Back in the forest, despite exhaustive debates on the limits of nonviolent action and to what lengths the group was prepared to go, a secret action, beyond the bounds of acceptability to the group, came as a political breakthrough. A small number of activists entered the forest at night, spiked trees with nails to deter cutting and identified them with spray paint. Logs lying on the ground were chainsawed into unusable lengths. TNFAGQ denounced the damage and publicly disowned the perpetrators. Privately, however, many agreed with the action: it halted the logging. As Michael Murphy said, "While I was in Sydney lobbying politicians, I left my chainsaw in good hands." The loggers could no longer hurriedly fell the forest. Nan Nicholson went straight to the heart of the matter, saying, "The most questionable act, and that which lost us most public support, actually saved the day."

Reaction was savage. The community was polarised. In the minds of the older settlers, law and order was paramount. Lismore City Council harassed the protest camp, and a group called the Concerned Citizens of the Channon District was formed, its primary purpose being to get rid of the new settlers. Police road blocks were set up and a blitz on defective cars netted many protesters. Trees planted by a Cabinet minister were poisoned. The council brought demolition orders against sixteen dwellings at Bodhi Farm (a nearby community). Many of its members participated at Terania.

Nan Nicholson was quick to point out the irony of the situation. "The sight of a local denizen appearing on television in filthy clothes, fly half undone and bare feet (a banana farmer in work clothes), denouncing the 'dirty hippies' for their depravity might have been seen as a joke to many who saw it. But the same man threatening to set fire to a forested ridge containing several dwellings was no joke. He was later elected to Lismore City Council on the strength of his antipathy towards new settlers and his vows to protect the community from them."

While political disaster for the new settlers loomed locally, political powers at a state level took notice. According to Jack Ferguson, spiking and sawing of trees gave Wran the ability to thump the table and demand debate on the issue. Michael Murphy noted that, "If we stayed with NVA [nonviolent action], the authorities would have walked all over the protest. A deeper political analysis recognised the nature of power politics and the fact that the threat forced the state government to talk."

Lin Gordon, the Minister for Forests, refused to move on the issue.

Wran, whose authority was paramount in the Labor Caucus after the 'Wranslide' in the 1978 elections, took the issue over and with the backing of his progressive faction set up a Cabinet sub-committee which reflected his views. They made a site inspection.

Jack Hallam was a junior Minister at the time and was later to become the Minister for Forests. He was one of the team whose job it was to inspect Terania. He relates, "When we arrived there was a fantastic atmosphere in the protest community. The meeting in the forest had an enormous impact on most of the politicians present. The articulate presentation of the leaders portrayed a deep emotional commitment. We came away from this meeting believing that the rainforest should not be logged." Conservationist Bren Claridge recalls, "The protest community had laid out a wondrous spread for lunch in the forest for politicians and media. Meanwhile, the pro-logging politicians were down the road eating bangers and bread."

A moratorium on logging was declared. It was a time of great celebration for the conservationists. The government declared an inquiry under a retired Supreme Court Judge, Justice Isaacs. But the inquiry was flawed. For one thing, Justice Isaacs was an old and frail man; he could not walk very far at all and his inspection of the forest in the rain was an horrendous ordeal for him.

Even more horrifying for Isaacs was the anarchy invoked by the protests: alternative people taking on the power of the state and seen to be winning. The anarchy was that of the protesters who thumbed their noses at all forms of authority, and Isaacs felt himself to be a symbol of that authority which was far more important to him than the rainforest. The judge ruled much of the conservationists' submission to be outside the parameters of the inquiry. This was despite years of research and months spent preparing their case. It became clear that Isaacs had little idea of the relevant issues. "He dozed off and couldn't keep up with the pages and kept losing his place, so the inquiry took twice as long as it should have, with double the cost," said Bren Claridge.

David Milledge, in his submission as a scientist, detailed the damage that would occur to the canopy during logging. Bren recalled Isaacs replying, "They are not taking the canopy they are just taking the logs and leaving the canopy."

Conservationists pulled out of the process before its conclusion. The inquiry cost an estimated one million dollars. Justice Isaacs' eventual finding supported logging at Terania. According to Jack Hallam, the Cabinet saw that "Isaacs was working in an iron lung." Premier Wran filed it, bottom drawer.

Hallam concluded, "The impact of that protest went well beyond Terania Creek and the bounds of government bureaucracy. It had an osmosis effect in the community. The younger generation, including my own, related to the protection of the forest. It had a massive effect. I realised as a politician that logging was an argument you couldn't win. The younger generation had taken a political decision that all logging was bad. In retrospect it was a dawning of an awareness of the damage we are doing to the planet. Politicians rarely lead, they react. However, it coincided with the views of the advanced radical thinkers in government. Wran, Ferguson, Landa and Walker are entitled to credit."

The forest remained at peace, never to be logged again. The issue slept until 1982 with the next explosive protest at Mount Nadi on the other side of the Nightcap Range. For the alternative community, Terania had set a significant precedent. It gave voice with awesome power to the ideals and aspirations of a generation alienated from mainstream society. The green fire ignited in the rainforest of Terania continues to burn to this day.

CHAPTER 2
GREEN DAWNING

I graduated from Fort Street Boys' High School, Sydney, in 1969. As a single sex male school it reflected the rats in the box mentality and survival in the schoolyard was not necessarily automatic. What I later learned however was that this public school gave myself and non affluent western suburbs students an opportunity of high quality education in the public school system for many generations and continues to do so up to the present day.

In fact, with a visit to the old school as a former Fortian of perhaps ill repute to some, I was impressed with the updating of the facilities, the calm reflecting its co-educational status and the serious intolerance of racist and bullying behaviour so prevalent in my boy's schooling of the 60's.

My first year at university in 1970 meant freedom and exposure to new ideas. I experienced a cultural flowering far in excess of my schoolboy horizons. Anti-apartheid and Land Rights issues and in particular the Vietnam War, were central to the concerns of my generation. After this century's shocking acquiescence to militarism and the hegemony of technological might, the Vietnam Moratorium movement came as a revolutionary event.

In May 1970 my first moratorium march saw the centre of Sydney grind to a halt. The major thoroughfares were packed with thousands of people who sat on the main road to listen to speakers. That afternoon the anti-war movement filled me with a sense of belonging and purpose. Here was a new way of acting, of making a difference. In September of that year came a second moratorium. This time there was violence, with police deliberately breaking up the crowd. Shopfront windows were shattered by the weight of bodies as police attempted to exercise crowd control. I received a first-hand lesson in the power of the police state and was traumatised. Yet in the victory of the Australian Labor Party under Gough Whitlam in 1972 and the withdrawal of Australian troops from Vietnam, my generation experienced a positive lesson – real change was possible.

Those days were the beginning of a new era. The political freedom we enjoy in Australia today, combined with access to modern communication technologies, has enabled the voice of the formerly dispossessed in society to emerge. As a consequence, the establishment has been forced to take heed. Convenient as it has been for the media to dismiss activists as a group of thrill seekers, or socially dysfunctional individuals giving vent to their frustrations, the media image of raucous 'anti-social' activity has disguised the truth of a cohesive philosophy which is about the health of society, of our planet and of our future.

Centuries of anthropocentric thinking have decreed that the earth is an infinite resource, existing only to serve humanity. Such arrogance has cast a shadow over our very survival. Global destruction of forests, extinction of species, the nuclear threat, mountains of toxic wastes and the poisoning of our air and waterways have imposed upon us stark lessons concerning the consequences of blinkered technological development. The folly of ignoring the interconnectedness of life has become all too apparent.

"In exploring people's individual journeys it is growing clear that global environmental issues are becoming an integral part of our sense of biography." So wrote Friedemann Wieland, author of The Journey of the Hero. Amidst the artificial constructs of civilisation, the faint memory of ancient precepts linger on the need to work with the earth, not against it, to belong to it as well as to each other. Wilderness resonates with a wildness in the hearts of many of us. In acting for the environment we make a personal journey, sharing with others along the way our conviction for social change.

In order both to survive collectively and grow individually, we must become agents of healing. We can then, as part of a great movement, change the world to match the wildest of our dreams. Wisdom and conviction, combined with an appreciation of nature in balance, provide us with the knowledge we need to make our stand. Our options are either to ignore the ecological crisis confronting us or to act in defence of the planet. The polarised realms of thought rely in the one instance upon denial and apathy and in the other upon the creative use of energy.

It is understandable, when we are daily assaulted by bad news through the media that our society still lives under the delusion that "it's all too big so why bother." Pervasive as that attitude may be, there are those in our community, however, who have refused to accept defeat. The anti-war generation has matured, and in many cases the much-celebrated 'babyboomers' have accessed positions of real power. With the lessons of Vietnam and the counterculture learnt, social control is no longer an acceptable concept. People and events have generated a formidable movement for social change.

Alternative ways of making the voice of change heard have chain – reacted, spreading from these shores to others; at American forest actions today they sing Terania protest songs. Unwittingly Australian environmentalists have pioneered, mythologised and impassioned certain attitudes, approaches and ideas which have echoed around the world, giving others the models and metaphors that they craved. The reverse flow has also been apparent. It has been a shared dreaming, a sense of ethic and awareness in a significant subculture which collectively felt disempowered by the paradigm.

As agents for social change we are breaking new ground, drawing on old traditions such as those of the American Indians and Aboriginal Australians as well as pioneering our own. In the words of Chief Seattle, "We love this earth as a newborn child loves its mother's heartbeat." As people from a dominant, destructive culture, we are proving ourselves capable of forging an alternative path, equipped with the technological competence of laptop computers and media know-how. With this amalgamation of the old and new we hope to create a 'survival culture' for the future.

Personal goals cannot be achieved in isolation. Our own identity and its growth happens in the context of family and culture. Beyond this, each individual's happiness is in the broadest and most profound ways intricately linked to the wellbeing of the planet. Hence we have moved from anthropocentric religion to an earth-bound understanding of the balance of nature and its changing tides. The goal is an harmonious world.

This book reflects on recent actions in which many thousands of individuals have participated, actions which have contributed to the growing tradition of environmental activism. Recent decades have witnessed a transformation of elements of western society; groups' and individuals' actions have succeeded in changing the course of history.

In the non-indigenous cultural context, Australia is, in the words of Hugh Mackay (Reinventing Australia), an "adolescent society... one of the youngest societies on Earth. Most of the societies with which we compare ourselves have much longer histories and much deeper cultural roots than ours ... It may be the case that Australia is only now approaching the threshold of its cultural maturity."

Despite Australia's relative youth, this country is at the forefront of environmental and social change. Once we recognise the value of ourselves, our anti-authoritarian past and our considerable political freedom, we have a rare opportunity to act with even greater power for the survival of our planet. In other countries we would risk the possibility of being gaoled or murdered for our efforts.

Agents for environmental and social change aim to create sustainable ideas – ideals for future generations. There are, of course, those who will profit by exploiting such ideals but in the case of the majority, integrity and a clarity of aims lie behind the words spoken and the actions undertaken. In the greater cultural context it can be observed that at a time when the planet is in crisis, an earthbound consciousness is emerging.

While participation in the green movement is strong, however, only mass awareness will prevent confrontation from becoming an endlessly repeated condition. When one evil has been conquered in the past, it has tended to reappear in another form elsewhere. But with sufficient involvement from the wider community, the need to continually fight essentially the same fire on many fronts will subside.

Hence political participation is vital. Politics is a valid arena for environmental and social activists; unless the political edge cuts deep, other modes of action can become a mere play in a sideshow. The mainstream political parties in Australia know that the growing green vote indicates a growing issues vote, not a mark placed on the ballot paper through the habit of generations.

With appropriate technology, mythology and personal example must lie our inspiration. We need to develop modern myth-making techniques to awaken the highest ideals in the community spirit. Activism as theatre is integral to the myth-making process and essential in building a movement. With a shared motivation, we reach beyond what is selfish and mediocre; freed from the constraints of society's paradigm, we seek the essential life energy. It is that sense of adventure, of a quest undertaken, which alerts others to the cause. and ignites within them a sense of mission. This can translate in many ways – from digging in a garden to participating in a revolution, from permaculture to politics. Striving for change, we seek the most effective methods.

These events and actions can represent an initiation, a first-step ritual toward global awareness. They give young people in this society's culturally barren wasteland the opportunity to dream again. Without our dreams and the ability to look outward and upward in life, we have nothing. Unless young people have a vision and a sense of social cohesion, we lose the human building blocks for a future 'heart society'. Confrontation with the support of people and ideals are an initiation by fire for those involved.

With the backdrop of river and ocean, police blue and forest green, gaudy boat and technicolour bulldozer, one has an exceptional setting for theatre. Theatre of the environment uses the vulture of the media (usually a tool of the establishment) to present the story; we dangle and perform, often in precarious circumstances, making ourselves and our act irresistible to the press. It is a play, an irreverent game, yet at the same time it provides a vital conduit for messages otherwise unable to be transmitted into a monopolistic realm. Lacking financial resources, we penetrate this powerful arena held as if by magic and in so doing create an alchemy for change.

For me, working for social change grew from a burning ambition to find something of consequence in my life. The automatic joy I derived from natural environments, combined with a sense of belonging with people from minority traditions – traditions that the dominant culture turned its back on – created a basis for personal action. This book evolved from injuries, both emotional and physical, resulting from the choice I made to strike a radical path. Recounting my experiences here is a form of healing, another stepping stone to being able to enjoy the successes won. I believe this is open to all of us; the choice as to whether we tread a pioneering path or stay with the conventional, lies with each individual. For those who search to discover a meaning to life beyond mainstream values or who suffer from a sense of meaninglessness, such a need can be a valuable driving force.

The strength of the environmental movement is not in organisation but in an anarchistic array of attacks on a monolithic establishment. To be sustainable, the activity must also deliver personal fulfilment. We can step away from carrying the mantle of personal responsibility and accept that it is too much for any one person, but collectively we share the capacity to find the answer. Those in control will take note of millions of people speaking with one voice.

The book that follows is but one tiny thread in a web of stories recounting the rise of a national movement representing a worldwide interest in conservation and human rights. The following story is the Australian instance of an international movement. It is the story of ordinary people, affected by the pervasive wrongs of society, acting in defence of the earth and in the process experiencing the extraordinary. We should take heart that ours is a powerful movement, just as the planet itself is strong in its regenerative capacity.

To quote the words of historian Manning Clark (History of Australia), "This generation has a chance to be wiser than previous generations. They can make their own history. With the end of the domination by the straighteners, the enlargers of life now have their chance."

CHAPTER 3
MIDDLE HEAD
Spirit Catcher

After five years travelling overseas I returned to Australia. Shortly afterwards I experienced an existential crisis of no small proportion. I felt there was little in Australia for me. I decided to leave again, but it was without the same sense of adventure and discovery of my first departure, it was purely an escape.

Before leaving, I spent a night at a campfire in the hills of northern New South Wales, listening to a stranger talk about protests against a coastal sandmining operation at Middle Head, a tiny beach south of Scotts Head on the mid-north coast. "The protesters seemed really naive, mainly locals without much political experience," he said. Then, in a different tone, "I don't understand why they would mine such a beach."

The explanation was simple: politics. An acute problem began for the sandmining industry when the Premier, Neville Wran, declared that all sandmining would cease in national parks. That immediately cut 70 per cent of the known reserves, making Middle Head a target.

Middle Head was an environment too beautiful to be bulldozed. The beach had been left alone in the past because it had been considered too short to be economically feasible to mine. All that was about to change.

As an 'alternative' beach, Middle Head was a place where people often frolicked naked. This raised the ire of the local council. The beach was in the northern part of Kempsey Shire but the people using it came from the neighbouring Nambucca Shire. It was their local beach, but they were disenfranchised by the decision makers in Kempsey, fifty kilometres away.

While parochial issues were causing a stir at Middle Head, greater powers were forging an industrial relationship which would ensure the rape of that little beach. Conservationists' research revealed that the industrial assault was part of a plan to source military and aerospace materials.

Unluckily for Middle Head, its sands contained three valuable elements: rutile, or titanium oxide, an insoluble powder used extensively in industry as a whitener for paint, paper and plastics and also for the manufacture of missiles, aircraft, nuclear warheads and reactors; zirconium, a raw material used for nuclear reactors and armour-piercing incendiary cluster bombs; and thorium, a radioactive element with potential as a replacement fuel for uranium in the nuclear industry.

The sandmining company Mineral Deposits was a subsidiary of the multinational mining company Utah (Australia), which had close links with Utah International, owned by General Electric. With such heavyweights operating behind the scenes, Middle Head in all its pristine beauty was destined to be sacrificed.

The easiest option for conservationists would have been to walk away and take comfort in the knowledge that there were plenty more beaches on the NSW coastline. In Sydney a number of conservation groups declared it was impossible to save Middle Head. "Too late," said Milo Dunphy of the Total Environment Centre. "Plenty of other battles to fight in the future."

I visited Middle Head in August 1980. A section of beach, along with its unique dry sclerophyll forest, had already been bulldozed, flattened and burnt. It was a wasteland butted up against a picture postcard coastal scene with high original dunes, gnarled coastal forest and patches of rainforest in the hind dune area. I sat on the frontal dune, which was ten metres high and ran the length of the beach like the wall of an ancient ruin.

There had been a few local protests after the first clearing. A local landowner, whose property had been bulldozed against his will for the mining of the beach, supported the protests and had manufactured and distributed an information sheet. The work stopped soon afterwards, and protesters left. When I visited the beach all work was at a standstill. Only one protester stayed on to maintain a solitary vigil.

As I sat on my perch on the dune, a sea eagle flew past at my height. It was like an old man; its wings beat the air with what seemed like a great effort. The sight brought tears to my eyes. Whether it was the imminent destruction of this beach, my own sense of futility or the strange beauty of this creature flying by so close to me, I still don't know. I returned to Sydney to prepare for my departure overseas.

One morning soon afterwards I awoke from a dream so vivid that I was sure I had been sitting up and awake watching that very eagle from Middle Head fly across my field of vision once again. The exact same dream recurred three nights in a row, just as clear and explicit each time. It was unnerving. Affected by this recurrent dream, I began looking for a positive approach on the Middle Head issue. My investigation led me to Robert Rosen, a Sydney businessman who in the 1980s lived on the mid – north coast. Robert had spearheaded the campaign against mineral sandmining, developing an in-depth body of research and educating many people in the region on the issue of coastal destruction. I was directed to an office from where he was lobbying government in Sydney at the time, and it was at that point I committed myself to supporting a continuing campaign. I cancelled my ticket overseas and headed north. My life was about to head off on a path I could not have conjured up in my wildest imaginings.

Robert and I decided to use Hiroshima Day gatherings in Sydney and Lismore to rev up the campaign. Bellingen was the first stop. Here I met with a local politico who considered our plan inappropriate and presumptuous. Perhaps he was right. I left the meeting, seriously deflated, and saw a distinguished Aboriginal man standing beside his broken-down vehicle. Giving him a hand to get started, we discussed Middle Head. He agreed it was an important place. He mentioned that a xanthorrhoea which grew there was many thousands of years old. The inspiring chance meeting with Burnham Burnham (who had been a major participant at Terania) instilled new-found confidence that our task was indeed valid. I rushed off first to Lismore for the Hiroshima Day march to stir enthusiasm for the cause, then to Middle Head some five hours away.

I arrived with a friend, Jim Benton, and in the bush behind the dune we set up a large army tent which became the 'Sun, Sea and Surf' Middle restaurant. Here, three dollars a day bought three wholesome meals if you could afford it; otherwise you got three wholesome meals a day. An office with phones was established in a banana packing and storage shed up the hill. Eight people worked in this building, while an ebb and flow of between 60 and 150 people occupied the protest site. Equipped with what I felt were considerable communication skills, I attempted to find a niche in the fast-blossoming hierarchy of the office. I was rejected by others with media communication in their sights.

Dejected, I returned to the beach and started to dig holes for the shitpit and compost. A new experience – soft, packed sand that kept its shape to a depth of four metres. Shovel after shovel, I carved it away like a sculptor. Young Jude, another protester, poked his head over the edge. I asked for a hand up and pulled him down. "Start digging," I said. It was the beginning of a lasting friendship. The rest of the camp came to witness the phenomenon of sand billowing out from the depths.

The group made an extraordinary campsite. Forty-four-gallon drums were brought in and ovens and hotplates were welded using coat hangers as welding rods. These were set in the sand walls by the kitchen tent. Nights saw hot food, campfires, music and a sense of community new to all. Mornings witnessed friends surfing together, with regular visits from a pod of dolphins. It was a far cry from the usual surfing dynamic of competition and aggression that was the hallmark of the Australian surfing culture. Life came to consist of meetings and discussions, songs and consciousness-raising circles and lots of holding hands, all blissful and unreal. Only Jim Benton, a local with a vast amount of practical experience, would occasionally comment, "Yeah, but what are you going to do to stop the dozers?" We felt strong in our numbers and thought we were invincible. Perhaps it was the titanium surrounding us.

The sandminers were constructing a dredge, a massive industrial monster which floated on a barge in an artificially created lake where the dune once existed. Once made, it started eating its way up the beach. A sense of urgency fuelled the debate about what to do for our first action. Some wished to stop the dredge, others felt the area had been destroyed already so there was no point, and others were just enjoying the party.

We decided to surround the dredge, some to exorcise it, others to make a physical stand, realising its assault would not stop without a major protest. We paraded out hand in hand, then sat in front of its working area. The operator in his cabin kept working. The blade, like a giant corkscrew, cut into the wall of sand. A section collapsed and three people slid down the bank, dangerously close to the working blade. There was screaming and pandemonium. The operator refused to halt his machine. One man sat cross-legged close to the blade and stared fixedly at the worker inside his cabin. Others, meanwhile, rushed around the artificial lake and across a pontoon walkway to gain access to the operator. The blade gouged dangerously underneath the protester, who dared not move for fear of losing his legs. Time was frozen. A group of people stared horrified as a piece of industrial equipment threatened to take the legs off a friend. Suddenly the machine stopped and cheers erupted as the operator shut down. Visibly shaken, the driver disappeared to another section of the plant. We sat on that sandhill for the remainder of the afternoon.

The arrival of renowned sculptor William Ricketts prompted us to further action. He had in the boot of his car a piece of his original artwork evoking Aboriginal and earth spirituality. We built three wooden crosses and stood them in the path of the dredge. To invoke the sense of a spiritual bond with the land, protesters tied themselves to the crosses for the day with Ricketts's sculpture set in the foreground. Around the base of the crosses people knelt; children, dressed in white, had flowers in their hair. The artist's concept was to dare the miners to bulldoze a nationally recognised masterpiece. If they wouldn't, how could they dare doze a natural masterpiece? The display was stunning, but the media was only interested in confrontation, danger and arrest. A federal election was on, which saturated the media, and Middle Head did not rate a mention.

In another action, a number of protesters slipped into the slimy green industrial wastewater surrounding the dredge. This was a brave act considering that none of us knew what chemicals the industry used and spewed into the water. The action stopped work for a short time.

Due to our inexperience, confrontation was unsophisticated. There was, however, a degree of social control. Anyone who wished to take direct action was roundly condemned. Those who, like myself were totally without experience in campaigning were led to believe that nonviolent philosophy was a new and perfect way, like some new-found religion. This doctrine often became an excuse for doing nothing.

An experienced campaigner arrived in camp. Graeme Dunstan had been politically active from the days of the Vietnam Moratoriums. He wanted to occupy the dredge. There were no police around, so he boarded the machine, confronted the worker and told him to stop work. When the worker refused, Graeme set about turning switches off. He saw it as an honest, open interaction with the worker. "Eye to eye we directly communicated," he said.

Most of us were horrified. Graeme's definition of nonviolent action did not accord with that of the majority of protesters at Middle Head. He left the camp and soon afterwards published an article in Maggie's Farm, an alternative environmental journal. Calling his article 'Lessons in Losing', this is what he had to say:

"The consensus at Middle Head was solid about nonviolence. That it was to be a peaceful protest was a precondition and a laudable one too. But nonviolent action is not a doctrine defined and fixed. Rather it's a concept for exploration in action."

"At Middle Head, dialogue about nonviolence was stifled . . . The protest got active when the police arrived. The way to win an action like Middle Head is to make it clear through effective harassment that the operation cannot proceed without massive and expensive police protection."

"When a mass of police did arrive the tactic was to lie down and get arrested. When the police were absent we all lay down and got a suntan. It was much easier to be locked in a Gandhian cliche of mass arrests (if only we had the masses). There is no shame in being afraid, but it is a waste of energy and time not to name it in oneself and work with it, then we can be organised for effective action. I'm weary of the loser mind-set. When will we stand and be brave for what we believe, taking the initiative to shape our future; to have faith in our truth and each other."

For better or for worse, harmony was the rule at the 1980 Middle Head protests. One indisputably positive offshoot of this was cross-cultural cooperation between the non-indigenous protesters and members of the local-Aboriginal community, who had set up a Land Rights embassy in the forest by the beach. Several months earlier, in a letter to the Premier, they had stated: "We, the people of the Gumbaingiri Tribal Elders Council, are not happy with the mining at Middle Head beach. This area is part of the sacred tribal lands, and for the Gumbaingiri and Dunghatti tribes, it is our birthplace. It is vitally important that this entire section of beach be preserved with the headland for us to retain our cultural heritage."

"Already many important elements, including significant trees and land formations, have been bulldozed and destroyed. We are concerned that if these works continue, we will lose the roots of our tribal groups forever."

"We also bring to your attention the serious matter that our peoples' representatives were not formally notified or consulted on this issue."

Middle Head featured in the Dreamtime stories of both the Gumbaingiri and Dunghatti tribes. In the Dreamtime, Aboriginal people migrated to Middle Head from another land. They travelled over a bridge made from the intestine of a koala, which was inflated by a little boy of the tribe. Once they landed at Middle Head, the boy's warrior brother cut the intestine with a stone axe. It floated up to become a rainbow. The seas were calm, so the warrior ran up and down the beach challenging the sea to chase him. It did, and waves started pounding up the beach.

Middle Head was a manifestation of the new wave of communal live-in protests which followed the tradition of the Aboriginal Tent Embassy outside Federal Parliament in 1973. For myself, other protesters and their children, this was our first real contact with Aboriginal folk in a shared purpose.

The calm was soon to be shattered. One sunny morning a caravan rolled onto the bare earth near our campsite, a huge fluorescent 'POLICE' sign emblazoned on its side. We raced to the frontal dune to defend the beach. Within minutes the police and industrial juggernaut began. People were herded together. Those in the trees behind the dunes hung on grimly as the dozer was brought in. The stunted coastal trees offered little protection, unlike the magnificent examples of protest refuge from the inland rainforests. They were dozed to the ground. Protesters saved themselves as best they could. Dangling like washing from a line, they dropped to the ground, narrowly missed by falling branches. Without trees to hang on to, we scrummed down, locking arms. We were pulled apart by the police teams.

Some police and protesters interacted in an entirely different manner. One protester, Felix, found himself hanging on as the dozer started shaking his tree. Eventually he fell . . . on top of a cop! Felix was dragged off and charged with assault and resisting arrest.

After several scrums I too was dragged off. The policeman wasn't altogether unsympathetic as he led me off for my first arrest, but I was dejected: I thought I had failed the team. Nabbed early, I was unable to defend the beach that I had grown to love. I felt like someone who had just lost all his possessions in a house fire. The door of the paddy-wagon swung open to let me in, and to my surprise I found it was packed full of friends. In the frenzy I had not noticed their absence.

Outside, the action continued. One protester, I was later told, jumped onto the dozer blade. The onlookers went wild as the driver ignored him and raised the blade for another attack. He jumped off in time to avoid being crushed between blade and tree and ran into the bush pursued by police. Late that afternoon, with the procedures of arrest completed, we returned and walked a broken wasteland that was once our little piece of paradise. Only the kookaburras were happy as they picked off worms in the newly upturned earth.

The following day the police presence was overpowering. We donned masks representing those animals which were being destroyed and headed out onto the dunes. Those who ventured too far were bowled over by cops who appeared to be keen on some football practice. Several more protesters were arrested. Our efforts, it seemed, were futile.

The dozer was working full tilt. It ran the entire length of the beach scalping the ancient frontal dune. As an act of dominance and a tactic designed to discourage any further rebellion, it worked well. I looked seaward to see that familiar pod of dolphins arching its way around the northern point, a thing of beauty amidst the destruction. It was short-lived; as soon as the dolphins cleared the rocky headland, the arching of their carefree swimming style flattened out in response to the vibrations of the dozer. In a flash they disappeared. A police four-wheel drive was busy patrolling, doing wheelies on the beach.

Hard as it was for us to comprehend, for the mining industry the central issue of the confrontation was pending unemployment. This fear gave great power to the bosses, who effectively targeted us as the enemy. Survival for the workers was the maintenance of a job regardless of its distasteful aspects. As one of the dozer drivers at Middle Head explained, "I'm due to retire in five years and I'd lose my superannuation if I retired now. Anyway, there are seven more drivers waiting to take my place. What would my resignation achieve?" Ironically unemployment also provided the potential for conservationists to act in defence of Middle Head. It enabled activists, accustomed to simple living and poverty, to undertake the powerful tactic of waiting in a world where time was money. We were patient, we witnessed events and attempted to get our story out via the media to embarrass the government into action.

We failed on that beach, but our actions did save Grassy Head, the next beach south along the coast, which was also earmarked for mining, right up to the border of the Yarrahappini ecology centre. Fearing further protests, the government gave confirmation of the fact that Grassy Head would not be mined only months after the Middle Head protest had finished. The loss of Middle Head was an important victory for many other beaches on the long New South Wales coastline. Due to the protest and further conservationist lobbying, after 1980 there were no new leases issued under the Wran government for sandmining on the New South Wales coast. Sandmining was also stopped on Fraser Island in Queensland in 1982.

No-one who spent time in the camaraderie of the camp at Middle Head left without the resolve to continue efforts to defend the environment against exploitation. Despite defeat and an overwhelming feeling of powerlessness, Middle Head represented for most an awakening of consciousness and an education in effective protest methods. Many of these activists continued on.

For me, the significance of Middle Head was immense. It represented my initiation into a love of the land and gave me a sense of community and purpose. I left physically wounded and bereaved, but with a sense of direction never before experienced in my life. From the bitterness of defeat rose a sense of mission that gave me no choice but to fully commit myself as an agent for change. There would be no more dilemmas concerning my life's directions. I had found something more precious than any bounty the establishment could ever offer; I had discovered a world – view that for me rang truer than any other doctrine or religion. Inspired, impassioned and freed in the knowledge that the authorities would regret ignoring our actions in defence of that special place, a sense of commitment coursed like a fire through my veins. I give thanks to the spirit that dwells at Middle Head.

CHAPTER 4
NIGHTCAP
A Win for the Wild

SONG TO MISTER WRAN

© Brendan "Mookx" Hanley circa 1979

verse 2: For a politician's pay-off will you let them take our trees,

And for multinational money can they do just what they please?

For the local country people, will you keep them in the dark?

For a handful of timber will you take our National Park?

verse 3: For the sake of your empire will you cut the future down,

For the history books to witness, will you be the criminal clown?

For the end of our forest will you give the word to start?

For a handful of timber will you take our National Park?

Transcribed: Bruce McNicol

It was three years after Terania, and the rainforest logging issue had still not been resolved in northern New South Wales. Terania remained untouched thanks to direct action, but while the government sat on a political powder keg, rainforest logging continued in the region. We decided to light the fuse and bring an end to all rainforest logging in New South Wales.

I visited Terania and was inspired by the forests and the direct action that had saved it. Knowing that I had missed an important historic event, I made a commitment to protect the forests by opposing the continuing destruction. I was ready to campaign. In my mind I was in a state of continual revolution to save the environment. The concept of rainforest as the 'womb of life' resonated with my desire to be proactive for the planet, to put my ideals into practice.

The conservation movement continued to pressure the government in Sydney, but things slumbered after the Commission of Inquiry with Justice Isaacs. The green movement feared that logging would destroy precious areas while politicians ducked the issue.

The radical arm of the green movement was not organised but came together when the call went out. It generally comprised those who were not otherwise committed and were able to undertake a long campaign. We ranged from scientists to local residents and itinerants such as myself – a mix of people, generally with alternative lifestyles and a wealth of expertise.

The Nightcap campaign, which incorporated two protests, the first at Griers Scrub and the second at Mount Nadi, was a continuation of political and on-the-ground action pioneered at Terania. These forests were literally over the hill from that lowland subtropical rainforest. As at Terania, local residents were the ones to escalate the issue, distressed by the rainforest logging occurring within walking distance of the largest alternative community in Australia. Like Terania, it was a people's revolution in the forest. The action was generally a peaceful one, but when confronted with authority, protesters acted with bravery, audacity and a measure of contempt.

Sustained lobbying of the New South Wales Labor government by a group of activists with the experience of Terania behind them and the knowledge that 70 per cent of the state's population supported an end to rainforest logging was effective. Unofficially Wran was annoyed with the Nightcap activists for pressuring him to act earlier than he wished. The conservationists, in turn, were annoyed with Wran for allowing logging to continue in other rainforests three years after the point had been made so unequivocally at Terania.

Our annoyance turned to action when the loggers were reported to be in Griers Scrub, a basin below the north-facing slope of Mount Nadi. Here among the tall timbers they could work unimpeded, protected by the sheer cliffs above them. The only vehicular entrance was a road some four kilometres long, closed by a locked gate. It was a deserted area, a safe twenty kilometres by road from the hippies of Nimbin.

A group of fifty protesters, myself included, drove to the logging site but were stopped by locked gates and an irate farmer. We turned our vehicles around and travelled to Murwillumbah, the nearest town thirty kilometres away, where we occupied the Forestry Commission offices. After a successful afternoon in town, we had won local media interest and departed without any arrests (the police were firm but friendly, setting the scene for further encounters). A smaller group decided to go secretly into Griers Scrub the next day, entering by foot from the mountain top. We believed it important to let the loggers know that we were able to descend the mountain and were prepared to confront them directly in the forest.

A dozen people gathered at a site near the transmission tower. We began the hike in a stand of montane subtropical rainforest. Our chattering voices grew silent as the first sound of chainsaws floated up the mountain; our pace quickened. We emerged from the rainforest on a drier northerly slope and from a lookout point viewed the logging area below. One of our group, Gummy, gave us a quick bushy's botany lesson as we viewed the forest's magnificence. "It's like a big bathtub and the pure stand of Bangalow palms is its plughole," he said. Thinner cover, identified by broken and separated canopy, showed the relentless advance of man and machine through the perfect mushroom explosion of intact canopy. We'd seen enough. Down the spur we hurried, driven by our determination to meet with the loggers.

Once onto the flat we passed along the fresh scar of roadworks, past huge stumps where ancient brush box trees once stood. The loggers came into sight. They looked up from their work, saw us and saw red. One big fat fellow marched straight at me, roaring abuse: "You fuckin' bastards, what d'ya think you're doing in this place? Dole bludgers, the lot of ya!" I was a few metres in front of the others, so I steeled myself for the initial impact as he came bearing down upon me. Like a train on rails he steamed straight past (much to my immediate relief) and stormed up to one effete young member of our group who was dressed in a poncho. To the logger it was a man wearing a dress in a forest.

The torrent of abuse continued. I must confess I was too logger – shocked to go to my companion's aid. In stepped Ian Hoskens (affectionately known to his closest friends as Bam Barn). He presented himself squarely to the logger, and in a voice as loud as his opponent's took the logger on in a debate of sorts.

The forest reverberated with the sound of two male voices, bellowing like bulls head to head. This continued until the combatants became decidedly hoarse. They took a rest as others in our group began asking questions, some as simple and personal as the names of our adversaries (the vocal logger, we discovered, was called Ned). It was, in a rough as guts way a 'get to know you' session. Beneath the bluster was a need to make some reasonable human contact.

A logging truck rolled into the clearing. The driver hopped out and hounded up to the top of the vehicle with a menacing cable adjuster in his hand. A superbly fit and muscular man, he moved like a cat as he checked the equipment on his vehicle, wordlessly stating ownership of the truck. His menacing body language was not lost on us. When they started to pack their gear, tension subsided almost as quickly as it had started. The working day was over. We bade a surprisingly friendly farewell to each other, the friendliness most likely a manifestation of the relief we felt in leaving each other. We said, pointedly, "See you again."

Thus began a consistent campaign of daily presence in and around the work site. We had little idea of the effectiveness of our actions. We simply knew that we were not going to give up and let the timber industry get away with the logging of this rainforest.

Tactics were developed to make us appear to be many times our number. The acoustics of the sheer cliffs aided us in our deception. If only a handful of us went down into the rainforest, each would call in different directions with varied calls. The work would stop as loggers listened to an invisible crowd of protesters descending. Often, when we arrived at the clearing, we would ask them to guess the numbers in the bush. Our ventriloquism was impressive.

But neither our actual or our supposed numbers proved enough: logging in the rainforest continued. What we needed was publicity, but the media required arrests before they would take up the story. Under a new law of trespass in enclosed lands, the forest was closed by the Wran Labor government. The offence carried a fine of five hundred dollars. We moved towards confrontation.

Four of us descended the mountain. Two of my companions were locals – Chris, an amateur botanist, and Frog, a musician and a mischief – maker. These two men ducked around the trees to foil the cutters while I entered the loggers' camp during their tea break. Charlie remained in the bush nearby as support. I confronted the startled workers saying, "Well, gentlemen, do you realise that you have the power to arrest me under this new law?"

They looked at each other, dumbfounded, and said, "What do you mean?"

"This forest has been closed and you as citizens can actually arrest me and call in the police to get rid of me."

Old Bill was rather confused. He went to the radio and said, "There's a bloke here that wants to be arrested – you'd better send the police down."

As he finished I said, "I didn't say I wanted to be arrested, I said you could arrest me, if you wanted to."

"Well that's just great!" grumbled Bill. "You've gone and got me to ring the bloody cops and now they're going to come all the way out here and blame me after you've pissed off into the bush!"

"Now then, I couldn't do that to you," I replied. "So I guess I really am under arrest."

"Yeah, right. You'd better not run away," he said. So I sat down. I was feeling at ease with most of the loggers. Alan Grindsell, who owned the operation, could see we were up to something. He came back agitated after a confrontation with Chris in the felling area and walked over with an axe in hand, waving it menacingly at me and saying, "Where are your mates now? We could do anything we like."

I looked at him and saw his gaze go past me. Just across the road at my back, my friends sat on a rock, like three elves in the greenery. Not so close that they could get caught, but not so far away either that they couldn't help. I relaxed a little and waited for the police.

My friends bolted when the squad car drove up. An imposing sergeant got out, looked at the loggers and then at me. "It really wouldn't be very pleasant for you to spend the night in the cells. They're pretty filthy over at Murwillumbah," he said.

"If that's the case I'll just have to put up with it," I replied. "How did you get in here?" he asked.

I pointed to the top of the mountain and said, "Straight down." From our position at the valley floor the cliffs looked impassable. Looking up at the sheer cliffs, both he and the loggers couldn't help but be impressed.

"Tough as mallee bulls, these blokes," he said to the loggers, gesturing theatrically.

It seemed he wasn't wholly unsympathetic to our cause. Yet he continued doing his job in an efficient manner. He placed me under arrest for trespass and sent his two subordinates into the forest to find the others.

Chris and Charlie managed to elude the police. Frog hid under a giant tree fern. From behind a nearby rock he heard the call, "The pigs have gone." Out he strolled, feeling pleased with his well-honed survival instincts, when up jumped a blinding blue flash and grabbed him. "Tricked you. You're under arrest," said the cop.

Mine was no ordinary arrest, either. On the way into Murwillumbah the squad car managed to get bogged after a near collision with an oncoming car, driven by the head forester. I jumped out and helped push the police car out of a rut. On arrival at the forest gates I was handed the keys and asked to unlock them. I climbed back in and away we went.

The conversation in the car turned to conservation. The sergeant related a public speaking experience he had taken part in on a crown sergeants' course. Everyone had been required to give a ten-minute lecture. His subject was the slaughter and eventual conservation of koalas. As a finale he recited to a hall full of budding crown sergeants a poem he had composed:

> Oh Koala, where are you?
> Leafy boughs obscure my view.
> Many a man has sought your track,
> Oh Koala, please come back.

Arriving at last at the station, I was processed and released. The police phone ran hot: the media had caught a sniff of forest confrontation.

The next morning I met with six local people at the top of the mountain and together we made our way down to the logging site. On the way I warned the others to take care, as they could be arrested. Carol Sherman, a resident from Nimbin, said, "This is our forest, we'll just go down and talk to them about that." A most impressive woman, I certainly wasn't going to argue with her. Downward we continued into the thick greenery. I dropped back, not wanting to be arrested again.

"Don't move! You're all under arrest," shouted a lone cop as he jumped out from behind a tree. I stood frozen, within a few metres of the group, unable to see or be seen. One cop, and they all allowed him to arrest them! From my position it was like an absurdist radio play acted out behind a curtain of green.

As my companions were being led away down the hill, I started to retrace my steps. Suddenly I felt very alone. I stumbled around in the bush looking for a radio I had foolishly set down. There was no way of knowing if there were other police in hiding.

A sudden coo-ee from up the mountain almost caused me to fall off a cliff. I called back, uncertain of my whereabouts. Voices answered, this time right below me. "Everyone OK down there?" I asked my arrested companions. They said they were fine. They told me later that a second cop had come tumbling out of the bush with scratches on his hands and face as I spoke. He hadn't seen me and was clearly as ignorant of his whereabouts as I was of mine. I had avoided him purely by accident. In the confusion of events I was earning an undeserved reputation as a bushman.

I had escaped, but the day had been disappointing, with too many of our people arrested. To avoid this next time, we decided on a night action. Evening began to throw long shadows as a group of protesters descended the mountain. Ungoaded by the sounds of bulldozer and chainsaw, we took it at a leisurely pace. We reached the bulldozer, which now lay idle. An air of peace surrounded the normally frantic worksite. Dirt was roughly piled where a rainforest once towered. Broken bangalow palms and ripped understorey stood as a silent reminder of the day's frenetic activity. There was silence, a peace of sorts. This was our chance to look around and take some action. Chains and padlocks were taken to the dozer; gears were locked to floor pedals and doors chained shut. The blade of another dozer, its fuel storage tank and a pile of logs ready for loading were graffitied with the words, "WORKERS' SWEAT = MILL OWNERS' PROFITS" We left the site, moving along the access road and building barriers as we went. At the access gate we used Superglue to gum up the padlocks.

Before dawn the headlights of a logging truck loomed in the dark, casting an eerie light across a blockade of cars and tents. We had decided to show the strength of our numbers. Stuck in front of a hundred bleary-eyed protesters, it became obvious to the driver that little work would be done that day. What's more, the truck was too big to turn around.

The police arrived. Their first priority was to remove the blockading vehicles, a task that didn't prove so easy as the blockaders grouped together and stalled the forward movement of the tow truck. A loud cheer erupted as the truck, forced to crawl along at a snail's pace behind us, boiled over.

Any triumph of people power over machines was always met with great excitement, primarily because it was machinery that so effectively destroyed the forests, but also because amongst us there were many with a strong fundamentalist hatred of machinery. The destruction of equipment was not far from the minds of these modern-day Luddites. While the Nightcap Action Group discouraged the practice, there were those who at times vandalised the machinery. Once, after a particularly nasty altercation in the forest, I arrived back at camp to hear it gleefully reported that one participant had poured sand into the hydraulics of the dozer the previous day.

It took an hour for the police to move our vehicles. The slow procession moved to the front gate and we scrummed down as the police moved in. They went for Eddie Buivids who, as an older man, they saw as a ringleader. One cop pulled his hair while another twisted his ear. A crescendo of complaint rose from the group. Eddie remained calm. The police pulled at his legs, the crowd held his arms. He offered no resistance, allowing himself to be the rope in a tug of war. Eventually he was hauled away, a wry smile still on his face.

With the example set, the remainder locked limbs again in a disorganised but determined scrum. The police continued to extract one person at a time, untangling arms which flayed around and tangled up again. The senior sergeant got particularly vicious with Gummy, who had his arm in plaster. I put my hand on the cop's arm.

"You'll do serious damage – that arm was recently broken," I said. "Tell him about it!" snarled the sergeant, and showed me a neat set of teeth marks on his forearm.

The blockade continued for several hours. Eventually the road was cleared and police wagons left the scene laden with the arrested. By 3 pm the loggers triumphantly reached the gate. They fitted key to lock, only to find it stopped by Superglue. Two sledge hammers smashed the frozen locks.

In drove the trucks at last. What happened beyond the gates none of us saw. Most likely they reached the bulldozer on foot to release it with heavy bolt cutters and welding equipment. Whatever happened, we had delayed work and brought about a short reprieve for the forest.

The loggers were determined not to be hindered from their operations any further. A caravan was moved on site. We presumed it meant a night watchman and decided to investigate. Chris and I climbed down the mountain and quietly walked along the forest road, ready to duck out of sight. We drew near to the caravan. Just as we were about to poke our noses over the rise, a loud voice bellowed in the distance. It was Sol from Tuntable, a charming and creative nonviolent activist. He yelled out to the night watchman, "While you're down there, I'm fucking your wife."

The caravan door slammed (our mission accomplished). "Fucking bastard hippie bludger!" bellowed the watchman. We decided not to look up to see who it was. This was just as well, as his furious words were followed by two resounding blasts of a gun. We looked at each other – this was the first time we'd been under fire. We backed away a few steps, as quietly as we could in the now very silent forest, and deciding not to leave a calling card, turned and bolted with the speed of frightened gazelles.

After a good distance and in the shelter of the forest we proceeded at a casual pace, chatting in order to relax our jangled nerves. It was almost sunset as we climbed the last section of rainforest on the mountain. A figure stepped out from behind a tree, an unrecognisable silhouette in the setting sun. "Fucking hippie bastards, I'm going to fix you this time!" he yelled.

I froze, real heart-attack stuff. What looked like a raised axe was in his hands. My imagination ran riot; all capacity for confrontation was depleted. So, the silhouette, laughed and said, "I thought I'd give you a bit of excitement."

After the shooting episode we decided to call the police. They investigated, but no gun was found. The night watchman insisted that he had hit empty milk cartons with the back of an axe. Next time we ventured down the mountain we invited him to give a demonstration. Surprisingly he obliged. The milk carton went pop. The display was like a toy gun emulating a cannon.

We welcomed support, but disaster sometimes loomed when new people on their first day acted in ways that made it difficult for the ongoing campaigners. One group of one-day wonders threw rocks at a passing dozer, then jumped out onto the road and abused the loggers – from a distance. Things were getting out of hand. Lunch came and I went up to the loggers and said, "Mind if I join you for a bite?" They did not reply. When they did talk, their discussion centered on the dangerous tactics that some of us used. They were pissed off. Suddenly a truck full of loggers skidded to a halt – they had been informed of violence over the radio. I bolted to a safer distance. The new arrivals and work crew gave chase as the protesters took flight, scattering across the fallen logs and crowns on a steep slope. I outpaced one young logger, a sullen fellow who was the son of the belligerent and boisterous logger we had sparred with on our very first descent. I scrambled up the rough slope to the top road and left him far behind. However, I felt vulnerable as I hauled myself up onto the road, imagining hairy knees at nose level.

There he was, my worst nightmare – the cat-like truck driver I had encountered days before – just thirty metres down the road and trotting up at a steady pace, a brick shithouse in boots. I kept running as he closed in on me. Two people were ahead. I called out, "Logger behind! Slow down!" A wave of panic sapped my strength; I needed the support of the others. With only metres between us, the logger suddenly veered off the road. He must have figured there were too many of us. One of our bunch was Aboriginal, which may have meant trouble in the logger's mind. He headed into the gully, pursuing another solitary protester.

We stopped to view the proceedings below. The forest had become a gigantic maze in a field of devastation. Loggers and prey could not see each other, but from our vantage point we viewed both. It was truly 'dress circle with Christians and lions'. We called advice: 'Logger below' and he moved up. Frantic waves and coded instructions were designed to conceal his position. At one stage the opponents were a mere fallen log apart. With our supportive grunts and hand signals, our player escaped. The nearest logger caught sight of him. We called in unison, "Run for it uphill!" The terrain was steep and strewn with branches and tree crowns, but he was able

to maintain his distance from his pursuer. We hauled him onto the road and made a beeline for the nearest forest and relative safety. Numbers were needed in the forest, as individuals were invariably set upon by the loggers. One was badly beaten. The loggers were nearing the end of their cut in Griers Scrub, so the exercise became our preparation for the impending assault on the other side of the mountain at Mount Nadi.

On our last day in Griers Scrub the loggers intercepted five of us on the steep slope. They stood above us, there was nowhere to go. The night watchman, an ex-mercenary soldier, came towards me with rope in his hands. He grabbed hold of my arms. I felt like I was in suspended animation; the rest of the participants became distant and strangely out of focus. Face to face we stared at each other. His was calm save for a slight twitch of his moustache and a glint in his eye.

I called out, "We're trapped by a bunch of loggers. Come back down!"

Ned yelled jeeringly, "Come up here, we've caught a few hippies!"

He was pretending, I was serious. Our friends appeared and sat on a rock ledge immediately above us. The man holding me tried to tie up my hands. Another protester came in close to help me but slipped. My captor grabbed him and wrapped the rope around his hands. Another friend grabbed the rope and threw it away. I remained motionless, not wanting to provoke the situation into a brawl. Out of the corner of my eye I could see fighting break out. Punches were flying on both sides. We outnumbered them, but they were a tough group of men who were used to a fight. "Stop, this is ridiculous!" I shouted at the top of my voice. They all looked my way, some with fists still raised. All were sufficiently scared, so they listened. "We'll get out of the forest now if you stop."

There was a sense of relief all around. The man holding me captive stepped back and smiled, a glint still in his eye. "Until next time," he said, and followed his workmates down the hill. We made our way up in high spirits, glad to have survived. Both groups had quit for the day feeling they had achieved a win of sorts.

We managed to gain media interest but we lost much of the untouched magnificence of the tall forest of Griers Scrub. We were familiar with the loggers and had gained recognition in the surrounding alternative community. We were now experienced and ready for the expected assault on Mount Nadi.

Our camp was on the only access to Mount Nadi, so we stayed on alert. Heavy rains interceded as we waited for the inevitable arrival of the loggers. The camp itself was hectic, with a sprinkling of unbalanced behaviour. One incident involved a jealous man who set fire to the tent of his estranged partner as she slept inside with their daughter. Both mother and child were dragged to safety in time. The community gathered to see the tent go up within seconds of the drama.

The perpetrator of the act was drawn into the middle of the community circle while it was decided what to do with him. Some suggested the police be called in. There was strong resistance to this course of action. Others wanted to tie him up until the morning. He was wild, angry and not entirely sane as the crowd gathered from across the camp.

He lashed out at the males who confronted him. Women stepped in. Against their power he was defenceless. In the light of the raging campfire they meted out community justice. There was no recourse to the authority of society; responsibility was clearly to stay within the tribe. Carol Sherman stepped forward first. Her flowing garments in the bright colours of peace and love masked the deep anger she felt in support of a sister abused by an unthinking male. She glared into his eyes. She spat in his face. He stood transfixed as woman after woman walked up to him and spat in his face.

The spittle hung from his beard and hair, glistening in the light of the fire. Not a sound could be heard save the fire's crackling. He stood there, head down and face stern, against a raging gale: the women of Nimbin.

During the rains we took shifts to guard the forest. One day the police drove up to find half a dozen vehicles blocking Newton Drive, the main road leading into the forest. Several of them had their axles chained together. The police were not impressed, insisting that as a public road it must remain open at all times.

So the next time we were more careful. We waved as the police continued on their way up the mountain road. Our radio contacts, meanwhile, informed us of two four-wheel drives containing loggers and chainsaws parked in the valley. The police cruised back down, satisfied that there were no more barricades on the road. We waved again. Everyone in the camp then trotted up the road and removed the cattle grid. The loggers drove by. We walked up after them. They braked hard to a stop, looked back at us, executed a perfect three-point turn, both vehicles in unison, and exited. Someone quipped, "The only thing missing was the music."

Over a period of several weeks we had effectively locked the loggers out of the forest. At some stages rain helped us in our task and at other times we made it abundantly clear that only a fully equipped police contingent giving around-the-clock support would allow logging to occur in the ancient rainforest of Mount Nadi.

One day about a week after the cattle grid episode, a wizened old man appeared on the top road where we kept vigil at the gateway to the forest. Uncle Lyle showed respect for the occasion by wearing a suit and tie, but it was another kind of respect that this Aboriginal Elder of the Bunjalung tribe had to share. He told us of his forebears who were buried on this mountain, and of its sacredness for his people. Thanking us for protecting it, he then performed a dance for the mountain.

While the authorities had a monopoly on technological communications, some of our information arrived in weird and wonderful ways. A message was received that a kindergarten teacher in Grafton had overheard one child saying to another in the playground, "My daddy is going up a mountain next week to arrest hippies." We went on red alert.

verse 2 : Cops and robbers early, stealing from the forest.
Getting in before us with the law and order freize.
Grim and never speaking. Gruff and all foreboding.
Treating us like criminals for trying to save some trees!

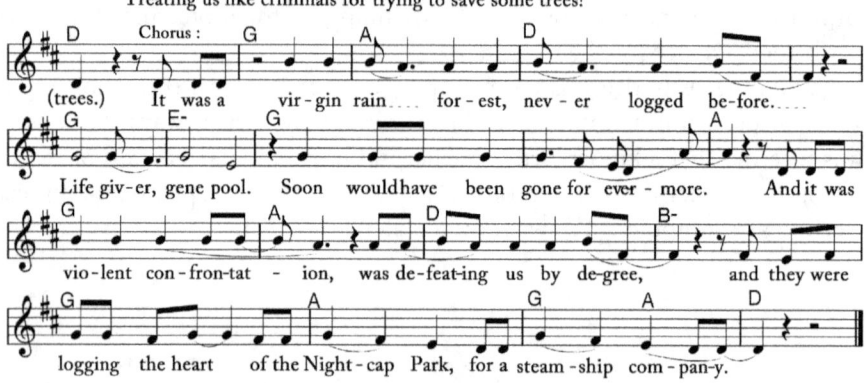

verse 3 : Little bit of mischief. Little bit of violence.
You know I couldn't get arrested ar all down there today.
And Premier Wran was watching. Voiceless in the silence,
Sometimes it seems we common people have no rights. We have no say. Chorus :

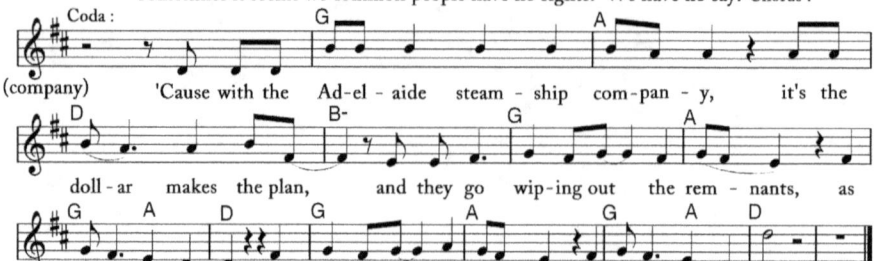

To hear this song, go to < bruce@brucemcnicol.com.au

Three hours past midnight the equipment convoy, spearheaded by a massive police contingent, pulled up at our first barricade on Newton Drive. Protesters drove an unregistered vehicle to a section of the road which was narrow and had a steep drop-off, broadsided it to a halt, locked up and disappeared into the bush as they saw the headlights of the convoy snaking up the mountain road.

Higher up the mountain, I was woken by a sentry shouting, "They're on their way up!" I jumped up, shaky from lack of sleep, hit the ignition and rolled my old truck out of the front gate, then headed downhill to the nearest cattle grid. I pulled up, locked up and jumped out.

The first police cars rounded the corner in a blaze of headlights to be confronted by a truck in the middle of the cattle grid. I approached the policeman at the head of the line and said, "G'day. It's a bit early to be working."

"Yeah," he said. "Sorry about this, but we really have to come on up."

I bade them farewell and ran off.

They tried to get into the truck with a crowbar but didn't succeed. Next they attempted to push it off the road. In all they spent nearly an hour trying to manually force it off the road. They were unsuccessful. The only good thing I have to say about English vehicles is that they're heavy.

Their next move was to get a front-end loader from down the convoy line. It lifted up the back corner of the truck and bulldozed it off the side of the road. My tactic had managed to hold the police and loggers at bay long enough to rouse the rest of the camp and allow them to create a large fire on the road as the next line of defence.

The convoy rounded the corner and was halted by an immense blaze. The camp stood behind the fire. It was still dark, and the flames leapt high, casting light on the fifty people. The front-end loader pushed the fire into the protest crowd, its headlights beaming through the smoke as it kept backing up and shovelling the barricade off the road.

The dozer completed the job as dawn broke. Police in four-wheel drives and on foot forced us back. They thought they were through until they encountered the next obstacle – the cattle grid, or rather, the lack of one. It had been pulled out and dragged off into the bushes for a second time. Too bad about the neat trail the grid ploughed into the ground. Far fewer hands dragged the railway girder construction back into place than had taken it away.

We gathered in front of the convoy and backed off as the police pushed us up the hill. They were not interested in arresting us; it would slow down their military-style juggernaut. Our plan was to hold them off long enough for media helicopters to land on the adjoining property in the morning light.

The loggers and police had six kilometres of uphill road on which to exhaust us. We hit a steep grade and decided to confront the lead vehicle, so we scrummed down and pushed against it. As the vehicle revved and tried to force its way through, clouds of smoke billowed from the clutch housing. People were pitted against machine and for the moment we were winning.

Fredericks, the head policeman, stood on the running board of a four-wheel drive, clinging on to the roof rack while directing operations. Finding himself getting pushed back, he called in reinforcements, who dragged us off the road. Job completed by his hit squad, Fredericks was about to continue, victory at hand, when the roof rack broke! He sprawled onto the roadside to the laughter of all present.

Recovering his composure, he had a laugh at himself and then continued to herd us up the road. All we could do was run with the vehicles, hoping that around every bend there would be a blockade.

Three-quarters of the way up the mountain Fredericks had the situation in hand. He had a formidable reputation: as a member of Z Force during the Second World War he had parachuted into Singapore. Once again he was playing commando in the field.

He was all smiles until we rounded one corner near the top, at which point his face turned to stone. A massive wall of flame belched black smoke from a vehicle right in the middle of the road. Fredericks kept his composure, but it was clear that in his opinion we had gone too far. The front-end loader was called in to push the blazing car into the bush. Our last blockade had fallen. The loggers erected a gate, moved the heavy equipment into a compound area and commenced building a barbed wire cyclone fence and mounting search-lights for night surveillance.

I ran down Googarna Road, which ran off Newton Drive straight into the forest logging areas, to take a look. Loggers, feeling confident after their successful ascent of the mountain, took after me. I jumped off the side of the road into the rainforest, pursued by swearing loggers. The thud of large rocks sounded nearby. I took refuge in the dark green of the forest and decided to stay hidden. I couldn't think of anything else to do; we were a spent force.

In a previous conversation with a few other greenies it had been suggested that a protester could disappear in the forest. Remembering this, I sneaked past the police encampment and took the old Nightcap trail down to Tuntable where I consulted with others that night. They agreed I should remain hidden. After the police had broken our defences so conclusively, it was felt by some that my deceit was acceptable. However, the plot came to an early end when I was spotted by the weed inspector the following day.

After many actions for which we could pride ourselves on our integrity, this was a desperate move, an act not in the spirit of our campaign. While some felt that working with police and loggers during the search was a good thing in that it put people on the same side, others accused me of having cut the energy of the protest. I was not overly popular in some quarters when I reappeared. It was debatable whether the tactic paid off.

I was delivered to Fredericks, who seemed only mildly concerned as to whether I was genuinely lost or not. He produced what interested him most: boards with four inch nails protruding from them, found on the road.

"With this you are directly attacking the police," he said without a smile. "We won't tolerate it. Tell all of your people, OK?" I replied that I would certainly pass his information along.

Loggers, trucks and police were now inside the forest and we were locked out. Word came from Sydney that our application in the Land and Environment Court was being considered, but that the judge would not grant a stay of work during the proceedings. Those who were not in the previous day's pre-dawn run went into the forest. The remainder, too sore to raise a trot, decided to sit on the road and hold up anything that passed.

A logging truck fully laden with one ancient brush box drove out. We sat tight, arms and legs tightly locked together – all except Rick, who had his legs stretched out, supposedly to block the rest of the road. The truck driver halted, then rode his clutch, thrusting the nose of his vehicle over the top of our scrum. With the weight of the load and the steep gradient of the slope, the situation was extremely dangerous.

A police four-wheel drive edged past our scrum. The steady hum of big tyres on the road was interrupted by 'Thump! Thump!' as if it were going over a speed bump. A scream rent the air. Rick's face contorted: "My legs! My legs!" He was taken directly to hospital. The remainder of us were dragged apart and arrested.

At Nimbin lockup the station was packed. Even with special facilities, staff and accommodation were severely overloaded. The scene was like an absurdist comedy with each of the arrested having his or her say in a highly original manner. These people were not the tidy greenies of future actions but the hard core alternatives who had dropped out of mainstream society many years before. One older fellow, John, was particularly reclusive, never uttering a word except in greeting. On this day however, he did make his statement. He was in the process line in front of me. I saw the harassed cop who was taking everyone's details look up and roll his eyes. Obviously he thought he had seen it all, but not this one. John stood, a silent statement of displeasure at social norms, with half his moustache shaved off. From that point on he was known to all as 'Half a Mo'.

After processing and release, we hobbled around town, beaten and weary. "POLICE RUN PROTESTER OVER!" shouted the headlines. A second submission before the Land and Environment Court at 1 pm that day saw a reversal of the morning's decision. A member of the legal fraternity paid the $10,000 bond and work was halted until the following Tuesday. It was a huge step towards victory. The logging moratorium was extended by further court action. Judge Cripps ruled that an Environmental Impact Study was necessary. Wran announced that the rainforests of New South Wales would be preserved.

At the next ALP State Conference, Premier Wran stated: "I know it was not everyone who thought it was a great thing to save the rainforest, but I make this prediction here today: when we are all dead and buried and our children's children are reflecting on what was the best thing the Labor Government did in the twentieth century, they will come up with the answer that we saved the rainforests."

Nightcap was a completion to Terania, and to a great extent the end of the logging of rainforest on public lands in New South Wales. The radical arm of the environmental movement gained an immense amount of experience and confidence as a result of this great and historic victory for the forests. The Nightcap National Park today incorporates Mount Nadi, Griers Scrub and Terania Creek, a testimony in perpetuity to a victory for the people, by the people.

CHAPTER 5
FRANKLIN
Heart of Wilderness

FOR THE RIVER

© Brenda Liddiard 1982

Mist on the river, the mountain and sky The wide ripples shimmer, as the boats wander by. The whole world is watching the wilderness war, but we don't have to ask, what are we fighting for?

CHORUS: We are here for the river. Here for the planet. Here for the forest, the place of our birth. We are here for the children, we are not an illusion. We will never allow them to kill Mother Earth.

Verse 2: Now you may think that this is some kind of game
Where the rules keep on changing, along with the names.
The faces are many. The spirits are high,
But if you think we're playing, just look in our eyes. CHORUS:

Transcribed: Bruce McNicol

In the summer of 1982, members of the Nightcap Action Group (NAG), some of whom renamed themselves the Nomadic Action Group, exited the Nightcap campaign with an historical victory and travelled to Tasmania's Franklin River Wilderness.

The northern New South Wales crew had rainforest action experience like no other group in the nation. We knew how to organise actions and deal with police. Having lived in the forests for months we descended upon the Tasmanian protest scene as experienced activists. The Tasmanian conservationists, and in particular Wilderness Society operatives, viewed us as wild people who had to be controlled. They wanted our support but were fearful of us.

The Franklin blockade was not the first protest staged over the Tasmanian Wilderness. The attempted defence of Lake Pedder in 1976 was an environmental campaign ahead of its time. Its failure and despair over the flooding of this magnificent alpine lake, gave birth to The Tasmanian Wilderness Society.

In 1982 Tasmania had a pro-dam Liberal government under Premier Robin Gray. The issue conservationists wanted to raise with the government was the proposed damming of the Franklin River by the Hydro Electric Commission (HEC), the same vandal organisation responsible for the flooding of Lake Pedder.

In June the government passed the Gordon River Hydro-Electric Power Development Act and in September it revoked large tracts of land from the Wild Rivers National Park and vested them in the HEC. These decisions outraged conservationists who in 1980 celebrated when the previous Labor government had announced that the Franklin River would be spared.

Federal by-elections throughout the nation witnessed "NO DAMS" scrawled on ballot papers. The federal Liberal government under Malcolm Fraser made a fatal mistake: it opted for states' rights rather than federal intervention to save the Wilderness. Fraser did make an attempt to assuage the Tasmanian government with a $500 million package to stop the dam. This was dismissed by Premier Gray as interference in Tasmanian affairs.

The proposed Gordon-below-Franklin Dam would inundate most of the lower Gordon River and about one-third of the Franklin River. The project would destroy the heart of the south-west Wilderness, one of the few remaining temperate Wilderness areas in the world. This potential for destruction galvanised the conservation movement across the nation.

The situation amounted to an assault on the established value systems of Australian society. Driven by a highly sophisticated media machine and charismatic leadership in the person of Dr Bob Brown, thousands of Australians from all walks of life came to the Franklin River to offer their support. Summer holidays meant that professional people, students and workers were able to participate, joining experienced forest activists and Tasmanian grass roots environmentalists, who came to stay for as long as it took to achieve victory.

The blockade was designed with a specific starting date of 14 December 1982. Protesters were instructed not to undertake any overtly illegal activities before that date. We camped on the river for several weeks and scouted the entire area, familiarising ourselves with the terrain. Some days were spent in frustration, unable to intervene as workers tore through the heart of the rainforest. We anxiously waited for action, keen to make a stand against the terrible destruction we were forced to witness in a Wilderness we were falling deeply in love with.

The first day of protest commenced amidst tumultuous media fanfare. Guides took a large number of protesters through the forest to Warner's Landing, the wharf on the east bank of the Franklin where HEC workers landed their equipment and which had been designated a prohibited zone. Our appearance did not elicit the expected reaction. The police simply kept their distance. With authorities and media afloat on the river nearby, we formed a circle in the forest to decide upon a strategy. A sense of urgency fuelled the discussion. With a quick group decision made, members of the group jumped into duckies and charged the police barracks to capitalise on the media presence. Some who intended to stay for the long haul joined in, despite pleas from those who counselled thrift. We did not want all our numbers arrested on the first day's action.

The assault on their territory sent the police into action. Amidst the roar of police boats, duckies were overturned and protesters soaked. The spray of water in that calm section of river launched an historical campaign. On the first day of the protest fifty-three people were arrested. At the same time support rallies were held in Sydney, Canberra, Bendigo, Hobart and Launceston.

Supporters started flooding the South-West of Tasmania. First stop for new arrivals was Strahan and, for those who had not completed it elsewhere, compulsory nonviolent action training at 'Greenie Acres'. This was undertaken as much as a screening process to assess the perceived suitability of participants' personalities and their equipment (according to the standards of the Wilderness Society) as it was to prepare individuals for the field. Those with children were actively discouraged from going upriver. Some activists were prevented from boarding the upriver boat, so smuggling ensued.

As one of the upriver coordinators I revelled in the vast numbers of protesters who presented themselves at the blockade site. Often it was a full boatload of fifty arrivals. The training we offered was different from that at Greenie Acres, with the emphasis on Wilderness experience. Upriver arrivals went through a quick orientation programme of a short bushwalk followed by some work to improve the camp, which had begun to resemble a wonderland. Sheltered under the full canopy, it had a network of corduroy tracks (straight sticks placed tightly together) to guard against the pervasive mud, which meandered from site to site. Tents were pitched throughout the greenery, and the more substantial camps of the long-stayers moulded into the soft surrounds of the rainforest floor. The radio shack sat on the barge which doubled as our landing area.

The function of the upriver permanents when confronted with vast numbers was to effectively utilise people in a way which best suited the fitness and sense of adventure of each affinity group. For those who were keenly intent on stopping work, an appropriate action site was the adits – the holes drilled into the side of the mountain at the dam wall site. Flanked by luxuriant rainforest ferns and trees, intermittent blasting and digging had created an ugly and barren scree slope down the steep mountain side to the river's edge, a poignant site for action. Getting there presented considerable logistic problems. Two boats were needed to foil the police; one would hide in an inlet with our volunteers, the other would take off at top speed upriver when the police water patrol came into sight. The police invariably gave chase. This allowed the hidden boat to slip ashore and off-load its human cargo. If observed, all were in danger of being arrested and having the boat impounded. For optimum effectiveness, a boat with media crews aboard was organised to cruise past at the appropriate time. From the vantage of the water a clear picture of the action was then captured for public consumption.

Fay Sutton, a long-time and well-respected activist from Sydney, was confined to a wheelchair, but with the support of a group of friends she was able to make it upriver. In a highly organised action she was boated upstream to the adit site in the early morning. With a rope around her waist she was carried from the boat and set in a strategic position on a fallen log near the tunnel. When workers arrived, Fay was atop that scree slope, surrounded by banners and flags. The police asked her to get on her feet.

The wheelchair was then produced. Getting her down seemed an impossible task. Finally a stretcher was ordered, and Fay was strapped in and transported to a specially convened night court in Strahan.

For the robust walkers of the group a favoured action was a hike to the helipads. These were landing areas which facilitated the daily arrival of HEC workers from their base camp to areas too distant for other forms of transport. For protesters, the end of the hike was followed by a magical night in the Wilderness. A short walk the next morning and the occupation of the helipad invariably led to arrest. A high tally of arrests was vital for media purposes in the overall campaign.

While high adventure and exertion suited some, there were many others who preferred to register their protest in a more genteel manner. For those supporters we had the connoisseur's arrest site: St John's Falls, a famous landmark on the Gordon River and a site which had been excised from the National Park and placed into the HEC forbidden territory. For many Tasmanians, particularly the older generation, it was considered the ultimate insult to be denied access. A favoured romantic haunt for arrestable couples, most took a picnic lunch to savour all that the site had to offer before the long arm of the law reached into their sanctuary.

Delivering these demonstrators to the site became a regular activity.

First we would cruise around nearby Butler's Island in a boat loaded with passengers, as if on a casual sight-seeing tour, and wait until the police were out of sight, or at least had their backs turned. We then proceeded with a discreet drop of passengers and their picnic hampers. That achieved, I would approach the police with, "Do you like lobster?" In response to their often quizzical looks I'd say, "Well, if you hurry you'll catch a bit of lunch before you arrest them." With a diligence borne of the quest for an easy arrest or an exotic tasty morsel, off they would go to capture their quarry.

The latter would be reclining on the smooth rock by the waterfall, blissfully relaxed. Some even had white lace tablecloths and fine glassware from which to sip champagne.

Late at night I would often help the adventurers settle down in what for them were alien circumstances. Few would have slept under, beside or in a fallen log before, but invariably these were the best positions from which to string a fly. Having settled them in, I would then head back to base. As a porter I did not carry my own sleeping gear.

One night, after leaving such a group, I made my way back to a rendezvous point for a ride across the river. All was going well until I came to an area behind Warner's Landing, normally a favourite location where a delicate rainforest stream trickled over soft, mossy terraces. Surrounded by giant tree ferns, it was an exquisite altar to the beauty of nature. On this night there was a transformation which hit me like a punch in the guts. The familiar landmarks were gone; the surrounds were alien and stark. I fell into a gravel ditch where once there had been that little stream. Ice-cold water cut at my thighs. I scrambled up the other side over a high pile of gravel and rotting uprooted ferns. A caravan was nearby with a green bulldozer parked beside it, silently mocking the beauty it had destroyed that day.

I escaped the destruction, relieved to find familiar forest tracks. In a thick maze of rainforest understorey my torch faded and inky blackness descended; I couldn't see my hands in front of my face. The best I could do was to scrape leaves around me and lie down on the forest floor to wait the night out.

At the first light of dawn I headed off I was moving quickly to warm up, but felt low. With depression sapping the strength from my body I climbed the last hill. From the summit a breathtaking riverine rainforest stretched out before me, with early morning mist entwined in the highest trees. The silent grey river was an artist's brushstroke through the intense forest green. My spirits soared as the first morning sun turned a distant perched lake into a shield of burnished gold. The far off cheering of greenies was the only sound. From my vantage point I heard another set of cheers followed by yet another further down river. Evidently the protesters were taking up their positions in a coordinated effort to stretch the police resources. I trotted home, laughing like a madman, alone in the Wilderness, restored.

Primed by the media campaign and the task of making it to the Wilderness camp, the protesters' enthusiasm was immense. Participants ranged from earnest, honest citizenry to so-called radical tricksters. Others were there to discover a new way of dealing with life by adopting the semi – religious processes of nonviolent action training, or NVA as it was called. These 'cadres' were appropriately equipped and anointed by the new elite of high priests and priestesses: NVA trainers. Their perceived task was to radically transform society, save the planet and be at peace with everyone and everything in the process.

The radicals, however, defined their purpose differently. Analysis of past political experiences taught them that it was important to deal with situations creatively and to maximise opportunities in defence of the Wilderness. The feeling was that thousands of years of destructive human – centred thinking needed a revolutionary about-face if an environmental holocaust was to be avoided. At best the radicals were a powerful extreme wing of the environmental movement, prepared to undertake tasks and survive for long periods in conditions which saw moderates head home after a few weeks. At worst they were a motley crew, abrasive and angry constantly overstepping the mark – a disruption to the hard-fought gains of the mainstream groups.

There were those of a strongly individualist bent. Rod from Victoria was one. He discussed his tactics but organised his own action, with attention to the smallest detail. One morning he borrowed a surfboard and sneaked over to Warner's Landing where he hid and timed the arrival of the bulldozer driver: early start, then a cup of tea as the machine warmed up.

Ten minutes would be just long enough for a greenie to slip inside the idling dozer and lock himself in. Rod worked diligently during the day to perfect the action. He didn't eat that night to ensure an embarrassing need would not arise during his anticipated occupation.

Early next morning he paddled off and stashed the board in the undergrowth. When the dozer started up, Rod, with the confidence of prior knowledge, trotted across the clearing, entered the dozer and proceeded to lock the doors with padlocks and chains. The dozer driver returned to find a smiling greenie behind the wheel. He was not happy. Rod's cheerful security was short-lived, however, as the fellow, as burly as Rod was thin, pulled out a penknife, removed the windscreen rubber, the windscreen and then Rod. The worker escorted him to the radio and reported the capture of a greenie. This time Rod's size worked to his advantage and he slipped away.

The skills available within the campaign were not necessarily amateur. The night before St Valentine's Day, Lisa Yeates was approached by an individual more experienced than the average greenie. "I can go anywhere and do anything you want," he said. At first, Lisa didn't quite comprehend, so he continued, "Anything you want done to machinery, plant, worksites or police equipment. I was in the SAS in Vietnam." Here, upriver, was someone trained for guerilla warfare and sabotage, offering his services. Lisa became interested.

She relates: "The blockade was well into its second month; we needed new angles, so I was loath to dismiss his skills out of hand, even though they contradicted our commitment to nonviolence. With St Valentine's Day approaching we thought it might boost morale to present the blockaders with a 'love-heart'. This required forward planning – after all, we were five hours by boat from the nearest settlement [Strahan] .

Having previously arranged for a reliable soul to send us red and pink crepe paper on the transport boat, the J-Lee-M, friends and I cut out chains of hearts. So I rushed to my tent, grabbed a bundle of hearts and returned to my co-conspirator. With face blackened and wearing camouflage clothes, he paddled upriver in a canoe towards the police camp and worksites.

Some time later he returned looking weary but elated. "Mission accomplished," he reported. At the police camp he had placed a heart on every moored boat, on the end of their beds and in their caps. At St John's Falls a heart was left near the police water supply inlet. Hearts decorated helipads, the adits and bulldozer seats. Our message was clear. "You fear us and accuse us of potential eco-terrorism. We could sabotage. We have the ability, but we choose not to," Lisa related. Expertise of another kind came with the arrival of Dr David Bellamy, a British botanist of international renown. With his ebullient personality he gave the camp great support.

While he was at the Franklin he shot a documentary which showed him popping out of hollow logs and giant tree ferns like a character in a Tolkien novel.

Bellamy had travelled to Australia with the publicly stated intention of getting arrested for the Wilderness. When it was time for his arrest, a plan to foil the authorities was hatched. We needed media directly on hand

to gain the international coverage Bellamy could generate. Deployment of a decoy seemed to be the most appropriate tactic. Finding a suitable look – alike amongst the mainly thin and young blockaders was no simple task.

One was eventually found who could pass as his son. With padding and grey paint generously administered, a functional look-alike emerged.

On land, synchronised groups moved towards the bulldozer. This distracted the police guard on the shoreline. While the Bellamy decoy motored around in the rain, flinging his arms and expostulating in a most professorial manner, another boat slipped ashore at Warner's Landing with a media crew aboard. The real David Bellamy was hidden under a tarpaulin. Out he jumped onto restricted land. He was grabbed by a police officer, a diminutive presence by comparison to the botanist. Bellamy told him to wait a minute (a rare criminal who says that to an arresting copper!) and turned to the now-assembled media to state his case to the world with typical effervescence.

The Franklin protest was primarily 'theatre on the river', and Benny Zable, our resident artist, revelled in this. His costume had become a familiar image of the Australian anti-nuclear and environment movement – a foreboding figure attired in black robes and a gasmask. The message on the front of his robes was chilling: "CONSUME, BE SILENT, DIE. I RELY ON YOUR APATHY." The colourful extravaganza of banners and flags which blazed across the world's media networks were, in great part, the result of Benny's labours. His banners festooned the communication barge, duckies and the J-Lee-M. Most spectacular were his visual arts displays on Butlers Island. With any major event, Benny and a specialist crew would decorate the island with banners. When the first dozer arrived by barge it broke a line of yellow duckies and passed by a riot of colour which proclaimed life in the face of advancing destruction.

When the protest camp was dark and silent and most participants asleep after a gruelling day, a faint shaft of light could be seen projecting from the art tent. A closer inspection would invariably find Benny, bent over in the poor light of the hurricane lamp, meticulously creating a banner. Often he would work until he was so exhausted he couldn't even crawl into his sleeping bag. One morning he was found wrapped in the unpainted section of his banner, which read: "IN WILDERNESS IS THE PRESERVATION OF THE WORLD." (Thoreau).

A handful of politicians made the trek to the Wilderness in a show of solidarity. The leader of the Opposition, Bill Hayden, visited the upriver camp and reaffirmed Labor's commitment to stopping the dam. Another Labor Party politician, Susan Ryan, motored upriver with explorer Dick Smith to offer support – in a fashion. That night it rained heavily. I approached the boat, which was moored at our barge. Soft candlelight shone through windows half fogged up from the warmth inside. I moved closer. Like a Dickensian character, saturated and shivering, I watched as explorer and parliamentarian in casual attire sipped after-dinner wine together – my first glimpse of 'civilisation' after a month in the Wilderness. I marvelled at their comfort, then trudged off in the mud knowing where I'd rather be.

Don Chipp, the leader of the Democrats, also spent a number of days living at the camp. I was asked to boat him to police headquarters; he wished to speak to the officer in charge. As police liaison, a few days earlier I had been angrily evicted from police grounds by the same officer, Inspector Chugg, under threat of arrest should I return. Chipp asked if we were acquainted and introduced me to Chugg. The inspector grunted an acknowledgment that we had met before.

On his first tour of inspection of the upriver site, Chugg had the 'pleasure' of meeting us. He was at the border of enclosed land. We boated over to complain about a track which had been senselessly chainsawed by workers a few days earlier up a previously untouched rainforest valley. I requested him to inspect the site where workers had broken the law by felling logs over creeks

Terania – Machinery under police guard rips into rainforest
(Darcy McFadden, Northern Star)

Terania giant
(Elsebeth Nielsen)

Terania –
A one-long truck
(Graham Riley)

Middle Head – Symbolic sacrifice

Middle Head – Protesters in dredge path
(A. Arnoldijs)

Nightcap – Stop-work meeting
(Edwin Buivids)

Nightcap – Cultural clash
(Graham Riley)

Nightcap Communications Centre
(Elsebeth Nielsen)

Franklin upriver base camp – Landing pontoons/radio shack
(Edwin Buivids)

Franklin – Heavy equipment barage runs duckie 'picket line'
(Edwin Buivids)

Franklinp – Frist bulldozer offloaded in Wilderness (Edwin Buivids)

Franklin – Daily duckie vigil
(Edwin Buivids)

Franklin – Police grab greenie flotilla
(Edwin Buivids)

as bridges for their convenience. He informed me that it was HEC property to do with as they liked, extinguishing our relevance.

In my role as police liaison I confronted the force with determination. Entertaining eyewitness accounts of my evolving relationship with the inspector established support for my position.

Unlike other campaigns, the drawn-out nature of the Franklin blockade, with its vast numbers of participants, stretched police resources to the limit. The Franklin action, more than any other in the history of the conservation movement, publicly challenged the state. It became a stylised confrontation between the police as the state's enforcement representatives and the conservation movement.

On 24 November 1982 the Tasmanian government amended the Police Offences Act in response to blockade plans, making trespass an arrestable offence. This was a similar move to that made in New South Wales just months before in response to the Nightcap actions.

The Tasmanian Police were mustered in huge numbers from around the state. They became a major focus for media and NVA participants who espoused their often newfound cause with missionary zeal. In short, the police copped the lot. They were, by and large, similar to any cross-section of male working society and exhibited a variety of reactions to a very new dimension of law enforcement activity – dealing with sincere and peaceful people in a social and political event of massive proportions. This placed immense pressure on their resources and on the personal realities of individuals.

It was, for many of them, an 'other worldly' experience. They had never encountered the nonviolent philosophy and accompanying forest strategies. The normally quiet backwaters of Tasmania reverberated with peaceful yet confronting communication.

On one occasion a cop was caught with his pants down – defecating in the splendour of the Wilderness. A greenie trespasser happened by, admonished him for not digging a hole and escaped from lawful custody.

Much of Australian society supported this greenie law-breaker. A deeply historic distrust of authority and an awakening of national pride in our natural treasures created the alchemy for social change.

Police and protester, face to face, represented the forced meeting of two groups normally poles apart. On the one hand were the upholders of the status quo, and on the other were the new flag bearers of a minority tradition in a society asserting itself as never before. The police squared off in a pose of distrust, backed up by their training. Experienced protesters similarly had an enormous distrust of law enforcement organisations and their role in the power of the state. The movement was, however, prepared to work with the police and respect them when appropriate.

We were pitted against a police force acting as functionaries of a conservative and antagonistic government. Our aims were to cost the state as much as possible, keep within NVA guidelines and maintain the interest of the media. Our survival upriver depended in great part on the success of the Tasmanian Wilderness Society's maintenance of national and international support.

The Franklin campaign was managed with an extremely tight rein by the Wilderness Society, but many events occurred which did not reach the media. At worst, rumours emanated from the upriver camp to surface as waking nightmares in the Society's offices of Strahan and Hobart. These politically coloured variations of the original deed were often carried out by self-interested and mischievous parties in the greatest traditions of palace intrigue.

However, such uncontrolled dissemination of information did work to our advantage at times. One undeserving casualty of our unscrupulous media behaviour was the officer known to us as the red-headed cop (an obvious yet superficial label for the man). We debated the merits of our respective roles. He had strong conservative views and presented them well; he expressed greater pleasure in fishing dammed lakes as the catch tended to be bigger and more plentiful. I likened that to angling in a fishbowl.

During one action, which involved blockading the equipment barge, I was foiled from delivering my eminently arrestable crew mid-stream by the cop in question. He towed us to the river's edge and pulled the bungs out of our inflatable raft. A spirited attempt by the crew to prevent him from removing the bungs caused him to lose his temper (that red hair again) and threaten to knife our ducky. The incident made headlines in the following day's media, out of all proportion to the nature of the incident. I had some regrets about being so Machiavellian. He must have regretted not arresting me after he read the newspapers.

Against superior police transport we were able to move to areas presumed inaccessible, travelling overland and often at night. Police resources were stretched to the limit when greenies appeared in three places at once – Warner's Landing, the dam site and the adits. The reaction was greater utilisation of resources to manage the situation. Helicopters flew into inaccessible areas to arrest protesters. This resulted in either long marches out or the possible return of arrestees by air. Often we simply set the scene; the boys with the toys added the extras which made the spectacle.

Life was often hell out there hiding from the ex-Vietnam copter pilot. His gung-ho tactics worked to our advantage at sites where people wished to get arrested. He was known to fly in low, lights flashing, hover several feet above ground as the squad of police jumped out in military precision to grab grannies.

One day the Challenger (an ocean liner) returned to Strahan virtually empty at huge expense. This was due to one policeman entrusting me with the function of efficient conduit for accurate information. I told him that we were going to have a major offensive, hence the arrival of the cruise ship.

Despite close media scrutiny and the active concern of our office counterparts, there were times that police action was inexcusable.

The day after the Challenger returned empty the police made more than fifty arrests, which swamped their more meagre resources. The weather was foul, even by South-West Tasmanian standards, and in order to relieve themselves of the burden of so many cold and hungry people who had to be transported to Queenstown several hours away, the police attempted to give them police bail and release them on the spot. The protesters decided not to accept that situation, fearing that it would set a precedent. The police threatened to drag them off to the protest camp.

Finally, those who were closest to hypothermia were taken by boat to Strahan. Without food, soaked through and exposed to abominable conditions on deck, they were furthermore subjected to the ridicule of a number of police. One officer, breaking a direct command, put his job on the line: he took those who were suffering the most inside and gave them hot drinks. Considering the mood of the police in charge, it was a brave act.

The Franklin action was set apart from all others by virtue of its size and duration. Instead of fleeting communication with police, as happens at every action, a pattern was set up over the months. Anxiety, alienation and formality characterised the arrival of a new police shift, often fuelled by propaganda and rumours. On arrival there was no reaction to our friendly but cheeky waves as we cooled our feet at the river's edge. Intense confrontation ensued. Their role and value systems were constantly questioned in a manner for which they were ill-trained. Personal contact with us as diverse people coupled with the all-powerful backdrop of the Wilderness broke down their barriers to the extent that senior police had to round up younger members who stayed too long communicating with us in the late afternoon.

Action was often punctuated by relaxed evenings, backdropped by Wilderness sunsets of inspiring beauty. A greenie, quietly canoeing at sunset, would wave to an off-duty cop idling by with a fishing line trailing from his police boat. Shifts were waved out with a considerable degree of reciprocated friendliness.

There were those hard cases in the force used to dealing with the seamier elements of society who had set one-liners to cut any communication. One such case was a sergeant from Hobart, unused to the bush and resentful that he had been removed from his inner-city tasks. He was extremely antagonistic. Every time I attempted to talk to him he would stare me down and cut me off in mid-sentence, saying, "You're wasting your time, we are different animals. We just don't belong to the same species."

One day by the river's edge, after numerous aborted attempts, the seemingly impossible gap was overcome. The issue was marijuana and the point of agreement was the concept of decriminalisation. I'm not sure who was the most surprised. Shortly afterwards he began telling greenies, "Call me Sergeant Tom."

The process was sufficiently expansive and creative to accommodate the personal growth of all involved. One such cop, nicknamed the Lone Ranger, was becoming the bane of the existence of those not wishing to be arrested. He was confronted one day in the darkest recesses of the forest by members of the most hard-bitten greenie crew from northern New South Wales, including Winniatta, a gay Maori warrior. The bush cop attacked Winniatta, who broke a guitar over the Lone Ranger's head. In this confrontation, far from the media's eyes, not the guitar but the highly charged communication broke the cop down to a state of tearful confession. He admitted that he felt intensely alone, alienated from his workmates. Unable to be a part of the social scene, and maintaining his rugged individualist image, he lived in an isolated hell.

The fate of the Franklin balanced precariously for the duration of the blockade. Protesters and police stood on the edge of that precipice. We formed unlikely associations, even friendships. All participants were feeling their way into the unknown. The growth of acceptance by authority structures regarding citizens' rights of expression was an essential step towards a sustainable future. Police and protester relations during the Franklin blockade made a small but significant contribution towards a society which could cope with the unexpected, was prepared to be disrupted and able to be transformed.

Few were more confronting than Celia, seventy years of age, tall and elegant, with long silver hair flowing over her black raincoat. She arrived at the Wilderness camp and set up a small tent by the river, lending lie to the notion that one had to be young to survive the rigours of the Wilderness. Blending with moss and myrtle, she spent several weeks by the river.

Often, bolt upright, she paddled her rubber duckie upstream for a kilometre and spent hours in vigil along with other new arrivals. The job of these supporters was to bear witness to the destruction and communicate information to the coordinators, where possible, as bulldozers gouged further into the area around Warner's Landing. At day's end, cold and wet, Celia paddled with the group back to camp.

Almost daily she approached me, requesting that I take her on a useful expedition. "I want to go out and stop the work," she'd say. "What about those chainsaw operators cutting tracks all over the forest?" My responses were often terse. I felt guilty; she was right. I was aware that while most of what we were staging was a clever media extravaganza, our actions on the river were not affecting chainsaw operators cutting into the Wilderness unhindered. I did not want to be arrested: my primary task was to guide people to various sites and we were constantly short of guides.

Experienced campaigners spent days showing prospective guides the routes to protest sites, problems with the terrain and the boundaries of the HEC's territory. Often, when this training was completed, the guides, in their zeal to witness the action, would end up arrested.

Commands arrived by courier from downriver. We were not to confront trackcutters under any circumstances. Rumours about these mavericks in the wild had sparked great fears in the Strahan Wilderness Society office. The cutters were contractors; any hold-up to their work schedule would directly cost them money unlike the waged HEC workers. The Wilderness Society felt that the likelihood of assault and injury was high and that this would reflect badly on the campaign. Those upriver were frustrated by what was seen as out-of-touch guidance from afar. We demanded a degree of autonomy.

I pondered the responsibility of taking Celia such a distance into the forest. When she approached me yet again with her request, to her
surprise and satisfaction I responded, "Celia, would you like to take a journey upriver?" We decided to confront the trackcutters. The controversial nature of such an action necessitated an infallible nonviolent strategy against these supposed hotheads.

Celia's excitement did little to assuage my doubts on many safety factors. Nevertheless, the die was cast. Celia and I would be part of a small group to hike to the chainsaw operators, who were cutting through the Wilderness at an alarming rate. This work was part of the HEC's latest project, which involved cutting a grid of 'transects' through the forest in order to survey the area for suitable drilling and helipad sites. All of this was being done in the cheapest, most efficient (and as a result most destructive) manner because, according to their plan, it was all going to be submerged.

We boated to Verandah Cliffs, our forward camp, and slept the night there. Our plan was to hike across country, find the transects, intercept the workers and halt their activities until they were picked up by helicopter at the end of the day.

Early the following morning the group set off. Through long grasses, muddy fields and dense scrub we pushed, guided by map and compass. Celia kept up with a pace that would have troubled many people half her age. We hiked for several hours until confronted by a massive wall of horizontal growth. This forest is a hazard common in the Tasmanian South-West. It consists of thick, maze-like branches which form a mass of impenetrable patterns, necessitating one to climb over the top of it, several metres above ground. What could I say to Celia? How could I ask someone of grand age to come swing in the monkey bars, performing climbing tricks in an area possibly never traversed by people of our culture? Lost for words, I looked at her.

"My legs are a little weak," she said. "I have trouble lifting them up high, but I'm really quite strong in my arms and can lift my legs over the branches as I go," she said. So, with Celia's reassurance, we clambered over nature's elevated pathway.

Midday passed us by. Our energies flagged as we wondered where we were; we did not want to retrace our tracks over the obstacle course we had just accomplished. Time was becoming a critical factor. We still had to find the transects and get back to the warmth and shelter of the camp within the day. Having previously (accidentally) extended a number of day trips into overnight stays, I did not wish to be responsible for a repetition of such an action. We stopped for lunch. As we ate, a quiet depression overtook the group.

A faint scream sounded in the distance. Was it wind? The faraway sound of chainsaws tearing into the Wilderness floated over us again. We jumped up, hurriedly packed and set off. Our target was at hand. I ran up the slope, meaning to save Celia difficult climbs in the wrong direction.

Instead I had to race to keep up with her. The shrieking grew louder. We could now hear the motor idling between cuts. Closer still and two deep voices could be heard calmly talking as they methodically went about their job, untouched by the controversy exploding nationally and even worldwide.

I moved ahead to warn the cutters of our presence in their felling area. I issued a friendly, "G'day how ya going," from the mossy depths.

"Bloody greenie bastard!" yelled one of the cutters. "Where are you? What the hell are you doing out here? I'll wring your scrawny neck!" I stepped out of the cool wall of green and politely said, "Now, gentlemen, be careful of what you're saying. I'm just here to introduce you to someone very special."

Chainsaw and voices stopped. Anger faded to dismay as Celia appeared, her hair stuck to her forehead from the exertion, twigs and leaves entangled like a wild crown in her grey wisps. She stepped out of the forest cover and across the broken earth. Twigs cracked loudly underfoot in the cool, now-silent Wilderness. The arms of a mother swept around this logger. She gave him a big hug, held his face in her hands and said, "You are such a handsome young man. How can you possibly do this type of work?" He swayed slightly, a boyish grin from ear to ear. A nervous chuckle escaped his lips as he looked for where to look. Six inches from her eyes he had nowhere to go. "Would you like a cup of tea?" he asked politely.

Soon we were all enjoying high tea for the matriarch of the forest. It was welcome relief and a moment of sharing after a gruelling journey.

Another member of our group extracted a string of paper flowers from her pocket. The men mutely acquiesced as paper garlands were hung around their necks and their pictures were taken beside the sleeping chainsaws. We talked the afternoon away: two loggers with families to support, fears for the future and a desire both for employment and community respect.

A helicopter zoomed in from nowhere to pick the loggers up. We greenies bolted for the bush in case of police. Once on our own again, the immediate problem became finding our campsite before dark. I ran ahead and found a midway camp staffed by a person who was none too keen to give over all his supplies to a marauding party of lost souls, so I asked him to keep them at the camp while I procured food and bedding from upstream.

Off I charged, a zealot on a life-saving mission. It was a race against the dark. Just as night enveloped me, the flickering light of the campfire appeared. Verandah Cliffs – an appropriate name as my foot stepped into blackness and found nothing solid underneath it.

Upon arrival at the camp I loaded up a boat and set off downstream with food and bedding. To preserve my torch I paddled in the pitch dark of a moonless night. The sky was overhung with heavy clouds, so not even the stars were able to show the way. I had asked my companions to leave a light at my destination. It seemed as if I'd paddled an eternity. Doubts crept into my mind as to whether they'd left a fire. Had I sailed by in the dark – heading, complete with pot of food and bedding, to the next rapids downriver? I heard the distinct sound of rushing water. The intensity of the Wilderness bore down with immense power on this little greenie. Would the river sweep me into its maelstrom, gone forever, with nothing but a floating pot to tell the tale?

Fumbling hands turned on the torch as the noise of roaring water and thoughts of impending personal tragedy exploded in my mind. Flotsam was passing by, the result of the turbulence that lay ahead. Penlight between teeth, I was ready. But wait, the flotsam was going the wrong way... No! *I* was going the wrong way. I had spent the last hour paddling upstream towards the rapids higher up. For the next hour of paddling I was able to contemplate the role of the hero.

When I finally arrived at the makeshift camp, my friends reluctantly emerged from a tent and ate a small amount of the food. I later discovered that everyone had been well fed and tucked up in bed together for warmth. Most did not want to emerge, but did so at Celia's insistence because I had gone to so much trouble.

The announcement of 'Green Day' on 1 March was designed to give an extra boost to media interest in the waning stages of the campaign. The publicly stated objective was to flood the Wilderness with greenies in such numbers that we would take over the HEC operations from that point onwards, stopping all work. I approached Inspector Chugg to discuss protocol for the coming event. He was of the opinion that the police were not there to protect demonstrators from danger, since we were deliberately breaking the law. I argued that it was the police role to consider safety as a primary concern with the option of arresting those who offended. He stated that as we deliberately put ourselves outside the law, our safety became an individual responsibility and original concepts of police function were not appropriate. l likened that to a policeman arriving at the scene of a road accident and taking to hospital only the driver who had the right of way. I was summarily dismissed from Chugg's court with the parting shot that anyone swimming in the river would be arrested. For us, arrests would be the icing on the cake of a successful day's media action.

One could well understand that Chugg was mortally offended at having to enter into negotiations with 'the criminal element'. We suspected that he was still rankled by the trap we had led him into the day before when we enticed him to chase greenies around the area of the proposed dam wall. We called in the media at the most compromising time for perfect footage of a clumsy inspector in a frenzy of pursuit in the lush rainforest understorey. As a media guide I remained respectfully quiet, of course.

Most arrests were made under the laws of trespass on enclosed lands. Except for Chugg's imposed conditions on Green Day. The rivers were free, a neutral territory where the best the police could do was some mild harassment of those in boats for breaches of safety regulations.

However, if one were so much as to step onto the bank declared prohibited zone, arrest was automatic.

Green Day saw waves of protesters rush ashore. Others roamed on the land, avoiding police and workers. A media helicopter circled, at which point a group dived into the drink to entice Chugg into action. He stood at the bow of his command ship like Bonaparte on the ramparts, signalling to his officers to arrest various people as they swam amidst the police and work boats. They captured some of us, but not all, as we forced the police boats in circles.

Chugg was oppressive, but beneath the authoritative exterior he was suffering from emasculation. His role was attacked in a radical fashion and

he suffered from a profound inability to laugh at himself or his newfound position in a society at least momentarily transformed.

Despite his 'stiff upper lip' attitude, Chugg was quite a dancer. On one day of mass arrests, Chugg appeared among the prisoners on the deck of the Challenger to check behaviour. One disrespectful felon tossed a packet of firecrackers under his feet. The consensus was that his sense of rhythm and timing was impeccable.

Our upriver actions were all-consuming, but we were constantly aware that the forest blockade was the major focus for the looming federal election campaign.

In a resounding victory for the conservation movement, Hawke's Labor stormed into office in March 1983. Huddled around a campfire upriver, we listened over the static on our transistor radio as Hawke announced that the Franklin Dam would not go ahead. We were euphoric – until we learned that the work would not immediately stop. In a shock announcement, the blockade was called off by the Wilderness Society, without any consultation with those involved at the ground level in the campaign. Those upriver knew that without the pressure of continuing protest, destruction could continue for months (and it did). The Tasmanian government challenged the new federal government in the High Court. The air force was used in a controversial move to spy on the activities in the Wilderness. It became a states' rights issue, destined to drag on.

Meanwhile, the industrial juggernaut continued. In a frenzy of defiance, bulldozers maintained their assault on the Wilderness. In answer to our pleas to continue the blockade, The Wilderness Society, forever fearful of upriver radicals, acted decisively. They sent up the J-Lee-M and loaded the communications barge with all their equipment. Like a nightmare, we watched as our life-support systems sailed downriver.

On 11 March I went to Hobart to present our case to The Wilderness Society. I was ushered into the office of the treasurer, who admonished me for not paying $750 lost in unpaid food supplies as a result of the forced closure of the base camp by the authorities. I apologetically told her I would attempt to collect the money. A few days later a short-term deposit of over $100,000 in the name of The Wilderness Society matured, paying all campaign expenses and leaving them with a surplus. This information I learnt later. I wrote an article pleading our case for a continued blockade in The Wilderness Society newsletter. Those involved had promised to include it in the next issue. It never appeared. They had lied to my face, and I was bitterly disappointed. Those upriver with a different but equally valid point of view were disempowered. We wanted to continue the campaign until the destruction ceased; the Wilderness Society preferred to suffer continued destruction than allow action to continue.

Hierarchical centralised power won, with devastating consequences. Upriver, in a rage against the Labor Party victory, HEC workers attacked a magnificent Huon pine, estimated to be between two and three thousand years old. From the ancient mound, built up over millennia of standing in one place, the tree leaned like a Tower of Pisa.

They cut into it with chainsaws. Too big to fell, they drilled holes, poured in sump oil and set it ablaze. The tree burned for weeks.

Eventually a vigil was permitted by the Wilderness Society. Those who remained documented the continuing destruction. They withstood worsening conditions as winter approached and witnessed snow falling on the Franklin. They hid from workers and police keen to 'bag a greenie'.

Their job was to photograph and document the continuing destruction, a task which was critical to court processes.

The final victory occurred at the highest legal level in the nation. On 1 July 1983 the High Court of Australia – in what has been dubbed by the media as the 'constitutional fight of the century' – ruled that the Commonwealth Government had the power to halt the construction of the Franklin Dam. Those at the vigil witnessed heavy machinery being barged back to Strahan.

The campaign concluded with monumental political momentum yet, undeniably it was a great victory for people power. Left in the hands of the politicians, the Tasmanian Wilderness was doomed. Conservationists had deftly moved the centre stage to the magnificence of the South-West; in the media, grey suits and bland political palliatives were replaced by heavy equipment, police uniforms and thousands of gentle people. It was a dance of life against industrial death on the glorious stage of the Wilderness. It was a lesson in the art of changing the values of society.

Environmentalists preceded mass opinion and ultimately succeeded in establishing that power.

At last, victory was complete. It was a time of rejoicing throughout Australia. Those upriver, with their camps of blockade leftovers and meagre little shelters held together with gaffer tape, had reason to feel proud. They, along with thousands of others, had worked long and hard, suffered under intense conditions and communicated with their hearts on behalf of the Wilderness. A wild river now flows free.

CHAPTER 6
DAINTREE
Paradise Lost?

Verse 2   It's time the people realised what's going on,

'Cause it will be too late when the last trees are gone.

Don't they think that it's important to their lives

Whether the Earth lives or dies? CHORUS :

Verse 3   So come and join us in our fight (don't be afraid).

Come and join us while there's something left to save.

People power is the greatest weapon yet.

Why don't we put it to the test? CHORUS :

Note : Originally written by Brenda as Save the Franklin   Transcribed : Bruce McNicol

Australia's last major expanse of tropical rainforest is found near Cape Tribulation in Queensland's north. Here, mountains more than 600 metres high fall directly to the sea where the luxuriant rainforest meets the coral reefs of the Great Barrier Reef. Two major rivers, the Bloomfield and the Daintree, define the northern and southern limits of this unique area which boasts two of the most complex communities on earth – the rainforest and the reef.

Until recent decades, the preservation of this region rested with the fact that the mountainous terrain and difficult access prohibited the cultivation of sugar cane and the grazing of cattle, the two rural activities most responsible for rainforest destruction in Queensland. In the early 1980s, however, real estate interests threatened to destroy what remained of the virgin lowland rainforest.

In 1980 a World Heritage Conference focused attention on the region. As the northern-most extremity of the tropical humid zone (the Wet Tropics) in Australia, the Daintree-Bloomfield rainforests harbour several plant and animal species unique to the transition zone between the humid tropics and monsoon zones. One mammal, the Bennett's Tree Kangaroo, is restricted to the area, and many birds exclusively inhabit the rainforests in the region. Of plants there are not only a great number but a huge variety of species. Many primitive plants found in the area are rare or non-existent in other rainforests in Queensland.

The Queensland government responded to the World Heritage findings in 1981 by setting aside a limited area to create the Cape Tribulation National Park. The concept of a Greater Daintree National Park was also suggested at the conference and later submitted by the Australian Conservation Foundation to the Queensland government; the proposal was rejected.

Despite the protection granted to the area, the environment remained under threat. The proposed building of a connecting road through the National Park from Cape Tribulation north to Bloomfield, which would rip up 33 kilometres of lowland forest Wilderness, saw the formation of the Cairns and Far North Environment Centre as a base for conservationists dedicated to protecting the environment. It was feared that clearing along the mountainous coastal fringe would result in land destabilisation, resulting in landslide sears and topsoil entering the reef environment.

The notion of building a road was not a new one. On five separate occasions since 1935 the Minister for Main Roads had been asked by the local council to investigate the road proposal. Each time the Minister had recommended against it on the grounds that it was neither technically nor economically feasible. By 1983, after nearly fifty years of petitioning, the Douglas Shire Council was granted permission to go ahead with the road, With full backing from the Minister for the Environment, Martin Tenni, the Minister for National Parks, Peter McKechnie, and Premier Joh Bjelke – Petersen. The reasons for its construction were unclear. In answer to reasoned arguments, Martin Tenni and Douglas Shire Chairman, Tony Mijo, stated that the road contributed to the military defence of Australia's north. This was despite the fact that the army had declined to build it. Tenni and Mijo's main claim was that the road had the potential to reduce the traffic of drugs, to control illegal immigrants and to stamp out the white slave trade.

The only hope for the rainforest lay in federal government intervention, and direct action was a tool to force their hand.

In 1983 a small number of locals decided to make a stand at Cape Tribulation at the southern end of the park. They were a mixed group – young hippies, respectable citizens, elderly conservationists – but in their determination to save the Daintree they formed a united community. They disseminated information to gain support, but little was forthcoming. The reputation of the State police meant that few conservationists were game enough to respond to the call for help from those in Queensland's deep north. Moreover the location was remote and the preparation time non – existent: bulldozers had already crossed the Daintree River.

From previous campaigns I knew what it was like to be in isolation hoping for support. Determined to get up north, I asked the Wilderness Society for an airfare to Daintree. "The situation does not warrant it yet," I was told. This was despite the fact that heavy equipment was being moved into the area. Luckily an activist, Liz Denharn, arrived at the office, listened to my story, gave me the money and wished me well on the trip. I flew to Cairns and hitched directly to the blockade site to link up with local activists.

For several days the work crew and police arrived, only to turn back when confronted by our blockade at the road which ended at the southern border of the Cape Tribulation National Park. During the stand-off the forest remained intact, but when the police arrived in force – an impressive display designed to scare the protesters – defending the forest became a task which required all our energy and ingenuity. On the first day of mass police presence, fortune was on our side. The council had neglected to place parking restriction signs at the end of the road and, as a consequence, tourist cars formed an unintentional blockade.

The next time workers arrived we challenged them regarding boundaries. It seemed extraordinary to us that while they were ready to attack the pristine rainforest with dozers they had not marked the boundaries between national park and private land.

Action at Bloomfield, at the northern end of the proposed road, was volatile. Without police in attendance, one belligerent dozer operator drove straight at the protesters, forcing them into the lantana. They had no choice but to hang on to the blade as they were pushed up the hill. The blade was raised and crashed from side to side in a furious attempt to dislodge them. When he stopped they hurriedly jumped off. A shaken group then attempted to communicate with the operator, who drove off in a fury. Police returned the following day and arrested the entire group in a brutal manner.

Back at the south end of the forest the pressure of confrontation slowly grew. Before long, all protesters were moved from the roadway and the bulldozers entered the rainforest. Hans had lived near the national park boundary for nine years on a property that became our protest camp. It featured bush showers, an open kitchen and magnificent offerings of tropical fruit and food from local supporters. Glorious as the conditions were, it did not alleviate the pain and anguish we all felt, and none more deeply than Hans. His response to the destruction, chronicled in the book *Trials and Tribulations*, was moving. "This forest had cared for me like a mother cares for her child," wrote Hans. "She had fed and protected me, calmed and healed my physical and mental wounds and had taught me many things, including tolerance and forgiveness."

"So, having developed a very special relationship with her, I was deeply affected when, after a few days of confrontation, police succeeded in moving away our blockade and chainsaws and bulldozers started to cut into her. In my mind I heard the forest screaming. It became too much for me. I ran towards the scene, ready to attack the nearest bulldozer, when I was grabbed by one of our people, taken back to safety and calmed down."

But all was not lost. We took to the trees to stop the dozers. For two days these tactics succeeded. The high canopy rainforest trees offered substantial protection to those who could scale them. For a time the authorities appeared to be beaten.

Our tenuous lifeline holding them at bay from the forest was one simple tool. "That bloody ladder," relates Rupert, another local. "We would have been lost without it. It looked much the same as any other ladder until it had to be smuggled to and from the blockade four or five times every day, at times up to a mile and a half from where it was kept at night. We could not leave it on site for fear of it being confiscated. Amazing how heavy it became after carrying it for a mile and how small it looked when it was propped up against a hundred-foot-high tree that blockaders were planning to climb. At times the 'fuzz' became too thick to risk moving the ladder very far. Bare hands were used to scratch a trench fourteen feet long and six inches deep to cover the ladder... Retention of our ladder became an obsession somehow symbolising our determination to carry on."

On day three of the campaign, the trees were amply filled with protesters. Only one skinny pole of a tree remained unclaimed. It was the worst seat in the house, right in the dozer's path. No-one claimed it, yet our defence was useless without its occupation. Jonno, who was already up a tree and feeling very smug, informed me of this fact. He was right. I had to get up there, and the ladder was far away. It was a six-metre scramble straight up a bean pole to the sitting board. Two – thirds of the way up I had to rest; my arms trembled with the exertion. I clung on, unable to make the journey of just a few more feet. Jonno, from the comfort of his perch, goaded, "Come on, old man!" I snarled unmentionable obscenities, regardless of elderly and genteel people below, and dragged myself up.

After only a short respite on my perch I became part of a surreal confrontation epitomising the clash between two cultures. Neville Tesch, the roading foreman, crashed through the forest armed with a chainsaw, determined to deal with the situation his way. He was angry. He swore at those on the ground to get out of the way and looked menacingly up at me. All eyes were focused on the chainsaw. He started the machine with one powerful rip of his huge paw. My friend Kevin picked up a lump of wood. Tesch lashed out with the revving machine; everyone scattered as the blade swung dangerously close to a vulnerable bare stomach. Tesch stepped up to my tree. Kevin raised his stick, ready to throw it in a last-ditch effort to save my life. The blade went to my tree. Screams and shouts echoed through the forest. Tesch was angry and confused; he swung the blade again and sank it into a log nearby.

Sergeant Turner, the most senior local policeman, appeared, strode resolutely up to Tesch and grabbed his arm. It was a brave act. If Tesch had lashed out in his fury without recognising the police uniform, the chainsaw could have been a murderous weapon. The shrieking machine stopped. Tesch's fury and raw power instantly abated. The chainsaw was confiscated and he was led away with the crestfallen look of a chastised child.

The reprieve was short-lived. The police cleared those on the ground with the threat of immediate arrest. With a dangerous situation defused, their attitude quickly changed. Those in the tree tops were instructed to come down. We unanimously refused.

The dozer started ploughing into the forest in front of us. National Parks personnel cut vines to prevent unnecessary damage as the interconnected fabric of the forest was torn. The driver and the police were going to disregard us, but I couldn't see how they were going to get through the narrow gap between my tree and the occupied one next to me. The police again demanded that I come down. I refused. The dozer blade cut across the base of my tree. With each pass the blade 'tickled' the roots, shaking me to my core. Nevertheless the work continued, heedless of my presence. Fearing that with weakened roots my tree could topple at any moment, I shouted to the National Parks man to cut the vines suspended from my tree to stop the forest crashing down. The dozer roared below.

Moving methodically, it cut a gash three metres deep into the floor of the forest, forming a flat road from undulating ground. I was left suspended looking over a precipice. The dozer passed. I watched helplessly as the full canopy, like a magnificent carpet, shuddered and tore. They placed a guard at the base of my tree with the threat of increased charges. Later I shimmied down, under arrest.

At the end of each day the bulldozers retired several kilometres away to a property called Camelot. Every morning they'd re-emerge like shining knights in a cavalcade to the forest. Their daily retreat, combined with the arrival of supporters from the south, who were starting to trickle in with the news of the rainforest destruction, gave us the opportunity for implementing a new strategy. We tied one person, John, onto a cross and buried several others in the ground up to their necks. The police arrived with a dozer and, seeing our blockade, went for the shovels. It was hard work digging through the packed clay. Halfway down, shovels were traded in for ice-cream containers to avoid hurting anyone. One protester was removed. They cut John down from the cross. The bulldozer rolled between buried bodies, compressing the ground dangerously as it passed.

Guarded by police, that night for the first time the dozer remained on the worksite, to the accompaniment of a trumpet-led forest ensemble. The police, falling asleep on duty the following day, voiced an angry protest. The entertainment was discontinued.

The next day an order was read out stating that reasonable force would be used to remove all who stood in the way. The dozer started up. People clung together in front of it. The police were outnumbered, but they charged like a football team. Slippery, writhing bodies churned up the already muddy ground. The dozer driver reversed into a group of people; mud and curses flew thick and fast. Police tempers flared and punches flew, but still our people gathered in front of the bulldozer. As we slipped and slid, police dragged one protester out as others dived into the mud.

One of the officers on duty, Sergeant Charles Chapman, complained bitterly, "It's all right to use a bit of roughhouse on the blokes, but can you get these women out of the way? The way they're dressed . . . You know, if we have to push them we will, but they'll complain, so move them off now."

"It's their decision to do and wear what they want," I shouted over the roar of the dozer.

"Don't you talk for me!" a woman shouted at both of us. The sergeant attempted to drag her off but she dived back into the fray.

As the bulldozer lurched forward, our people were pushed back. The nose of the dozer extended over an embankment. People were below. Glen, a local, waved frantically at the driver, but the blade ground forward. In an act of great courage he jumped at the front of the blade, grabbing hold of the protrusion used for pushing down trees. The dozer lifted him high, roaring like an angry beast, and shook him as if he were its prey. For long and frightening seconds everyone stood transfixed before a life and death struggle in the forest. The dozer crashed the man to the ground. The police ran over and stopped the driver. Police and protesters alike were visibly shocked.

A tense silence reigned, with only the crackle of communication equipment to be heard. One protester whispered, "I thought he was finished." Another muttered, "That woman copper throws a mean right, in close."

Minutes later the radio reported a low pressure system on the way; more rain. Fearful that the dozer could be trapped in the forest for the entire wet season, the loggers retreated under police escort. A loud cheer burst forth in the forest.

After a festive dinner and the cessation of heavy rain, we walked to the original blockade site at the southern end of the park. We worked hard in the cool of the evening placing log blockades across the road. The sound of digging and hammering was accompanied by an orchestra of frogs rejoicing. It remained wet and peaceful for six months.

Finally the wet ended, and along with it the protection for the forest. Protesters came in a convoy of vehicles from northern New South Wales to support the locals. The police presence was upgraded in response to the numbers. Local authorities were supported by Brisbane police, who brought with them the dog squad. While we chatted amiably with those local police we knew, others on the sideline waited for blood. One way or another, this action would be conclusive.

In the early stage of the protest, our side held strong. People were dug into the ground once again. In addition to the logs assembled at the end of the earlier blockade, which formed a maze of defences, people were chained to cement pillars deep in the ground or to bolts nailed through logs.

The north end of the proposed road was our weakest defence.

Having learnt our lesson from the earlier blockade, we sent experienced people to the north, who set up a camp near Woobada Creek and built defences. We expected the road builders to move in simultaneously from north and south.

The police had a monumental task before them. The Bloomfield River only allowed crossing at low tide. We had one yacht which we were prepared to moor in the middle of the crossing and allow to be beached at low tide. At another crossing site, 'elephant traps' (enormous pits) were dug to stop dozers crossing the river.

One evening there were reports of police patrols at the north of the Bloomfield River. Action appeared to be imminent. We had heard that the bulldozers were being slowly driven out of storage. The machines would take twelve hours to reach us and were likely to arrive early the next day. That corresponded with low tide. We decided to obstruct the crossing using a tree trunk with a small platform built on top. As it was my idea, I was duly selected to be the person to sit atop. The night was spent constructing a

platform in the fork of a seven – metre pole. An old boat with the bottom torn out was placed on the roadway, a hole excavated and the installation lifted upright. We piled a cairn of stones in the middle for support.

At dawn I climbed a rope ladder. With food, warm clothing, a sleeping bag and a can on a string for hoisting up drinking water, I figured I'd be able to maintain a vigil for a number of days if necessary. Everyone was enthusiastic. We thought we were engineering a successful campaign at the notorious north end.

From the perch I welcomed the misty dawn on the river. I waited.

The sun rose and all was quiet. We were on tenterhooks, expecting the dozer to round the corner at any moment. Instead, a local appeared; he was on his way to work. Here I was, up a pole, stopping a local going to his job. He withdrew.

Still no bulldozer. Rumour suggested that it had been taken to the old loading wharf at the mouth of the Bloomfield and barged to another location. We decided to stay in position, however, as we had built a good defence. Then the unexpected happened: the entire mission arrived, a group of some four hundred Aboriginal people. One drove a front-end loader across the weir and stopped in front of my pole. There were all manner of people dressed in bright colours. Some played in the water; however, one group of men was deadly serious. They wanted me down off that pole.

The mission police demanded I withdraw or face arrest. I refused to move. They backed off and discussed the matter, quickly finding a solution to the dilemma of this idiot up a pole: the front-end loader would be chained to the pole and upend it.

In consideration of the latest proposal and the no-nonsense manner in which it was delivered, my group conferred. It was becoming increasingly apparent that no bulldozer was going to appear, so it was agreed I would quit. I climbed down from the pole, expecting to face the music, but the mission people were jovial about it. They put the front-end loader into gear and did exactly what they said they were going to do – upend the pole.

Whether or not due to our plan of defence, the absent dozer had, it turned out, been barged south to Cape Tribulation. There, protesters sat in position night and day. Confrontation was inevitable. The police were specialists, as were many blockaders, and the potential for violence was real.

Months before, with the end of the dry season, we had achieved a significant win, but the police weren't going to let us get the upper hand this time. Queensland politicians planned to crush the blockade and put an end to this greenie nonsense once and for all. A number of us hiked south to the major blockade site at Cape Tribulation.

The police brought in a front-end loader and used it to dig out buried protesters, scraping the bucket down within inches of people's bodies and faces – no ice-cream containers this time. Those chained to logs remained passive while timber around them was lifted by the loader in a giant game of fiddlesticks. When that first line of defence fell, we moved deeper into the forest.

Gummy, that tenacious defender of the forest, had been up a tree for several days. He'd succeeded in holding up all work, but now he needed fresh water supplies and moral support. A number of us had tried but failed to get past the police patrols.

Jonno and I decided to sneak out late at night in an attempt to supply our treetop friend. We made it to the road and crept along until behind us we heard the sound of voices and saw bright torches – the type that double as riot clubs. They were in the distance but coming our way. As they were climbing over fallen logs we heard the tinkle of a dog's choke chain. It was hardly likely to be the pampered family pet out for an evening stroll. I bolted up a dry creek bed; police with guard dogs in the middle of the night brought out the acute coward in me. I was relieved that everyone ran in the other direction.

Jonno, meanwhile, gathered up the gear and ran down a different path through the bush. He could hear the rattle of chain fast approaching. He recalls, "I kept saying to myself, 'No copper could run this fast.' I dumped the stuff and ran out onto the beach. About thirty metres down, the dog lunged at my arm, which threw me to the ground. It stood over me with my forearm in its jaws. Every time I made the minutest movement it started to growl menacingly. I could see its eyes reflected in the faint moonlight, staring into mine. I yelled to the dog handler, who at that stage was a hundred metres away, to get the bastard off me. He retorted, "Come over here and I'll get the dog off you."

The dog let me go, but as I tried to get up it grabbed on and shook me down again, growling. It was a big dog and the handler was quite drunk. I was scared. I'd been arrested the night before and had seen that the dog squad had two huge pallets of beer stacked outside their caravan.

The cop called the dog off and told me to come over, as I was under arrest. His voice was slurred. I picked up a big rock and said if the dog came at me again I'd use it. He came no closer as I retreated down the beach.

People could see no method of effective action under conditions such as these, so I suggested what I thought would be a nonviolent action – a candlelight procession with the whole camp in attendance. Candles and singing seemed like a perfect solution to our impasse. What's more, it would provide an opportunity for us to slip some food and water supplies to Gummy.

Fifty people walked the beach on a beautiful moonlit night. At the edge of the forest we lit candles and commenced singing gentle forest songs. In single tile we made our way through the forest to the road. We were confronted by a single cop menacingly wielding his torch and holding his dog on a tight lead. Above the singing he yelled, "Don't move any further down this road!" We gathered around him, still singing our songs, and swayed as one entity. We did not physically touch him.

Trained to deal with enemy crowds, the cop was worried. To him, a mob meant violence, and he was grossly outnumbered. We said we wanted access to walk along the newly dozed section of road. He refused. He had the dog on a half lead and flicked the animal out at people as they moved. It snapped at the faces of people; some were bitten and started to bleed. A few of us, attempting to defuse the situation, called, "Let's stop! Let's move back! It's time to go."

I attempted to talk but the cop did not respond. He was a brick wall of fury and trained hate. I suggested that if he stood back I would move everyone along in an orderly fashion without confrontation. However, his training said he had to violate us to get obedience. He worked himself into a frenzy and like a dog sensing fear in a retreating opponent became more violent as his dominance grew.

Another cop arrived from the other side armed with club and dog. The two of them worked in a pincer movement, driving us down the steep slope with dogs and batons. The dogs kept jumping and biting at people.

Despite the horror, dust and panic, it was amazing to witness the rapport between trainer and dog. The animal became an extension of the man's personality and body; according to the amount of lead it was given, the dog responded appropriately in terms of savagery. With a short lead it nipped, jumping around like a puppy wagging its tail, yet still drawing blood. A slightly longer lead and it snapped hard and growled. Full lead instantly catapulted it into a vicious attacker, a killing machine aimed with precision by the handler.

The second cop cracked and lunged with a forward thrust of his controlling hand and put his dog on a long lead. In an instant it had grabbed someone by the calf and was mauling, shaking its head from side to side. It started to savagely drag the victim along the ground. Someone picked up a piece of wood to hit the dog over the head: we slid into the abyss of violence.

The crowd asserted itself. More people picked up weapons. There seemed to be an instantaneous, collective realisation that these monsters with their animals had to be stopped. They were beyond reason. The dogs were pulled back as the police sensed the crowd turn. For a moment we were in the eye of the storm, and in the brief calm we picked up the savaged man and made our way down the hill. His injuries were so serious he had to be rushed to hospital.

As we retreated, the police started again. They threw the 20 litre water containers we had carried up to re-supply the tree sitters, bowling us over like ten pins on the steep slope. Then they picked up rocks from the side of the road and started tossing them into the crowd. I tried to reason with them, saying, "Look, there's no need to do this. People are going, can't you see?" We got a torrent of abuse in return. They swung their torch clubs at the heads of those retreating. We kept together as a group as best we could, trying to stop people straying where they might get nicked off by the police, and made our way to the beach. It had been an unsuccessful nonviolent action.

Our people were extremely depressed and oppressed but weren't particularly angry. We all knew and understood the attitude of many Queensland police. Instructions had been given from on high to break the blockade. They didn't want to see a repetition of the successful Franklin campaign or the earlier Daintree blockade.

Gummy remained up in the tree, sending us reports via radio. He was too high to arrest. Momentarily the police were foiled, but Gummy couldn't last indefinitely. Eventually he came down and met his inevitable fate – arrest. Others bravely continued to build defences further up the newly dozed road and to set up camps in nets strung between trees. Late at night drunken police threw rocks at the people in their perches and terrorised them. Those in the nets received serious wounds but were unable to come down or give themselves up for fear of further brutality.

The media support we so desperately needed was not forthcoming. We felt isolated, and a sinister air of danger pervaded the action. The issue of police brutality was not reaching the media. Our people at Cairns wanted to talk about rainforest preservation; they didn't want to pursue a human rights issue with the Queensland police.

At that point the relationship broke down between our group at the action front and the people who were representing us nationally. We were told that the Wilderness Society and other conservation groups had asked people to attend, but the numbers did not materialise. Appeals for support were not put into full swing. As had occurred at the end of the Franklin campaign, we were considered to be dispensable. The blockade crumbled. The successes of the Franklin River and Nightcap campaigns were not, it seemed, to be repeated. The road, all 33 ugly kilometres of it, went through.

The unbridled police brutality was effective. They found the holes in our defences and exploited them ruthlessly. It was indeed a very sad time. We were forced to recognise that small people who banded together were unable to successfully act in defence of the environment where the police were sanctioned by the state to use vicious assault.

The great victory for the Daintree and for conservation came much later. In 1987 the Federal Labor Government created the Greater Daintree National Park, and World Heritage status was gained for the Wet Tropics. The issue reached the international media.

The road through the Daintree remains an environmental nightmare, but vital refuge areas of the inland valleys, where new species continue to be discovered, were saved by the World Heritage listing. Shire Chairman, Tony

Mijo, was inadvertently our greatest ally. He admitted to conservationist, Sue Wilke, that he pushed the confrontation with the conservation movement in order to prove himself: he wanted the National

Party pre-selection for the federal seat of Leichhardt, which he had been refused previously on the grounds that he was not tough enough. This Machiavellian act of destruction to gain a political career backfired when he failed to get the pre-selection he desired.

The environment was the clear winner in the long run with the furore that followed. The Federal Government stepped in with a controversial package to compensate the timber industry but lock up sensitive areas. Political successes have since seen a leading conservationist, Mike Berwick, elected president of Douglas Shire Council. None of these historic developments would have been possible without the explosive confrontations of the Daintree blockades.

The treatment protesters endured in the forests of the Daintree at the hands of the police were a far cry from that of the heady days of the Franklin. The campaign had lacked the resources and numbers of the Franklin, yet it had been the culmination of a long history of opposition, both locally and nationally.

Conservation groups now have an ongoing programme to buy threatened rainforest for its protection. The struggle continues for the rainforests of North Queensland.

CHAPTER 7
ERRINUNDRA
Protest Division

Daintree was a demoralising event but, driven by a sense of urgency to save as much as was left of the Australian forests as possible, I and many others were prepared to continue to act upon our concerns until those in power woke up and took notice. For me, campaigning for the environment had become a way of life, and the summer of 1983 presented an opportunity to act upon the forestry issue in what I felt was a more sedate and politically liberal climate than that of the state I had just left. Victoria would never dish up the excesses of Queensland, I thought.

Agreement had been reached in the radical green movement to stir up both the forestry and conservation establishments. The plan, presented by Milo Dunphy, was to move around the state, protesting at a number of sites to draw attention to the damage being done by logging and the ineffectual attitude of those in power in slowing or stopping the destruction. The concept excited me.

The journey to the forests of East Gippsland was one of discovery. Appreciation of our forest heritage enhanced the flames of my burning desire to continue efforts to halt the destruction. I was inspired and educated as I travelled through those magnificent forests.

The warm temperate rainforests which once ran down the eastern seaboard of Australia met their southern limits in the Errinundra Plateau in East Gippsland. Here, cool temperate floras of southern Victoria and Tasmania found their most easterly distribution. While this region occupies only 4 per cent of Victoria's total area, botanically it is very rich, with one third of Victoria's total plant species and about half of Victorian eucalypt species found here. It also boasted some of the tallest hardwoods in the world. Some of the mature forests of the Errinundra Plateau are up to 500 years old and have never been burnt. These forests are unique in Australia, and the world.

Rare marsupials including the long-footed potoroo and the tiger quoll were also to be found there. Significant birds included the powerful owl and sooty owl. Despite the well-documented scientific evidence of very rare fauna and flora, the Victorian Forestry Commission had not recommended the founding of a single reserve for the protection of rare species. If cutting was to continue at the rate current in 1983, these forests would be substantially destroyed by the turn of the century.

Errinundra was the site of the first public protest to focus on Old Growth logging. As a radical group we launched into action, without backup from the mainstream conservationists, in order to impact on Victorian forestry issues, but also to assert ourselves against a conservative and timid Victorian conservation establishment.

The groundwork for the Errinundra protest was laid at the Wangaratta Festival, an annual music event held in the township of Wangaratta, which serves the East Gippsland plateau and its tributary valleys. Here we invited people to come with us to help save the tall forests of this beautiful area. A group of some fifty people responded. With several trips in two small trucks, we transported a bunch of young, naive revellers from an indulgent party scene to one of the largest and heaviest industrial logging regions in the nation. We arrived to find magnificent shining gums with a lush rain-forest understorey in the process of being clear-felled, burnt and regenerated into a blue gum plantation. The uniform regrowth meant a high fire risk, while the fabric of the forest itself was degraded to an irreparable state.

Fifty greenies camped under the tall gums on bare earth. The understorey had been removed by bulldozers in preparation for the timber harvest. Scientific reports within the Forestry Commission itself classified this portion of forest as a conservation area. Despite this, acres were ready to fall to the chainsaw. It was here that we decided to make a stand.

Small groups of workers came to see our camp. Invariably, arguments developed and little communication was achieved. We were culturally poles apart. Unlike many areas of forest confrontation where interaction had achieved some level of understanding and a begrudging mutual respect, the loggers were tough and intransigent. No less so were the 'fundamentalist' greenies, who pushed a one-dimensional extremist line which aggravated loggers and damaged our cause. Yet the very fact that we had the audacity to be there was enough. Lacking clear direction for a constructive campaign, we had only a fervent desire to empower ourselves and save the forest. The rest was held to be in the lap of the gods.

The programme unfolded as if rehearsed. Without the time – consuming nuisance of group consensus, one member of our thoroughly individualistic, anarchistic 'organisation' produced a leaflet which most (but not all) considered to be a wonderful piece of inspired eco-creativity, thus to be followed through with. It was an invitation calling on all interested parties to attend a public meeting in order to discuss the future of the Errinundra Plateau. One hundred of these notices were dropped off at the Bonang Post Office, the only building in town except for the Bonang hall, where the proposed meeting was to be held a few nights later.

From this simple beginning, rumours ran amok in the region. Gus Gearson, the Forestry Commission local chief, spread the word that the meeting would decide the fate of logging in East Gippsland. Unbeknown to us, the industry sent out the alarm signals.

That day, in the tranquility of our forest camp, we made our preparations. Three of us would speak. At 4 pm we headed off; two small trucks full of greenies. Once out of the forest it became apparent that something special was about to happen. Barbecue fires, log trucks and beer drinkers lined the Bonang Highway. A rough honour guard, or a funeral retinue? The loggers had clearly expected hordes of conservationists. We rode along, waving regally. I felt like Czar Nicholas just prior to 1917.

We reached the Bonang hall while it was still daylight. A rapidly swelling crowd of loggers and their mates sat outside the hall on a natural, grassed amphitheatre, drinking heavily. Our decidedly tiny and shabby trucks wove through a traffic jam comprised of modern, heavy equipment. Deeming it too dangerous to leave our meagre transport on the outskirts, we headed for centre ring, counting on greater safety in the public eye.

I rolled my truck onto the flat area in front of the hall. As I stepped out, a burly logger staggered towards me, bottle in hand. I braced myself for the worst and was relieved when he said, "How d'ya like me T-shirt, mate?" "Not bad at all," I replied, a grin on my face, gut churning as I read the caption, "GIVE BIRTH TO A GREENIE: SHIT IN THE BUSH". Impressed, I offered to trade my nifty three-colours-on-green "SAVE DAINTREE" T-shirt, but he wouldn't be in it and staggered back to his mates on the hill.

Meanwhile some thirty greenies were spilling out of our trucks, dressed in dazzling (if a little dirty) rainbow brilliance and many with flowers in their hair. To the swelling crowd of loggers and their supporters, we were creatures from another planet. At a loss what to do next (a somewhat magnified feeling of walking into a party, not knowing anyone and wishing to take root with the pot plant by the door), our group closed ranks and formed, of course, a circle. The loggers glared and there was a momentary silence. It was broken by a prime mover which drove into our people's backs, pushing them forward on its bull bar. The circle crumbled and the mob roared with delight.

Approaching twilight cast a more serious aura over the scene. The proposed master of ceremonies, the local newspaper editor, appeared and introduced himself. The hall was too small to accommodate the growing crowd, so a public address system was set up outside. The MC introduced himself. Loggers even clambered on top of our vehicles to get a better view. The first speaker was called. "Would a representative of NAG [Nomadic Action Group] please start the proceedings."

No-one approached the microphone. The MC repeated his request. It would hardly do to have no-one volunteer at this point. With a feeling of resigned desolation I fronted the microphone. Slobbering drunks jeered at me as I passed. I surveyed the scene: the sun had set (on possibly more than the day) and floodlights threw surreal shadows across angry drunken faces. Media later estimated 700 pro-loggers had rallied. We greenies numbered a mere thirty. Across this sea of antagonism not a single blue uniform was to be seen.

At that point a personal calm descended upon me. Beatings, even death, was a reality at the hands of this mob, but there was nowhere to go. I couldn't hide or run, stranding my friends or the vehicles. There was no choice but to stand and weather the storm. I accepted my fate and launched into an aggressive speech on the rapacious nature of the logging industry and the strength of the conservation movement. Drowned out by jeers and catcalls, I was only audible to the first few rows of people. An occasional empty beer can flew by my head. I faltered. What was the use? Friends who had managed to worm their way to the front called out, "Keep on going, Ian!" I took heart and kept talking. The crowd roared. A barrage of cans whistled past my head.

Doug Ferguson took to the microphone next. A crescendo of abuse greeted him as he approached the stage. He was neither dressed for the bush nor resplendent in the bright alternative garments of the others but stood before the crowd instead in striped men's winter pyjamas. He let them have it.

Jules Davison came on next. He too was given little chance to air his views, despite the fact that he faced the crowd in his wheelchair. Debbie McIlroy was the last to speak. As a local she expected to get a hearing, but the abuse and jeering reached dangerous proportions. She and her family left the region shortly afterwards. Harassment of her children at school, and the fact that one night someone poured petrol around the family home, were prime reasons. The Forestry Commission representative, Gus Gearson, took to the microphone with relish and whipped up the crowd. He blasted dole – bludging greenies and passed motions to continue logging the entire region.

It was definitely time to retreat. I manoeuvred Jules in his wheelchair through the angry and drunken crowd. Someone shouted, "You're just hiding behind his wheelchair, you gutless bastard." I freely admitted that to be the case and wheeled onward. We reached the truck and started to load people in, Jules first. Kerosene was poured over someone's hair. "You need a good wash, you filthy greenie shit," a voice snarled.

Exit preparations were further delayed as we searched the floor of the truck for foul-smelling blocks thrown through the window, which turned out to be toilet disinfectant tablets. "That'll get rid of you fuckin' scum," someone yelled through the window. Others rocked the car and tore the tarpaulin off the back door. Fortunately it was only there to stop dust; a securely locked door stopped them entering. Shot with nerves, I could hardly get the motor started. One of our people warned me not to back up, as the loggers had placed stakes poking into my back tyres. My clutch foot, trembling, made the truck lurch forward into the black mass of people. One angered worker leaned through the passenger window and punched one of us several times in the head. Meanwhile, I contended with abuse on the driver's side. I left the truck's sliding door wide open, reasoning that my vulnerability made them less likely to attack. "Piss off ya bastards and don't come back!" they yelled. I just kept agreeing with them.

Press and TV cameras were revelling in the growing violence. By shining their spotlights on our vehicles they protected us somewhat. The crowd realised this and began to push and punch the media crew. Injuries were mounting. The scene grew uglier.

At that point the violence began to turn on the media and a group of sober men moved in. They strong-armed men out of the way.

"Are you police?" I yelled.

"No, union and management," one replied.

These men were alarmed that a bloodbath would injure their cause.

They threw a cordon around us with the deftness of a trained police contingent. Next they locked arms and formed a human wedge, allowing my vehicle to slowly reverse. We had to keep stopping as members of our group stumbled into the surreal, floodlit area, desperate to jump aboard. I had over twenty people in the back of my truck.

Only one of our group was not fazed by the melee. David Rainbow, as a Tasmanian born and bred in a logging town, thoroughly enjoyed himself. He leaned on his crutches (a consequence of another greenie misadventure) and complained that he didn't want to leave the 'party' just as it was hotting up. Eventually we dragged him aboard, arguing with both him and the belligerent drunks. We escaped into the night and the forest.

Our blind stumblings stirred a media storm in Victoria. TV and press crews descended on us in the forest. However, the consensus of the group, led by Jules and Doug, was to refuse to communicate with the media but rather to stand apart and act as wild tribal people. The group, manipulated by them, would not permit me to speak to the media. So instead of discussion and explanation, they were treated to an extravaganza of naked, painted bodies, ritual dancing, totem pole construction and primitive revelling. After a few days of this the media decided to quit. An historical opportunity was lost to communicate our concerns for the forest.

A small number of the group, including myself, wanted to secretly disappear from Gippsland under the cloak of night, then reappear and set up camp in another sensitive forest area of Victoria. This, we considered, would be a high quality piece of environmental theatre. It was also an arrangement that I had worked out with Milo Dunphy prior to the Victorian campaign. The intention was to protest at all the major sites around the state. The group decision, however, was to dig in till we won at Errinundra.

Destruction was being allowed to continue while all was quiet on our immediate site, so late one night we shifted camp to where the cutting was taking place.

To the beat of drums, two huge bonfires were set up on the access road to provide light while barricades were constructed through the night. Work continued until dawn. In the early morning we stood by the smouldering ashes of the tires, ready for the arrival of workers and equipment. A bulldozer appeared with a heavy-set old guy at the controls. His thick 'bottlo' glasses were taped to his head. He drove the bulldozer straight at the barricades and the people in front of them.

Davy Dubens, as light as a jockey, leapt onto the dozer blade to avoid being run down, and rode it like a wild horse. The dozer driver bore on. Driving with one hand, he lifted the high pressure tire hose attached to the dozer and let Davy have it in the face. He was another who judged we were in dire need of a wash, for he'd mixed phenol into the water. The acerbic smell bit the air. Davy was obviously distressed but could do little more than hang on as the dozer crashed onwards through very rough terrain.

Our people were quick to react. Tarne, slender and agile, climbed onto the rear towbar. Holding onto the side of the driver's cage, he stepped gingerly along the moving caterpillar track and grabbed the driver by the arm. The driver was shocked to find someone up there with him. He stopped to push the intruder off. Tempers flared as others jumped up and grabbed his glasses. The rest of us had our hands full calming friends. Once we were clear of the dozer, the driver roared off over the hill from the direction he'd come. The forest returned to calm.

Back at the campfire it was difficult to relax: we knew the crunch was coming. More loggers were expected. Instead, police paddy wagons and media crews arrived. The head cop read out our rights. I announced the reasons why we were there, but before I had finished I was summarily grabbed and thrown into a paddy wagon. People tried to scatter, but the huge police contingent had us under control.

From inside the wagon the scene looked and sounded like a roundup in a chook yard. Before the dust had settled, about forty people, myself included, were jam-packed in almost pitch darkness inside one police wagon. Deep breathing was the only way I could cope with the intense wave of claustrophobia which flooded through me. I wondered if things could possibly get worse: locked up, squashed up, our camp and vehicles unattended, angry loggers roaming around and several hours of travel to the nearest police station. Such musing came to an abrupt end when a number of our earth-sensitive, planet-defending 'friends' started and refused to stop smoking cigarettes within the wagon, despite desperate protestations. They eventually stopped, but thought we were unreasonable.

The trip to the nearest police station became a journey of epic proportions. We were arrested early in the morning and arrived at the town of Bairnsdale in the late afternoon. It would have been a comprehensive scenic tour of East Gippsland forests, as we drove along every rough track imaginable, if only the vehicle had had windows.

We were dejected. In a single action the police had managed to break our blockade. They could not have known of our internal divisions but they must have been aware of a lack of support from the mainstream conservation movement. Their action was ruthlessly efficient. They disregarded our basic human and legal rights and treated us like animals, yet not a murmur of protest was raised by the conservation establishment or legal circles regarding our treatment. The Victorian Herald reported on 3 February 1984 that "Others ran for the bush chased by loggers eager to give police a hand." The combined illegal action of loggers acting with police was successful: our blockade was broken.

Meanwhile, the media trumpeted the successful police operation. They claimed we had caches of supplies hidden in the forest and that we'd planned to stage 'hit and run' raids on logging operations. Specialist police squads on trail bikes were used in the hunt, said the report. The operation was directed by the Assistant Commissioner himself who was flown to a specially constructed helipad. Assertions that the police believed protesters had buckets of excrement hidden in the bush which they planned to hurl over loggers was nothing more than media hype.

Logging continued under police guard. An amendment of the Forests Act was passed to make it illegal for any person to go within 200 metres of a logging operation or obstruct such operations. A Melbourne – based conservation group, the Native Forest Action Council, publicly stated that it did not support the protests. The loggers headed back to the bush.

We were in disarray. The group split, and I and twenty others travelled to the Otways area in south-western Victoria to continue the hit and run campaign as originally intended. The remainder went interstate.

It was the opinion of the mainstream conservation movement that the Errinundra campaigners put the anti-logging cause back by many years, pushing the government from a position of communication to one of defiance. The government trumpeted measures to guarantee the industry jobs and a secure timber resource. We were sick of political compromises. We saw well-paid armchair conservationists, whose ineffectiveness was appalling in terms of the destruction of Old Growth forests, preferring to side with the establishment and attack us as extremists. They missed the opportunity to utilise the moment when we had the state media focus on the issue of forest conservation.

On both sides grave errors were made. For the radical activists, the Errinundra campaign represented a serious defeat. We were our own worst enemy; consumed by our sense of mission, we stumbled. Our actions were flawed and fundamentalist to the point of primitive, but people were risking their lives in support of an ideal. They did not deserve to be deserted yet again by the power brokers in the movement.

The resulting backlash in the Victorian media and in the conservation movement pulled many wild heads into line and proved to most (but not all) that we could not take on the power of the state without a properly run, media wise campaign. For the sake of the very forests we were defending we needed to integrate with other elements of the conservation movement.

CHAPTER 8
ROXBY DOWNS
Radioactive Crucible

THE THREE WITCHES

All – 'All hail, Bob Hawke,
That shalt be Prime Minister hereafter
Until the women from their bonds do break free
And gather in the desert to denounce thee.'

Witch 1 – 'Thrice the war-burned babe hath cried.'
Witch 2 – 'Thrice and once the children whined.'
Witch 3 – 'People cried. 'Tis time, 'tis time.'

Witch 1 – 'Round about the cauldron go
In the poisoned power throw.'

All – 'Double double toil and trouble
Uranium burn and reactor bubble.'

Witch I – 'Spectre of mutant child unborn
Burnt and blistered earth deformed.'
Witch 2 – 'For a charm of powerful trouble
Like a hell broth boil and bubble.'
Witch 3 – 'Nose of missile, trigger of death
Bomb blast mummy, dragon's breath.'

Witch 1 – 'Root of power digged in the dark
Burst from this cauldron, strong and stark.'
Witch 2 – 'Liver of blaspheming politician
Make this gruel thick with fission.'
Witch 3 – 'Cool it with the people's blood
Then the charm is firm and good.'

All – 'Double double toil and trouble
Uranium burn and reactor bubble.'

(Adapted from Macbeth) Roxby Action Theatre, 1983

In 1983 the issue of uranium mining took the protest movement to a forgotten corner of South Australia where a number of controversial mines were being commissioned, including the world's largest uranium mine, Roxby Downs.

Roxby was not the first mine in the area to receive attention from the protest movement. In May 1982 the Honeymoon mine, located north – west of Broken Hill inside the South Australian border, had seen the first nationally coordinated occupation of a uranium mine in Australia. The leaching process planned at Honeymoon involved pumping solvents deep into the earth to the stratum containing the uranium ore. The uranium-laden solvent solution was then to be pumped to the surface for processing.

The great fear was that the solution would percolate to the ground water and contaminate the inland water supply, the Great Artesian Basin. A similar project in the United States, the Iriguay uranium project in Wyoming, had been closed after chemical leach solution percolated through fractures in a supposedly impenetrable rock layer into the underlying aquifer. This had sent shock waves through the industry internationally.

Though it had attracted only a small number of protesters, and very little publicity, the Honeymoon campaign achieved the closure of the pilot plant at the mine. It set the scene for the major action that was to follow at Roxby Downs.

From August to September 1983, thousands of people from across Australia came to participate in a civil disobedience action at the Roxby Downs mine site. Much was stacked against the anti-uranium movement: the South Australian and Federal Governments had invested financial and political capital in the project. The police stationed 250 officers, the mounted police, the dog squad, helicopters and planes.

It was understood from the beginning that on-the-ground protest action alone would not stop mining at Roxby, but that the events there would provide a useful springboard for the overall campaign. On the ground we aimed to hinder the mine's schedule by protest, while media exposure highlighted the dangers of the project. The presence of people, peaceful or protesting, was threat enough to an industry which relied on secrecy. The attack was also directed at ALP hypocrisy in supporting the nuclear industry, contrary to its own policy. The threat to the Great Artesian Basin against national farming interests was the final straw giving weight to an action which was a statement of widespread opposition to the nuclear industry throughout Australia.

Roxby is a mixed deposit of copper, gold, silver, rare earths and uranium. The ALP federal Caucus decision of 1983 claimed that uranium deposits were incidental to the project. In fact, the Roxby deposit consisted of 1.2 million tonnes of uranium ore – the largest deposit in the world.

Uranium at Roxby represented 30 per cent of the western world's reserves. Within the peace movement, for many who had supported the ALP since the era of Vietnam and conscription, there was a deep sense of betrayal.

The ALP had deserted its policy of no more uranium mining with the paltry excuse that the world's largest uranium mine was primarily a gold and copper mine.

This deception failed to convince the protest movement. Many felt that to stop the mining would be the Australian people's contribution to the breaking of the global nuclear chain. In the international climate, still in the grip of the Cold War and the resultant nuclear stand off, it represented an issue of global significance.

Organised by CANE (Campaign Against Nuclear Energy), activists assembled at Port Augusta and set off through the desert in a cavalcade of cars, trucks and buses with banners flying. The private security agency boasted continually in the media that it would be impossible for demonstrators to breach their defences. Our camp was outside the security gates, several kilometres from the Olympic Dam site. Much debate ensued in the camp between those satisfied with a symbolic protest, and militant groups hell-bent on storming the fortifications. The campfire debates raged late into the night.

By morning it was decided to line up vehicles at the gates to obstruct the entrance to the mine. Two lines stretched back half a kilometre from the lead vehicles. I parked my truck, which had a motif of a nuclear bomb and a huge skull emblazoned on the side, next to the front vehicles. Benny Zable climbed atop in full regalia of gasmask and black robes to perform his mime. All seemed set for the 'theatre of survival'. A sense of the surreal pervaded the milling throng as uniformed security guards watched from behind the gates. Negotiations were under way between mine officials and demonstrators, with us arguing that according to law the authorities had no right to bar our access.

The previous evening, while we gathered at the camp, our representatives had given an ultimatum to Premier John Bannon to explain the relationship between government and the Joint Venture Management. Failing an adequate answer we would test the legality of the agreement by moving onto the site on mass. The deadline we had set was 11 am that day. We did not receive an adequate reply from the Premier.

At the main gate the security officers, in some confusion, decided to let pedestrians through – a grave mistake, particularly since they had trumpeted in the media that their defences were impregnable. A heavy chain, which passed through girders at the road's edge, lay on the road.

With a concrete block at each end ready to drop as a counterbalance, it looked like a medieval drawbridge.

Protesters marched in single file through the main gate like good little sheep. As the crowd gathered inside, someone passing through pushed in front of the guard and swung the gate wide open. Others jumped to hold the gates open. Stirred by a surge of adrenalin, I hung out of the door of my truck, cheering the impossible breakthrough.

Then Megan, a diminutive woman dressed in nuclear holocaust black bandages, called, "Get moving!" Reality hit: I was at the front of the line. The motor roared to life. With a shaky foot on the clutch, my van lurched forward. People ran alongside, banners whipping in the chill wind. Out on the gibber plain, with a clear blue sky as a backdrop, I was surrounded by the brilliant colours of life. Cheers rippled up and down the long line of vehicles. There was a whiff of revolution in the desert air.

Protesters wrestled with a guard to prevent him activating the chain barricade. The chain writhed like a snake on the ground. I drove the truck over before it ripped into position. The next barrier was a four-wheel drive vehicle parked across the road. Someone jumped in and bumped it out of gear, then the crowd pushed it down the embankment. In pandemonium, we rolled onward until stopped by a semi-trailer straddling the road. A woman jumped in and threw it into neutral; people power pushed it off the road.

When a police car arrived, the crowd attempted to push it out of the way. As they rocked it, one policeman pushed a woman off. The crowd surged around him, demanding his ID number. *The Age* later claimed that some started to unzip his jacket in search of the number. "Anti-nuclear demonstrators stormed into the Olympic Dam site yesterday like an invading army smashing down the defences of a fort," it said. "Their determination was frightening. At times it bordered on hysteria. Chanting, singing, clapping, shouting, goading the police and frequently tangling with them, the demonstrators got past several barricades on two main roads that led to the site."

Arrests started to mount. One person, who had jumped into a company truck, was dragged off. Another went when he tried to knock a police vehicle out of gear. A policeman was hit on the leg by a rolling protest vehicle and the driver was arrested. Other drivers took to the sand hills to avoid police, pushed along by crowds of supporters. Any stoppages meant the entertainment started, with music, dance and juggling. When the police and security personnel became confused, the protesters made another dash for it. In the wild and frenetic atmosphere, the rest of the world did not matter. That day we were winning.

With several of our cars in convoy, I kept driving as police attempted to wave me down. Behind me, barriers were being thrown up. I pulled other protesters into the van and decided to advance as far as possible. Our puny cavalcade, with people, feet and flags poking out every window, moved on unopposed, past fenced areas with massive stockpiles of drums. Lines of police stood on guard, strangely motionless. As we sailed by my cheeky 'royal' waves elicited no response. It was odd, particularly as they all seemed to be staring at the air above my vehicle. We motored on without any interference until two police cars dashed past. I sped up. 'Bang! Bang! Bang!' A deafening noise reverberated through the car and from the roof Benny yelled, "Slow down!" Flags flying and in full protest regalia, he was still hanging on. In the excitement I had forgotten about him. We hauled him down and continued to Whenan Shaft, the mine entrance. Here we established a camp which was to survive four or five days, with all the other protesters eventually joining us. Our numbers were too great for police and security personnel to remove us; for the moment we had defeated them.

Back at the access gates, however, progress had slowed to a crawl. Vehicles detoured to avoid hastily-constructed roadblocks. Police and security personnel were not the only ones trying to stop us. The mine workers used our tactics against us; in many instances they sat down in front of our vehicles. One potentially explosive situation developed when workers blockaded a protest food truck. Eventually, negotiations allowed it to pass.

As night fell, exhausted groups trickled into the main campsite near the mine. We had a convincing victory that day. The media gave us saturation coverage, though nearly all of it was unsympathetic. We were accused of violence. In the melee tempers had flared, and there were elements in our large and diverse group who had been hell-bent on smashing the barriers. Yet, ironically, we would not have gotten through the front gates and won media attention without them. Despite the media's portrayal of us as a violent mob, our actions were tame that day compared to the authorities' treatment of Roxby protesters and Aboriginal custodians in the ensuing months. The atmosphere had actually been one more of exhilaration than anger.

Each new day saw repeated actions at the front gates, timed to coincide with shift changes. Information was printed and distributed to the workers explaining the health hazards of their jobs, but they weren't interested.

A stylised theatre developed between police, protesters and workers. Painted demonstrators gathered at the gates at shift change and made human pyramids in the hope of jumping the fence but were dispersed by police. The Sleepy Lizard affinity group, one of the many groups at the protest, bound themselves together as one lizard unit and flopped at the most inauspicious times under the wheels of the shift bus or police vehicles. Each day the number of arrests rose.

We had the numbers and the diversity to operate at night. Affinity groups cut through the fence and made dashes into the mine area. Others ran over the sandhills, pursued by police helicopters with searchlights blazing.

One night, music at the front gates created the Roxby Disco, timed to coincide with the late-night shift change. As we were dancing the night away a message of panic arrived: a busload of workers was about to descend upon us, intent on violent confrontation. In the settling dust from the disco, a meeting was hurriedly assembled. Many wanted to call off the planned action and return to the camp. Feeling that the threatened confrontation was unlikely I urged the group to stay together and go through with the action which, according to our plans, was to end with arrest. I didn't let them know that the safest place to be in the event of an attack by workers was in gaol.

The shift bus arrived under the eerie floodlights. We scrummed down in front of it and were duly carted off to the local squash courts-cum – gaol. Packed full, it turned into quite a party The busload of belligerent workers never materialised.

Action escalated, with seventy-five arrested in one day; fifty were women who bound themselves together with strips of material in a passive protest, symbolic of the interconnectedness of life. On that same day, Star Force, the South Australian riot police, went into action. They ran into the cleared area in front of the gates in a phalanx, pushed protesters to either side and dragged a number of them off under arrest. The shift bus appeared from an unexpected direction. Then, in a cloud of dust, police horses escorted the vehicle out with police running alongside. The whole process was over in a matter of minutes: it was an action done with crack military precision and ruthlessness. Those of us who were not stunned or injured were impressed.

Right to the end of the allocated blockade time we worked hard to upgrade our media profile. However, all participants knew that we could only sustain such activity for a short time. When the designated time arrived, the main blockade packed up and dispersed. There was a feeling of a job well done, despite the bruises borne both physically at the hands of the authorities and mentally at the hands of the media. In the course of two months, 300 people had been arrested. The goals of the blockade were met: the profile of the issue had been raised.

All left except for a small group determined to maintain a vigil in this inhospitable environment to monitor the activities of the operation. They wanted to gain first-hand knowledge of the area in preparation for an action expected the following year, as well as learn from the local Kokatha people.

The miners, it was discovered, had drilled the main Whenan Shaft directly through an Aboriginal sacred site. Without any consultation, a plaque commemorating the mine was affixed to a rock of great significance to the Kokatha people. Elders had been on their way to inspect a sacred site when their car had broken down, but Roxby Management Services (RMS) refused to wait even one day for them. The site was destroyed. RMS also refused to acknowledge the Kokatha's requests to reroute a road marked to run through Cane Grass Swamp, a wetland in the desert fed by the surfacing artesian waters. The Kokatha had to set up a camp in order to stop work in that area.

Mound Springs, where the miners extracted water, was another place of significance to the Kokatha people, as were local claypans – depressions in the ground which retained water.

It is suspected that the unconfined aquifers forming the sub-surface water of the central desert are supplied by the upward moving waters of the artesian system. For millions of years, water under great pressure seeped through rock, finding outlets in cracks and fissures – fault zones such as that at Mound Springs. Tappings in recent times revealed that the Great Artesian Basin was in a fully charged state. However, water drawn for the purposes of the mining and agricultural industries had resulted in a drop in head pressure across the entire Basin.

This draining of Australia's major inland water supply was paired with another concern, that of radioactive effluent being sprayed onto the road to settle dust. After each application and resulting evaporation, radiation became concentrated. The fear of those in the vigil camp was that it would eventually re-enter the artesian basin. Roxby management's environmental impact statement actually admitted that the usage would extinguish some springs in the region.

Despite so much evidence of the violation of the Great Artesian Basin, the South Australian Government, in its controversial caucus decision of 1983, granted RMS the most extensive right to underground water ever seen in this country. Activists were determined to take their protest to the nation's capital, right to the doorsteps of those who had made the decision.

The Lakeside Hotel in Canberra was a far cry from the desert and Roxby. It was July 1984 and the National ALP Conference was being held to make a decision on its 'three-mine' uranium policy. It was an arbitrary position, hard fought by the ALP left and the anti-uranium movement, to control Australia's uranium production. The Nomadic Action Group turned the conference into a visual event.

Activists were drawn from across Australia – in all, over a thousand people attended. Each group painted a banner which was installed on scaffolding constructed by the Builders' Labourers Federation. This surrounded a stage donated by the Canberra Arts Council. It was the middle of a Canberra winter; fingers stuck to the scaffolding as they tied the banners on.

The week-long protest witnessed a variety of techniques to draw attention to our concerns. One day was a women's action, another was a children's action. Babies were let loose in the foyer of the hotel with anti – nuclear slogans on their nappies. Artists, meanwhile, performed street theatre outside the building with Hawke effigies. Arriving delegates had to run the gauntlet of banners, post-nuclear mutants and the Social Action Theatre, which stormed the entrance of the Lakeside Hotel on stilts. The scene was a riot of colour and absurdist theatre. Politicians were forced to wade their way through the masses; for once they couldn't avoid the issue. With everyone inside the hotel, the manager refused to allow police to clear the protesters for fear of damage to the building.

Calm times were interspersed with waves of wild energy. Amidst the madness, an alternative conference took place in the foyer while the ALP conference was going on inside. Jim Cairns, left-wing anti-Vietnam activist and Treasurer in the Whitlam government, counselled people to join the ALP and effect change from within. A Green Alliance was suggested.

Dr Michael Denborough from Canberra wanted a party to run specifically on an anti-nuclear platform. Activists felt betrayed by the ALP; their voice was being ignored, despite massive mobilisation against the nuclear industry. The Nuclear Disarmament Party was born soon afterwards, with Denborough as its founder. It was to haunt Hawke in the 1984 federal election.

Members of the ALP Left walked out of an emotionally charged conference. They joined the demonstrators and announced that they had quit the Labor Party. Meanwhile, some protesters who were also Labor members had infiltrated the conference. One such person, we later learnt, walked down the aisle, made an anti-nuclear announcement and burned his ALP card. Eric Early, another member, stood on a balcony and made an impromptu speech to the assembled delegates. He spoke about Roxby and being a grandfather. Someone shouted, "Shut him up!" to which Neville Wran responded, "Let him go, he's speaking more sense than we are here."

Eric relates the events which followed. "I felt a tug on my trouser leg and the man on the door said, "You told me you weren't coming in here to do this." I just went flat. I got down and walked out with him. He didn't manhandle me; he was one of the honest, misguided souls who believed in the ALP. But we both knew that the ALP had ratted on their uranium policy."

The licence to allow three uranium mines to operate in Australia was given the go-ahead at the conference. The ALP Right declared that the uranium found at Roxby Downs was incidental to the process of mining gold and copper. In a tumultuous argument and media extravaganza, the anti-nuclear movement divorced the ALP.

Meanwhile, the vigil at Roxby stayed on, its participants victimised by police in the harsh but beautiful desert environment. Fraught with problems of survival, they continued to collect data, which they then forwarded to the conference. One inappropriate work practice they discovered was that workers carried breathing apparatus underground which they did not know how to use. Management stated that radon, the toxic gas released during blasts, could not cause problems to the workers, as the wind blew it away. Yet virtually no wind was recorded from 22 March until 30 June. Other objections raised by our people included the fact that fumes were observed emanating from the pilot plant, workers did not have breathing apparatus and the plastic lining of the tailings ponds was torn in places.

On 4 August 1984 the authorities returned to Roxby Downs and gave those assembled an hour to remove themselves. Upon refusing to leave, and with the hour up, Star Force dragged off the entire group in a brutal manner. The mother of a week-old baby was not even allowed to collect nappies from the line. Maxi Thomas, a Kokatha elder, was dragged from his land and thrown into the back of a police wagon. The South Australian Minister for the Environment had signed the eviction order.

The vigil people stayed in the area, despite continued police harassment. However, their accumulated knowledge and local expertise was to prove vital when protesters started gathering, in August 1984, for a second blockade at Roxby. This time the authorities were prepared. They fortified the perimeter of the plant, determined that we would not get away with the successes of the previous year.

One day the whole protest camp gathered at the gates to welcome bike riders who had travelled hundreds of kilometres to join the protest. A number of Star Force officers were present. Doug, the vigil leader and a NAG radical, denounced Star Force's previous actions to the media, shouting his accusations three inches away from poker police faces. He was a marked man.

With the arrival of the riders, two police buses drove in directly behind. The inspector refused to speak to protesters, ordering that the road be cleared. Consequently, everyone sat down on the road. The police moved in and picked their targets. All those arrested had been members of the vigil camp. When the word was given, five officers swooped on Doug, bashed him and dragged him off. He was charged with assault, hindering police, resisting arrest and abusive language. It was a violent endgame for those who had suffered ongoing police harassment over many months.

Police control during daylight hours was brutal and absolute, so people made long treks at night to action sites. A group carrying a letter explaining our arguments against Roxby set out at night through the perimeter fence to the mining camp. One of the group, Eric Early, related, "We had to guide ourselves by the lights in the sky from the village as we hiked over high sandhills. It was easy to get lost. We arrived at the mining camp and began letterboxing. The security swooped and told us to stop." At seventy, Eric, forever the rebellious Irishman, proceeded to the next letterbox. As a result, he and his companions found themselves in gaol for the night.

In search of an effective day action, we went further afield. It had been observed that trucks laden with water made regular trips from the bore fields to the mine site. Workers had warned us that the trucks needed a great distance to pull up in case of an obstruction on the road. A strategy was planned. A dozen people chained themselves underneath a cattlegrid on the borefields road. Makeshift signs were placed on the road to stop the vehicle. Others ran a kilometre up the road to warn the driver. He came into sight, trailing a plume of dust in the distance. The driver realised something was amiss and slowed down before he reached the cattlegrid. The tactic had worked. Police were called but, given the huge distances, the freeing and arrest of the protesters took most of the day.

Across Australia, people joined the Roxby blockades in the belief that our political culture would allow the collective voice of dissent to be heard. This was not to be the case. The authorities bludgeoned activists at the mine site and attacked them at gatherings in Adelaide. CANE was decimated after working for years on the issue. For the Aboriginal people it was another step in the ongoing experience of dispossession and cultural genocide.

In the ALP dissent was crushed and the right wing of the party bullied their way to a uranium future. It was a bitter defeat for the anti – uranium movement. People were disillusioned, but the determination was still strong. The next challenge was to be at the federal elections later that year, where activists across the nation rallied against the two-party system under the banner of the Nuclear Disarmament Party. Jo Vallentine became the first NDP senator, and rock star Peter Garrett only just missed out in New South Wales due to the fact that the ALP placed him low on their preferences.

It was a resounding defeat for those who campaigned for an anti – nuclear future, but the overall movement was strengthened by the experience and the resolve to continue campaigning was maintained.

Perhaps most important of all, the Roxby campaign marked an important coming together for the protest movement. The anti-uranium protests saw forest activists working with mainstream conservationists, with the support of religious organisations and many concerned citizens nationwide.

CHAPTER 9
BUGA UP
The Writing's on the Wall

SUBVERT THE DOMINANT PARADIGM

© Brendan "Mookx" Hanley circa 1980

verse 3 :
    Now the dominant paradigm, ego inflated. Paranoid, schizoid, triangulated.

    Not free. Guilty. Triple X rated. Subvert the Dominant Para * - * digm. * * *

verse 4 :
    Now the dominant paradigm, * such a consumer. *

    Inflate, rebate ** No sense of humour.

    Eating the world like * a cancerous tumour. * *

    Subvert the Dominant * * * *

The Paradigm is subverted by the clapping. Have fun.

verse 5 :
    If you're wondering what * * * * * * * * * the paradigm might be,

    It's not a thing * * * you can hear or see *

    It's a mind space * * * Simply consumes and doesn't replace * *

    Off its face * Subvert the Dominant Paradigm.

Notes: You'll find a lot of Mookx songs on Reverbnation. Have a listen.
         This was also on Silly Symphony's album "Walkabout" in 1984,
         and Gregarious Chance choir's version in 1998.
         Contact bruce@brucemcnicol.com.au for the choral score and mp3

Frustration and a sense of failure pervaded the peace movement following the uranium mining debacle. A number of long-term activists felt the need for a change in style.

A problem facing agents for change in mass action was often with the inflexibility of the group dynamic. We were, at times, no better than the system we confronted, with our obstinacy and divisiveness, but the disillusionment was with the means, not the goals. A short-term solution was to work in small affinity groups or completely alone. Sporadic individual action, I was soon to discover, could be as powerful as the major organised events.

The anarchistic actions of BUGA UP (Billboard Utilising Graffitiists Against Unhealthy Promotions) gave a legitimacy to act powerfully on the issue of inappropriate advertising. The artful refacing of tobacco and alcohol billboards was one way of giving individuals an opportunity to express themselves freely while continuing to maintain a social change momentum. The city environment provided an ideal backdrop for such expression.

As in many local actions, the global environmental implications, while not so apparent, were of major importance. At the time of the actions, every hectare of tobacco cultivation in Third World countries required the timber from a hectare of forest to flue-dry the product, the woody flavour increasing its value. The finished product was then sold back to countries on a cash payment basis, where many could not afford to feed themselves. Tobacco production represented 30 per cent of global deforestation annually.

BUGA UP was a loose-knit movement of social, political and environmental activists, and a significant number of medical practitioners. It issued written campaign information, newsletters, catalogues and calendars showing the very best examples of 'billboard artwork' but activists working on changing the advertising culture in a city-scape were unknown to each other. The activities of BUGA UP participants gave the individuals concerned a sense of personal empowerment, offering them another way of taking control over their local environments. The proliferation of corporate advertising, particularly of hard drugs, was and is a vital urban environment issue.

After leaving Roxby Downs and the stark desert landscape at the end of 1984, I began the search for something that I could do anywhere to something that was everywhere. Hence BUGA UP.

I had met the founder, Bill Snow, at Middle Head. Back then his pursuit of smokers had been dogged and had inculcated a sense of urgency into the issue. Inspired by Bill's actions I launched into a campaign of my own. So, a word from our sponsor:

"I was driving a Koori to court. He had a badly damaged lung from smoking. I'd offered him a lift on the condition that he would not smoke for a few hours. A spraycan rolled around the floor. I mentioned that it could be great to jump out of the car and stuff the Marlboro man up. When I asked my companion what to write he said 'Poison might do it. Come to Poison country.'" That was the first word of protest on a tobacco billboard.

"My main aim, after the original euphoria of attacking the tobacco industry, had been the vilification of cigarette advertising, which was accepted as part of the culture. The word 'poison' became a trademark. It well expressed what the advertisers were promoting".

"We discovered humour to be the most effective medium of communication. Our conceptual thinking progressed and we learnt to consider the location and social environment of our artwork. Near a school, graffiti was designed to appeal to kids, near a technical college it targeted that age group. Where a church was nearby we tried to give parishioners a jolt. Then the billboards became more political. BUGA UP was exposing injustice and the rape of the planet," concluded Bill.

From the rainforests and the deserts, I returned to Sydney and the streets of the central business district. I got myself a bicycle, an industrial gasmask for the filthy inner-city environment, and a set of spraycans, which fitted snugly in my water container racks. Traffic jams and red lights, far from being an inconvenience, became a source of great challenge and artistic expression.

Taxis sported advertising mini-billboards on their boots, where cigarette advertisements predominated. First strikes on them at traffic lights were invariably a sloppy affair. The limited time of stoppage and the high degree of nervous tension meant the spray hit hands, clothes and even face before a line could be slashed across the tobacco ad. Before long, however, I deftly sprayed dollar signs on taxis in traffic and at red lights (a full stop I would execute with an expertly inverted nozzle – clean and off). Even the last cab at the rank was a target. Within weeks the results were well distributed, clearly visible, and mobile.

Such activity was not without its drawbacks. Some cabbies welcomed it; others noticed me, but not in time. One day I was caught in the act by a large and aggressive driver. Eyeball to eyeball in his rear vision mirror, I sensed that my time was up. He was out of the cab before I could replace the can in the rack. It was a steep hill. From forest pursuit experience I'd learnt that one always retreated uphill, but there was no opportunity to do so on the bike, so I tried to circle around him while avoiding oncoming traffic. The traffic didn't get me but he did. With one hand at my throat and the other on my steering arm, he sent me crashing into the gutter. A spraycan rattled forlornly down the hill. As I struggled up, he threw a punch. Fortunately it hit my helmet. "Fuckin' ratbag!" he yelled.

"Who's the fuckin' ratbag?" I yelled back, too nervous to think of something original. I was starting to get indignant (I am, after all, an anti – smoking fanatic). "You're the fuckin' ratbag, cruising Sydney with hard – drug advertising on your boot."

By this stage I had managed to stand up and, with the help of the helmet, was as tall as him. My soreness translated into a decided meanness When I saw my bike lying in the gutter; a broken derailleur dangled, the wheels and handlebars pointed in opposite directions. Whether it was my anger (fortunately he was unaware that words were as far as I was prepared to go), my helmet or the fact that this confrontation was costing him time and money, he jumped into his cab and sped away, leaving me to drag my broken bike to the nearest repair shop.

I saw cabs as the ants of the city, busily transporting people and goods from nest to nest, each of which was a gigantic building covered in corporate advertising. The most offensive of these advertisements, to my mind, were those by the tobacco giants, who pumped neon flashes into the unwary brain. Indignation arose further at the thought that tobacco grew where forests once stood.

Tobacco is the major cause of avoidable death in Australia. The industry costs the Australian tax payer millions of dollars annually through related medical expenses. Just as galling is the fact that greenies smoke in huge numbers.

'Anyhow have a ...' We all knew the rest, and so would almost 100 per cent of thirteen-year-old smokers who had taken part in extensive health surveys in New South Wales and Western Australia. The results showed that children were directly influenced by cigarette advertising. So much so that over 50 per cent of kids who smoked chose Winfield, nearly double the proportion of adults. Most of the remainder smoked Benson and Hedges, Alpine and Marlboro.

These brands, more than any others, promote images that appeal to young people. Alpine promises the gateway to womanhood, sexual activity and confidence; Marlboro offers freedom, potency and masculinity; Benson and Hedges suggests sophistication and status. Most insidiously there is the nonchalant, ocker indifference and fatalism of Winfield's "Anyhow ...' It took two years' legal lobbying of the industry's self-regulating council before it deigned to remove Paul Hogan (an acknowledged cultural icon) from the Winfield ads.

According to a 1991 *Western Mail* article, "Health awareness amongst adults over thirty has meant an increasing number are cutting down or stopping smoking altogether. Cigarette companies are replacing this lost revenue by redirecting their advertising towards children, 75 per cent of whom are unaware of the associated health risks."

Cabinet documents as far back as 1965 showed that Cabinet had repeatedly resisted the advice of its health minister and the National Health and Medical Research Council to put strict controls on cigarette advertising with a view to a complete ban. Warnings from the Council about the links between smoking and cancer had been issued as early as 1957. The Menzies government did not believe it was their responsibility to warn people and refused to finance educational films.

The BUGA UP fraternity certainly had its share of colourful characters. None was more dedicated than Fred Cole, who worked closely with Bill Snow in the early days of the campaign. Fred has been confined to a wheelchair in recent times. This should have been enough to end his career as a high-flying BUGA UP artist, but not our Fred, a tank driver for the British army during the Second World War. He recently purchased a cherry picker, and with wheelchair secured is still able to hit those heights with spraycan in hand. Fred has been graffitiing by this method from Sydney to Perth.

In campaigns of such a clandestine nature, all sorts of rumours run amok – a bit like the 'fish that got away' stories. One adventure, however, to which reliable sources can attest the truth, deserves to be set down in words so as not to fade into the mists of time, remembered only by a few. It involved two members of the BUGA UP fraternity, a billboard of substantial magnitude, and an ingenious planning process. The individuals, who wish to be known as BUGA and UP for obvious reasons, performed one of the most adventurous actions in the short annals of graffiti art history. To some they were ratbags, to others heroes. Whatever their status, no one could deny the daredevilry of their adventure.

The site they contemplated was a series of billboards atop an eight – story building which dominated the skyline of Sydney's lower city. On the side facing Broadway and visible to several suburbs was a Peter Jackson tobacco advertisement sporting a massive cigarette packet six metres high. Fosters beer beamed out from the other side towards George Street, the city's busiest thoroughfare.

Roxby Downs – Protesters storm the front gates (Melbourne Age)

Roxby Downs – Peaceful confrontation at the main mine shaft

Daintree – Locals on front line

(Wilderness Action Group, Daintree Rainforest Foundation Ltd – Trustee)

Daintree – Thin green line agains Daintree road
(Wilderness Action Group, Daintree Rainforest Foundation Ltd – Trustee

Daintree – Council worker threatens to cut occupied tree
(Wilderness Action Group, Daintree Rainforest Foundation Ltd – Trustee

Errinundra – Loggers vote at the Bonang meeting (Melbourne Age)

Peace protesters in warship vice (Leigh Howlett)

Benny Aable, 'Theatre of the Environment' Master
(Leigh Howlett)

BUGA and UP recall their adventure of a lifetime: "The interior of the building was being renovated and doors were left open for tradespeople. We decided that a closer inspection was in order before organising equipment for an assault on the billboard. If caught, fines and costs would be monumental, but we thought the attendant publicity against hard-drug advertising would make it worthwhile. The fact that Harris Street police station was directly below the billboard added a fatalistic air," said BUGA.

"We headed into the building, up the stairs and passed men laying carpet without being noticed. On the top floor we found the trapdoor unlocked, so we climbed onto the roof. A construction of scalable iron girders supported the billboards. It seemed all too easy. I climbed up the twenty-foot-high supports and peered over at the procession of beetle-like vehicles and tiny creatures below," UP recalled.

The two then retired unseen and made their way to a bicycle mechanic's, where an effective spraycan extension apparatus was manufactured, guided by BUGA UP's 'Catalogue of Handy Equipment'. The following day, with a backpack full of spraycans and a dowel rod in hand, they stood at the traffic lights below the building and surveyed their canvas.

"With the next green light we decided to go for it," said BUGA, continuing the story. "We stepped off the footpath as part of the crowd, nervous but determined. Halfway across the road – shock, horror – we sighted an elderly man inside the foyer, sitting behind a desk. We veered off our course and retired unseen to the Social Security office across the laneway. Peeping over job-application cards, we checked his movements like bank robbers ready to strike.

"He went out the back and began to hose down the garage. We looked at each other: time to go! Once through the front doors we moved silently across the thick carpeted foyer and up the stairs, figuring that the workers would use the lifts. As we neared the fourth floor the voices of carpet layers at work in a nearby office drifted down the stairwell. We slipped by them unseen and proceeded to the trapdoor access. The heady exhilaration of success was fleeting, the trapdoor was open and men's voices echoed down from the scaffolding. I cautiously peered up through the trapdoor to find that they were repairing lighting equipment on the billboard itself. They could well be coming and going all day. We retreated to the top business suite and quietly discussed the possibility of hiding out in the building for the remainder of the working day – seven hours," UP said.

They decided to retreat until the late afternoon. A return at 4:30 pm would allow access during office hours and would mean that they'd get locked inside the building, unstoppable for an adequate period of time even if police were notified.

"We quietly ran downstairs to the fire-escape exit, where we huddled for a murmured debate: close the door and leave no trace of our having been there, or leave it ajar, giving us an alternative to the chancy bolt across the main foyer. We left the door discreetly ajar," BUGA said.

Late that afternoon they returned. Their immediate task was to gain access, unseen, through the hopefully still unlocked door.

The lane was empty. They bee-lined to the door, discovered it was still ajar, and stepped inside. Alert to hidden pitfalls and imagined dangers, two frail agents for social change ducked and wove their way around a disinterested world going about its normal daily business.

UP recounts the next stage of the artistic experience. "We ran lightly up the flights of stairs and locked the trapdoor by wedging timber offcuts under the door handles. If the worst scenario did occur, the police would have a hard time getting to us before we completed the job. We waited until 5:45 pm to guarantee the guard had left. The sun was still shining. I wrote a message on BUGA's forearm so that when over the edge, inverted, painting letters three metres high, ten floors up, torso dangling and blood rushing, he wouldn't get disoriented and paint an 'E' back to front or commit some other such slight to the artistic standards of the BUGA UP fraternity."

"We had no argument as to who would actually perform the task: UP was terrified of heights," said BUGA. "I was only marginally less frightened. What a team! I climbed the scaffolding. He handed me the equipment and over I leaned, my lust for multi-national destruction overcoming my fear of heights. The late afternoon sun reflected on car windscreens as they crawled along, bumper to bumper, in peak hour traffic. I could see up Broadway as far as Sydney University, a whole suburb away. I hoped that the cops had better traffic sense than to be stuck in such a line – up."

"My lettering was shaky at first, but I was into the swing of things by the third letter. Choking on the overspray I went through a can every two letters. The dark blue background of the billboard was soon emblazoned with 'VOTE GREEN' in brilliant white."

"Far below, little blue ants moved in and out of the Harris Street police station. One pedestrian stood with his finger on the walk button while the traffic lights changed several times. I stopped working as a policeman approached him. The fellow at the button just kept leaning there, looking upwards. Eventually he moved off, in the opposite direction to the police station."

"I positioned myself so as to reach the artwork itself, a giant Peter Jackson cigarette packet with enticing cigarettes poking out the end. This wonderful example of corporate beauty was some five metres high and bolted onto the billboard. I drew a large cross on it and sprayed a 'NO' below the cross," BUGA related excitedly.

"By the time I got to spraying the Fosters ad on the other side of the billboard I had become quick and proficient. I wrote 'DRUG – PUSHER' and attempted to pour a can of yellow paint over the beer cans, but the updraught sent it back up all over me. My ability to melt into the crowd if police were around was looking rather dubious – for, of course, we'd forgotten to bring turps. Spillages and accidents were not on our agenda."

"Once finished we considered the consequences of our actions. We were prepared to get arrested, possibly abused, and spend a night in gaol over the issue. Yet with the job done, the possibility of a clean escape and freedom tasted sweet indeed. To that end I climbed around the scaffolding, looking for constabulary in wait. With no-one in sight, we decided that it was as good a time as ever to depart. Empty cans rattled in my pack as we descended. In the silence of the narrow ground floor corridor we looked at each other and the closed exit. As partners in a ludicrous act, we pondered the world beyond."

"UP nodded. Noiselessly I turned the handle and slowly opened the door wide enough to poke my head out: a deserted street. Like merry pranksters, we danced down the laneway and onto the main road – free and guilty, just like the perpetrators of those criminal ads. However it was unlikely that any tobacco industry executive had gained anything like the same satisfaction from their product as we had. We walked down Broadway to view our conquered billboard Everest. I leaned on my extension sticks and for the first time in my life was able to remark, 'I am an artist,'"BUGA recollected.

The artwork stood unsullied for several days. A team of two painters finally rolled over the graffitied areas on the blue surface, but the lettering started to show through the covering coat, projecting a subliminal message to the heart of the city. Another week went by before the painters returned to finish the job properly on both ads. The cigarette box was all that remained of the deed. Cranes were moved into Harris Street, forcing the closure of the thoroughfare. The crane remained there for several days until the repaired box was returned and hoisted up into position again.

That could well have been the end of the saga, job well done, but messages began filtering through that debate raged in the public service offices overlooking the Fosters billboard. The morality of the action was not the subject of discussion; support was overwhelming, according to reliable sources. Attitudes ranged from full endorsement of the message to the sentiment that any graffiti was a welcome respite from the boring alcohol advertisement. Debate centered around the imagined methods by which the deed was perpetrated. A descent on climbing ropes was the favoured theory. When the correct method was explained to a worker in the building, word quickly spread. The delight in having inside information was compelling evidence of the occupational poverty of the public service.

An explosion of graffiti occurred soon after these events, and with it came a clamp-down on all graffitiists. The consequent reduction of BUGA UP activities was not, however, the result of a tightening of the laws entirely, but was in great part due to the belief in the atmospheric destruction wrought by spray cans. Many in the movement argued that the best course of action was to let BUGA UP peter out. The impact of its messages had been undeniable: cigarette billboards were removed from railway stations and billboards became increasingly bland, proving that such radical action had been effective. Activists moved on to other issues and BUGA UP never got the chance to grow old and conservative.

A decade later, active promotions against alcohol and tobacco are commonplace, with cigarette sponsorship dying out rapidly. Opposition against the tobacco industry has now become culturally acceptable and government supported. The efforts of a handful of activists had helped change the mindset of a nation.

CHAPTER 10
WARSHIPS
Give Peace a chance

TURN AROUND

© Brenda Liddiard 1985

Verse 2: Now we have listened to their promises, and we have listened to their lies.
Now we must listen to what our heart says, 'cause we know we are running out of time.

CHORUS: So turn around ....

Verse 3: We are growing discontented with the generals who play chess with our lives.
No! We don't want to be connected with the maniacs who plan our suicide.

CHORUS: So turn around ....

LAST CHORUS: Turn around. Turn around. We don't want to be a target.
This must be neutral ground, before we are the sunset.

Transcribed : Bruce McNicol

The time had come to take the nuclear protest to the water. Australia's harbours were to become the scene for the next phase in the fight against the nuclear madness. Anti-nuclear protest events unfolded in quick succession in the early eighties. They were part of a strong anti – authoritarian reaction, typical of Australians vexed by this country's one – sided power relationship with the United States and other nuclear armed nations. The Roxby Downs protests, the women's actions at Pine Gap and Cockburn Sound, the 1984 National ALP Conference demonstrations and the 1984 Nuclear Disarmament Party election campaign had matured and politicised the anti-nuclear movement. It was out of this revitalised movement that the Peace Squadron evolved.

With rock star Peter Garrett heading the ticket for the NDP, and with anti-nuclear feeling riding high, the gathering of activists at election time was an ideal opportunity to mobilise for further action. Operation Sea Eagle, a joint military exercise between the United States and Australian navies in our waters, was due to take place at the end of 1984, and I was pressuring for action in the harbour against nuclear-armed ship visits.

On a personal level, my knee had clapped out due to running around in the wet and mountainous Franklin River terrain, and I despaired at not being able to run in the forest and escape the loggers and police. The arrival of nuclear warships offered me a new lease of life as an activist.

Crews from visiting warships landed on our shores to spend money on prostitutes and grog while the media feted them as heroes. I believed that people would recognise the folly of allowing into our ports the ships which brought these men when the vessels had been banned from many ports of the US, including New York, Boston and San Francisco. In my enthusiasm I invited various peace groups to attend meetings. I even happened upon Peter Garrett in the street and asked if he, as a surfer, would be interested in becoming a participant. My idea was to hold a press conference at Bondi Beach and have Peter, with a board under his arm, declare that he was in training to paddle out and protest. He agreed to come to the next meeting at the Greenpeace office. At the meeting I presented my concept. It was not appreciated. Peter thought it irresponsible and proceeded to give me a dressing down, saying that people would be injured, that the group was preaching to the converted and that we had to appeal to the conservative sections of the society. There was certainly truth in what he said, but I saw another perspective. To that end I encouraged people at every public opportunity to take to the water when the nuclear-armed ships arrived.

Greenpeace was supportive, giving the fledgling Peace Squadron office space for meetings. Michelle Sheaver, a Greenpeace coordinator, was competitive in a friendly way. When I encouraged others to participate on boats, floats and zodiacs, she retorted, "What do you intend to use when the time comes?" She had a valid point. Without organisation, funds or equipment behind me I was sounding increasingly like a lot of hot air. Still, enthusiasm had to count for something. I looked at her sheepishly and said, "I'll be out there on my surfboard." I didn't have the faintest idea what I would actually do in the middle of Sydney Harbour on my surfboard.

The first arrival was the USS Buchanan, a nuclear-capable destroyer which had catalysed the closure of New Zealand's ports to nuclear ships after a vigorous campaign. The US military, in response to our questions, employed a policy of neither confirming nor denying the nature of their arsenals. They stated that to do so would give away vital information to their enemies. It was hard to envisage ships like the Buchanan entering friendly ports unarmed for public safety only to race back to their US home-port for weapons in the event of a global nuclear alert.

The early hours of the morning of 7 March 1985 saw the first of what was to become a traditional harbourside routine. I found myself on a yacht captained by a nonchalant fellow from the Hawkesbury River. The last thing I wanted to do was relax as I clung to his rigging, holding on to a wrapped-up sail which resembled the state of my stomach. The warship loomed through the Heads.

"Aren't you going the wrong way?" I yelled.

"I'm the captain on this boat," he replied, patient but annoyed. In excruciatingly slow waltz-time, the ship drew closer. The yacht tacked gracefully to pass the port bow of the Buchanan at a safe but defiant distance. The captain, cool as ever and laughing under his beard (yes, he had one) said, "If you're going to take a leap you'd better do it now. This is as close as I'll be getting."

Landing with an ignoble bellyflop on my surfboard, I felt the warm, calming water wash over me. I paddled hard with no idea about conditions near a large ship. Obviously I should have practised on harbour ferries. I paddled across the bow two metres away and marvelled at the churning currents. I turned and paddled, feeling the push of the vessel as it slid through the water. A police boat drew alongside and a cop yelled, "Come here, you idiot!"

"I'm paddling as hard as I can," I replied, not knowing whether I was in any real danger or not. The police boat drew closer. "Get in!" a young officer yelled. I let them haul me aboard. I was taken to a boat which lagged behind the protest fleet. In the distance Greenpeace zodiacs zapped around the warship. It was a forlorn ending as I sat in a slow boat. After all these weeks of preparation, it seemed I was to only see the action from afar.

We all gathered at the Greenpeace office that evening to catch the news. "What happened to you today?" Michelle teased. "Get lost on the harbour?" She described the action-packed chase in powerboats, the adventure we all dreamed of. The pre-news highlights flashed onto the TV screen: "One protester narrowly escaped death as he paddled dangerously close to the USS Buchanan on a surfboard this morning." An image of yours truly paddling in front of the ship accompanied the report. Of all the material generated that day, the newsroom had chosen the image of my tiny surfboard in front of the vast ship to highlight the coming news. The adrenalin rushed through my body just as it had earlier that day. The juxtaposition of small and mighty had caught the attention of the media.

The very helplessness that I had felt, overawed by the immensity of both ship and task, turned out to be just the image the media wanted to portray. My mind raced with the potential of a vulnerable person on the smallest of craft in front of the mightiest of vessels. How to progress with the image which caught the media's attention became an obsession.

Some see God; for others, enlightenment is a blinding, beatific flash of light. Me, I meditated on the grey steel nose of a warship. Late one night, I peeked over my bed sheets and there it was, my very own vision – spectacular, ridiculous, an illusion of danger, a dance of life on the very nose of death, indisputably a nonviolent action in the classic sense. To hold on to the nose of a warship and surf a great, grey wave up the harbour was the ultimate statement; Aussie surfboard diplomacy.

Another activist, Dean Jeffries, had an adventurous plan of his own. When the Buchanan departed Sydney, we followed it in protest boats ablaze with rainbow colour. The police were extremely touchy and shunted us off forcefully. With glee I shouted to one of the more belligerent officers, "Don't worry about us, we're just here for the pleasure cruise. We've got the air force out today! Look up!"

Thirty metres in the air and heading for the warship was a motorised hang-glider. Dean, playing World War I ace, at the helm! The ultralight swept across the front of the ship, turned and came in low for a run, dropping a yellow package as it passed. It missed the ship and landed in the harbour: a paint bomb, which splattered like a giant bird shit on the water. (The media were good enough to mention that it was water-based paint.) The episode hit media networks worldwide.

With the success of that event, a core group formed and the Sydney Peace Squadron officially came into existence. Nuclear ships were entering ports on the east and west coasts of Australia and activities proceeded to grow in size and enthusiasm with the arrival of each ship.

From the north of New South Wales I travelled to Brisbane, where seven warships were due to dock. I hid in an isolated section of bush on the river. In a thunderous storm I donned my wetsuit, which was glaring red for maximum media exposure. With police helicopters overhead I crawled through the bush and hid, like a red crab in a garden salad. Then this not – so-camouflaged activist bellyflopped into a thicket and waited.

A grey US warship loomed in the calm river like a skyscraper. I hit the water with one aim: midstream. Police and media helicopters sighted me and moved in. I manoeuvred backwards and forwards, almost causing the police boats to collide. I paddled for the ship, but it sailed past, out of reach. Faced with growing police antagonism, I surrendered. A cop, nicknamed Flash, was my captor. It required some adaptation on both our parts to achieve a level of congeniality. I was handcuffed to the boat rail like a Roman galley slave, with Flash, who pocketed the keys, my sole source of salvation. His mood mellowed remarkably with his increased level of control.

I was delivered to the water police station. Here I found myself alone with a dozen police. Each took it in turn to ridicule me. The officer in charge entered the room and there was silence. To assert his authority, his performance had to be masterly. He stood close, leaning over me as I sat in the middle of the interrogation room, and barked, "They shouldn't let your type breed!" Appropriate answers flooded my mind. Charged and released, I retreated to northern New South Wales.

It was still my aim to ride the warships, and other surfers shared my ambition. The confusion generated by the arrival of non-nuclear French ships in Sydney provided us with exactly that opportunity.

After a twelve-hour drive from the north of the state, I arrived in Sydney with a vanload of activists and surfboards. It was the middle of the night, and the news which greeted us was that the Sydney Peace Squadron had publicly stated that they would not protest as the ships were not nuclear-capable. We were ready to secede, and declared that the decision was not the policy of the Northern NSW Peace Squadron. Some Sydneysiders joined us to display their commitment to action.

Fishermen and demonstrators lined up at the Rose Bay boat launch in a protest peak hour. Zodiacs were pumped up and banners hung from all manner of small craft. Surfers donned wetsuits as the first of the sailing boats tacked out to the shipping channel. "Glassy conditions for a surf on the harbour," quipped one of the surfers.

The two French ships were due to dock at 8 am. As we reached the shipping lane the first of the vessels was already through the Heads. We positioned ourselves in the expected pathway. The ship headed slowly but directly towards our flotilla. Late stragglers joined us and the Paddlers for Peace came off Bradley's Head in kayaks. A police launch roared straight towards the port side of our yacht. I hid on my surfboard behind the hull, along with Ashley, another surfer. With police attention on the beleaguered yacht, we paddled off unnoticed.

The bow of the Jeanne d'Arc surged slowly past. I grabbed onto the rounded edge. Ashley, on the other side, attempted to do the same, but he disappeared into oblivion behind the grey mass of metal. I maintained a hold and was towed along at a constant pace. The surfboard managed the small bow wave with comparative ease. The police launch sighted me and drew alongside.

"Get away from that boat, you idiot!" yelled the driver.

"I can't!" I shouted in reply. "I think I'm stuck here for the entire ride."

"Get off or you're under arrest, you bastard," he said.

"Is this really time to discuss the finer points of law?" I shouted back.

The police launch came closer, but backed off as my board buffeted against the warship in the surge. Peter Hale appeared on his surfboard with a grin from ear to ear. He grabbed for the other side of the bow, but smile plus Peter slipped away. Meanwhile, I was still hanging on, trying to maintain both my balance and a conversation with the sailors leaning over the side.

Danger lay ahead. The figure of Colin Charlton, a Peace Squadron activist, loomed larger than life in the water. On the nose of the warship I was surging directly towards this protester, who was paddling furiously on an airbed (you get one out in every surf). Crash! Squash! The airbed almost folded double on impact, and Colin disappeared after a valiant attempt to hold on. Airbed between his teeth, he exited the same way as the others, almost taking me with him in the process. (A subsequent occurrence with another protester, Murray Matson, on a similar craft, saw him actually go under at the bow. This near-death experience, spiritually uplifting as it may have been, prompted the banning of airbeds in future actions.)

The warship slowed as it approached port. The police moved in on me again, boathooks at the ready. They managed to hook my arm off the bow. I washed alongside the ship, still on my board, to be picked up by the Peace Squadrons zodiac. A new chase now began, the police boat in hot pursuit. With Jenny Ryde at the controls we outmanoeuvred the larger craft. In a race around the warship, her skillful driving forced the police to give up.

Peter and I again launched ourselves out on our surfboards. The police helicopter swooped low and tried to blow us away with the wind generated by its propeller. We kept paddling as the wind flattened us and whipped up the ocean for extraordinary media visuals. The winds only ceased when the helicopter pilot looked behind to see a warship relentlessly bearing down in his direction. Meanwhile our press boat got so close to the action that it collided with the French ship.

The police contingent was too small for effective control. This advantage was compounded by the increased number of active small craft, particularly kayaks and surfboards. They required only one person each to operate, were highly manoeuvrable and necessitated the use of a police boat to control each one.

With the ships berthed and all the hard work over, the police were given little respite, for our protests went underwater. At a distance of twenty metres from the Jeanne d'Arc, Jon, a professional diver, put a 'diver below' flag onto the water and jumped overboard. Several naval divers took to the water to investigate as the potential saboteur proceeded to do nothing more than clean the underside of his boat.

By June 1986 each arrival into our ports met protest flotillas of increasing size. Water actions allowed people to directly confront the machines of war. Instead of feeling disempowered from the sidelines, activists taking to the water described their experiences as spiritually uplifting, like a baptism. The tactics of the naval crews varied, but they continually lost points in the propaganda war as small craft and swimmers created spectacular media theatre with the picturesque backdrop of Sydney Harbour.

The entry of the USS Joseph Strauss into Sydney Harbour ran a gauntlet of large numbers, on surfboards, kayaks, yachts and power boats. The authorities had not found the key to dealing with us. As the police presence grew more sophisticated, the simpler our protest vessels and style became. Police helicopters successfully disabled sailcraft with their propeller downdraught. They came in low over the surfers, whipping up the calm waters like a gale. We paddled on, flattened to our boards, yelling "surf's up". We were an unstoppable armada of water fleas as we paddled towards the ship. Sailors ran along the decks with water hoses and let us have it, making us wonder at the naivety, or arrogance, of those naval commanders who could so blatantly thumb their noses at public opinion.

For Dr Peter Hale, our spokesperson, it was a day of hard knocks. He was kicked in the head and hosed off the deck when he tried to board the ship. He was later to report in the media, "I intended to speak to the captain so I climbed onto the mooring buffer. I wanted to explain our concern about the dangers of nuclear weapons. They were guests in our country, yet I was kicked and fire-hosed."

Dean Jeffries' casual approach confounded observers as he sat on his surfboard while being pounded in the crossfire of hoses from two ships moored alongside each other. The ships were slowly moving together; Dean sat contentedly between them, his arms raised and fingers extended in peace signs as the ships closed in like jaws of a giant vice. Fortunately he managed to overcome his zeal for proselytising in time and escape unscathed.

That night's television images made it look like a scene from 'Apocalypse Now'. Water cannons blasting at people in the water looked as if demonstrators were being (shot'. It was fun for us on surfboards; we would be pushed under only to pop up again. Both protesters and the media revelled in the scene created by the authorities.

The reputation of Queensland police, however, made Brisbane River actions another matter to those in Sydney. Here, people demonstrated on the docks but were not keen to venture into the water. Brutality was expected. In September 1986, myself and three other demonstrators found ourselves in a launch on the Brisbane River facing an incoming US destroyer. The USS Paul Forster moved steadily upriver in the brilliant morning light; in the dead calm conditions, the surface of the water reflected a ghost ship mirror image. One police launch prowled nearby.

As the warship drew nearer we had to make a quick decision. Given that there were no media craft in sight, was it worth the risk of police attack, unfettered by media surveillance? Fools that we were, we decided to go for it on principle. James and myself dived overboard on our surfboards. The police boat, also aware of the lack of media backup, zeroed in on James and bashed him over the back with a boat hook. With the police busy elsewhere, I headed for the slow-moving warship. Another police boat roared up with a lone operator. I had thought I would be reasonably safe, but obviously the Queensland police had taken a page out of the Canadian Mounties' rally cry, 'We always get our man'. The police officer stripped down to his underpants (in a flash, I might add), wrapped a length of rope around his wrists and launched himself off the side of the boat on top of me. With rope around my throat and fists behind my ears, I was dragged under. I broke the surface gasping. The cop hauled me over to the boat, swearing at me all the way.

In future actions on the Brisbane River I dreaded meeting him again. Of course, it had to happen. He stripped as his boat made a beeline for me, then jumped and landed on me. I was more prepared this time. I held onto him, looked him in the eye and said, "You know, we really shouldn't go on meeting this way." He cracked up laughing and I was saved from brutalisation. He still arrested me.

The media coverage mobilised larger protests later that week. The HMS Illustrious, a British aircraft carrier, was the target. I hid in the bush on the south side of the river with two others. The Illustrious was unmistakable: with its decks bristling with jets and armaments, it was huge. We broke from our hiding place as it loomed into view. On a long malibu board, I was first into midstream. A police shark cat pulled up in front of me.

"Get out of the way or you're under arrest!" yelled the driver as he nudged the boat closer.

I kept paddling. The twin hulls were on either side of me as he revved his motor. "Look behind you!" I shouted, and pointed upwards.

He slowed the motor and yelled, 'What?' "Look behind you!" I shouted again.

He looked over his shoulder to see a massive grey wall moving inexorably towards his craft. Throwing the boat into gear, he charged off to harass other paddlers.

For me it was an unfettered run at the approaching ship. I lined up on the side without the tug boat. As I turned the board and stroked before the oncoming hull, I felt as if I were about to catch the perfect wave. I grabbed the bow and glided upriver, an easy ride in the glassy calm.

There's always someone to spoil a perfect moment. A policeman, the same delightful fellow who was in the habit of ramming our boats up launching ramps, approached in an outboard motor with an upraised boathook in his hand. He cracked it across my knuckles, manoeuvred his boat back into position and caned me across the knuckles again. I moved my hands below the edge of the surfboard, which deflected the boathook to a certain extent. Under the full force of the bashing my fingers could easily have been broken.

I continued to hang on grimly, every hit steeling my determination. All else, even the warship, paled into insignificance as a Queensland cop moved through a stylised battle. Nothing was more important than hanging on. My antagonist picked up an oar and tried again to bash my hands. Then he went for the boathook once more, positioning his craft between me and the shore to shield the act from media eyes. He speared me in the heart with the blunt instrument, winding me momentarily, then scraped the hook down the side of the ship in an attempt to push my fingers off the bow. By alternating my hands as they gripped the nose of the boat, I managed still to hang on. It was becoming like a chess game. Finally he tried a new tactic: he pushed the hook onto my board to dislodge it from under me. It worked. I lost the nose of the ship and the board at the same time.

The ship was moving so slowly by this time that I swam a few strokes and grabbed hold once again. The ship slowed and came to a halt. While I could lay claim to having stopped the pride of the Royal Navy with my bare hands, I was far more involved with my one-to-one interaction with the cop. "You've proved your point and gotten plenty of media. Get into the boat," he ordered. I was too exhausted to do much else, and bleeding profusely from my knuckles I grabbed onto the rail of his boat. As he hauled me aboard he said, "I'm proud of you, mate." One minute he bashed me, the next I was acknowledged. The 'duel' cast a line between two opposites. It was a recognition, albeit unconscious, of a man's striving for meaning. The media images portrayed a protester being bashed by Queensland police.

The Peace Movement was effective in highlighting the issue of nuclear war and global destruction, yet the seemingly death-defying actions undertaken by its participants continued the myth of male heroics. It was mostly men who were seen to be opposing the 'boys with the toys.'

Our actions led to the inevitable discussion about the perversion of the male role through the history of patriarchal domination. To avoid a defensive reaction to the justified aims of the peace movement, it was recognised that men needed to find a new, more aware identity: strength with compassion. With men and women working together as allies, crossing established gender roles, there was the potential to create a powerful movement for social change.

In the late 1980s, people in the Peace Movement were breaking new ground with the best of intentions and there was unanimous support of women taking on erstwhile male roles. The yacht Hysterisis was crewed by women. With regular training days, more women became involved. This prompted Di Ingram to get her boat driver's licence. Due to her diligence and the shortage of licensed boat drivers, Di became the mainstay of the Peace Squadron's zodiac fleet. "It led me to attain skills that I would never have acquired normally to the extent that I now have blue water sailing experience and a competence recognised by the active peace groups," she said.

Women in the Peace Squadron often bore the brunt of police and military prejudices. At one action, Di piloted the zodiac, making obstructing circles between the mooring ship and the wharf. A police launch charged in and rammed the zodiac, sending it skittling along the side of the warship.

"There was a look of horror on his face as he drew close," said Di. "I could only presume that he recognised me as a woman. His face set hard and his launch sped up drastically crashing into me at a speed that could have caused serious injury." Di was reported in the media as "a man in an inflatable acting in a dangerous manner."

In 1986, Sydney was the major venue for the Australian Navy's 75th anniversary. This included the arrival of the largest international assembly of allied vessels in a foreign port since World War II and the presence of the Duke of Edinburgh to take the official salute.

The media was primed by the supposedly violent confrontation on the Brisbane River. It appeared that reports of a protester being bashed by the Queensland police somehow meant that the victim must have been violent to deserve such treatment. This debate dominated the media prior to the arrival of the international fleet.

Despite the policy of neither confirming nor denying that US and British ships carried nuclear weapons, Admiral David Martin of the Australian Navy blundered and admitted that such weapons were aboard visiting ships when they entered Australian ports. He tried to retract the statement but the media seized upon it.

The issue of port safety in the event of nuclear accident was pushed by our side with spectacular success. The media ran several documentaries highlighting the dangers of radiation escaping and spreading on the prevailing winds over the central business district and beyond. This concern was supported by Scientists Against Nuclear Armaments (SANA).

Activists on the water were unstoppable. We too had our secret weapons, from waterwings to a little dingy with a sign on its sail reading, "When I grow up I Want to go to Moruroa." When a contingent arrived from Brisbane with a high-powered zodiac, complete with a planing wing to maximise manoeuvrability, our fleet was able to boast a 'catch us if you can, coppers' state-of-the-art protest boat.

On the day of the navy's sail-by, the peninsula at Mrs Macquarie's Chair was a sea of protest flags. There was also a sprinkling of American and Australian flags in support of the military exercise. Senator Bronwyn Bishop staunchly defended the establishment, her loud-speaker system overpowering our megaphones. A protester's cup of coffee in the generator fixed that.

The first ships entered the harbour to be greeted by a large banner on North Head reading: "No DEATH SHIPS?" As the warships convoyed in, our boats announced over the megaphones the arrival of these nuclear – capable ships. Motorised vessels played cat and mouse with the ships. With protest vessels approaching from the side, one warship tacked and blocked our advance on the following vessel. In a scissor motion our target ship disappeared behind the mass of the ship in front. An elegant manoeuvre was performed, if the movements of such a hulking machine of war can so be described. Clearly, some careful strategies were being worked out and communicated from bridge to bridge to neutralise the protest fleet.

Relying on well-developed tactics of our own, Gerry Smith drove the zodiac a distance away from the main fleet but manoeuvred directly in front of the approaching ships. For a few nervous moments we sheltered beside Fort Denison, Sydney's historic fortified island – the nearest thing to hiding in the bush out in the middle of the harbour. With a nod and a wise smile from Gerry, our forever-calm pilot, we skimmed down the harbour straight at the oncoming destroyer, the USS Oldendorf. When we were about 50 metres in front of the warship we stopped dead in the water. I jumped off. Gerry executed a quick U-turn and disappeared before the police realised what was afoot.

I paddled for the ship. An armada of small support boats in front of it was bearing straight down upon me. The boats could not break ranks for fear of collision, and if they stopped they were in danger of being hit from behind by the warship. I paddled my way through the lines until nothing separated me from the warship. I turned and paddled hard. In the choppy conditions it was imperative that I had momentum at the point of contact. I grabbed hold just as the ship appeared in my vision from behind. As I strained, the nose of the ship began to propel me along.

The hardest part over, I was positioned for the ride of my life up Sydney Harbour. I waved to police and protest craft alike, smiling from ear to ear. That is, until I sighted a boat ten metres in front. On board were cameramen with monstrously large lenses pointing at me. I pulled an excruciatingly intense face; after all, nuclear warships were no joking matter. A large police launch motored past. The bow wave crashed over me, but I managed to hang on. The police came no closer, unwilling to repeat the negative publicity of Brisbane one week before.

The captain of the Oldendorf was aware that he had a problem. He later stated in the media that he had seen me jump from a boat directly in front of the ship and disappear under his line of sight. The ship slowed down appreciably. This, I assumed, was the normal practice of a ship approaching port. Just as I began to relax, the ship began to surge forward. I hung on as the speed increased, stretching my arms out of joint. It sped up and slowed down repeatedly. Either there was a miss in the engine room or someone was attempting to dislodge me. The surfboard nosed into the growing bow wave and ripped away from under me. I grabbed my board midship, pushed away from the hull and paddled hard to avoid the propellers, uncertain whether the stories of propellers sucking under those who ventured too close were a reality or a rumour spread by the police to control our actions. I paddled off looking for a friendly boat, but the police were in hot pursuit and so I surrendered.

I was taken to the Darlinghurst police station where I was processed and released two hours later. Still in my wetsuit, I ran down Crown Street with my thumb out, desperate to get back into the action. A car pulled over: "Mrs Macquarie's Chair, I presume?" said the driver. Upon arrival I jumped once again into the zodiac. The police were instantly onto us. They didn't dally with the niceties of a reason for our arrest, and so it was I found myself incarcerated for the second time that day.

I couldn't help myself; I was possessed by an energy so positive and strong. It was a meditation. In the ocean I felt protected. As I headed towards the bow of the advancing warship there was no questioning the logic of my actions, no ifs or buts, no 'perhaps I should be doing something else'. Rather, there was absolute conviction and belief. With it came a focus rarely experienced in my life. In stark contrast to my personal brand of spiritual upliftment, the authorities slapped bail conditions on me, prohibiting me from entering the 'waters of Sydney Harbour'. I was neutralised.

That night I was berated by members of the Peace Squadron for hogging the limelight. Bow riding became a major internal issue and discussion papers were circulated, most of them criticising the activity. One such paper by Kel Dummett stated: "Bow riding is seen by many in our ranks as an important way of focusing media attention on nuclear ship visits, but many Australians see it as a dangerous, thrill-seeking activity. It gets the front page but often it is the issue of the dangers surrounding bow riding that is raised, not the issue of nuclear ship visits. Sooner or later the danger of nuke ship visits to our harbour must stand up on its own and make front-page news without the questionable bow riding 'antics'.

"Only when this happens will we in the peace movement know if the majority of Australians are with us or against us. While we continue with bow riding we present another distracting issue, one which is much more easily addressed by middle Australia. We can't let them continue seeing us portrayed as ratbags."

Another perspective was that the photo of yours truly holding on to the bow of the Oldendorf hit the media headlines worldwide.

The next day the harbour sparkled. Swimmers, board-riders and anything that floated hit the water. The previous day's positive media coverage meant that the taboo against action was broken. It was like a giant religious festival, a sight to be expected on the banks of the Ganges. People splashed, swam, stroked and sank, all except me. I stood wringing my hands in anxiety, unable to do anything but watch the proceedings. Any entry into the water invited instant arrest and harsh consequences for breaking bail conditions. I lent my beloved surfboard to another 'demonstrator', a big guy with an American accent. I should have known better. The surfboard and its rider disappeared. Despite earnest investigations I could only conclude that it sailed back to the US, adorning a ship's locker room.

The USS Missouri ('Big Mo') appeared through the Heads. The destroyer dwarfed anything that had arrived the previous day. A floating dinosaur, its decks had been the stage for the Japanese surrender at the end of World War II. In later years the ship had been refitted to become a floating nuclear arsenal, a propaganda machine representing the awesome power of the US fleet. Protesters attempted to get close to the bow of the great ship but were ferried aside by water police. Seven people were arrested in the water, and after a harrowing day on the sidelines I became coffee boy at Darlinghurst police station.

Our media antics were designed to win over public opinion, but what followed the berthing of Big Mo was a sobering experience. Two hundred and fifty thousand people arrived to visit the historic battleship. In what was a serious underestimation of public enthusiasm, five times the anticipated number turned up. More than 40 people were injured in the harbourside chaos; 18 were hospitalised. Tactical-response personnel were called in and mounted police were used to clear the crowds from the roadway. The authorities were forced to close the dockyard.

After that event, sailors raided our camp. Their favoured booty was flags, whisked off to their ships as trophies in the dark of night. It became sport.

One day they flew a rainbow flag from a porthole. On Saturday's sail-past, Prince Philip was to take the salute. Weekend crowds celebrated with Sydney boatspeople turning out in their thousands. As protesters hit the water they became targets for a hail of beer cans as the Sydney 'slobberati' vented their anger against anyone out to spoil their day of fun. Boat owners flagged down police and gave away our positions. One protester, Jon Jacobs, had his barge mocked up as a coffin. The crew of a women's boat were dressed in black with a banner reading: 'IN THE MIDST OF CELEBRATION THERE IS DEATH'. These people received the worst response from the assembled crowds. A group of activists descended from the harbour bridge with a banner stretched between them. Suspended on climbing gear, they were high enough to be clear of police boats yet not so high as to allow the passage of warships that intended to sail under the bridge as part of the grand parade. The police cut their ropes. Two hapless protesters wrapped in a flapping banner plummeted into the harbour to be scooped up and arrested.

While we as an organisation were faced with the depressing reality of massive public support for the military, Dean Jeffries once again was to be found assembling his rickety ultralight for a flight over the departing Illustrious. His preparations were hurried forward by the arrival of police. Before they could stall his planned protest he took to the controls and blasted off, trimming some of the nearby shrubbery in the process. Once in the air he headed for the ship but was intercepted by a police helicopter which attempted to block his progress and shepherd him away. An aerial dogfight ensued. Dean flew low over the ship's deck to escape his pursuer, making several runs over the giant carrier. At one point it looked like he intended to land. He gained height once again and in his final pass dropped a wreath of flowers and a message of peace – which, appropriately, landed in a missile bay. He returned to Dobroyd Point, where the waiting police swooped on him.

In court the magistrate threw the book at Dean for what he considered to be dangerous tactics. Indeed they were, but the action had created a spectacle that reverberated around the world. Dean was sentenced to a month in Long Bay Gaol.

To some in the Peace Squadron, things were getting badly out of hand; to others, things were delightfully out of hand. The debate raged between the opposing factions, discouraging some activists from participating in a number of events. The media, spoilt by the high drama of recent events, quickly lost interest, until, that is, the arrival of the USS Sterritt in June 1987.

The atmosphere was rather casual on Jon Jacobs' barge. All the old hands on board had decided not to act until the second day. I casually remarked as the warship cruised past, "You know, I could board that ship without too much trouble."

"Is that so?" said Di.

"There's a screw guard that isn't high off the water level," I replied. "Too bad we aren't doing anything today."

"Lots of our boats, but it looks pretty quiet out here. We may not get any media at this rate," chimed in Jim Dixon. Jon, the pilot, was consulted. He replied, "I'm just driving."

As a professional salvage operator, Jon was a skilled boatman. Despite the fact that the police were shadowing us, he drove his barge at high speed, executing a neat U-turn around the stern of the warship, and parked the nose of his vessel directly under the screw guard.

All I had to do then was haul myself up. Our boat stayed in position in case I slipped (we were directly above the propellers). I hopped up onto the deck. "G'day, gentlemen, I've just dropped in to let you know that there are a growing number of Australians who don't like the idea of nuclear arms coming into our harbor," I announced.

The crew of the Sterritt tried to haul me out of sight from the media helicopter overhead. I grabbed the guard rail and held on, not keen to disappear from public view. An officer appeared and ordered sailors to surround me. I became locked in by a human barrier of huge sailors pressing against me in silence. They just stood there like bars on a cage.

I was held until the ship berthed, handed over to New South Wales police and locked away for an interminably long time until one rather disgruntled detective returned and informed me that they were unable to charge me, as the US ship in Sydney constituted US territory, beyond the authority of Australian courts. This piece of information was of great significance to the Peace Movement, with relevance to the status of US bases in Australia. As official US territory on our soil, foreign control meant that Australian authorities would have no right of access in the event of a nuclear accident.

The Peace Movement had significant success in holding the media spotlight. The bicentennial celebrations of 1988 loomed as the largest event for both the navy and the protest movement. Townsville hosted the first media blunder for the military: a nuclear ship crashed into a vessel tied up at a wharf. In Brisbane, people blockaded buses full of sailors as they left the wharves, and a group of Christian anarchists boarded a ship on open day to pour their blood on the deck in the shape of a cross. The event and the protest captured the attention of the media Australia-wide.

Activists gathered in Sydney for the big one. The first day witnessed a great armada of warships entering the harbour. Each nuclear – capable ship was 'greeted' by zodiacs and fast runabouts; closer in, graceful sailing boats cut across their bows. The spectacular display of painted sails and flags was enhanced by the Auckland Peace Squadron, which had sailed across the Tasman to support us. As the ships berthed, several protest ferries bedecked with banners and flags listed precariously as passengers gathered on one side to view the action. One ferry carried Sydney councillors against nuclear warships. Another was loaded to capacity with university students.

On shore, Benny Zable, with his anti-nuclear show, focused on the huge protest crowd at Mrs Macquarie's Chair. Tugs assisting the warships to berth flew anti-nuclear flags and banners – an important step in an anti – nuclear alliance with the unions.

A week later, in the freezing waters of Melbourne, masses of swimmers appeared from under the piers and swam to an incoming vessel. The Seamen's Union refused to assist the HMS Ark Royal to berth in adverse conditions. After the ship had circled for two days it was forced to depart, with 2000 frustrated sailors on board.

The nuclear issue in its many manifestations has mobilised millions throughout the world. The task to decrease this threat to our survival is still monumental, but change has begun. Water-borne actions were part of this global reaction to the nuclear Armageddon scenario created by the leadership of the United States and the Soviet Union. These adversaries agreeing to point their weapons away from each other may be an incomplete symbolic act, but it has been a move away from the doomsday position evident at the height of the Cold War. The Soviet Union has been dismantled and relegated to history, and former member states are decommissioning their nuclear arsenals. The United States has removed nuclear weapons from its surface fleet. Despite these positive moves there still exists enough fire power to end life on earth. Maverick nations such as North Korea, Israel, India and Pakistan continue to assert their right to bear nuclear arms.

The Peace Squadron revitalised the anti-nuclear movement in Australia, after the defeat at Roxby Downs. Strong international links were forged with New Zealand, which had successfully defied the US by barring nuclear-armed warships from its ports. The anti-nuclear debate raised by these actions made a mockery of so-called safety regulations in the nuclear industry and sent a strong message to the international community that, after the sinking in 1985 of the Greenpeace flagship, the Rainbow Warrior, the peace movement was able to bounce back with added dynamism.

The collective global effort to halt the nuclear madness has been monumental. The contribution of the Australian Peace Movement and those who took to the water around Australia as part of anti-nuclear peace fleets, played a vital role in an international movement by ordinary people to turn the tide of nuclear destruction on earth.

Paddling in before connection (above)
Riding the bow (right)

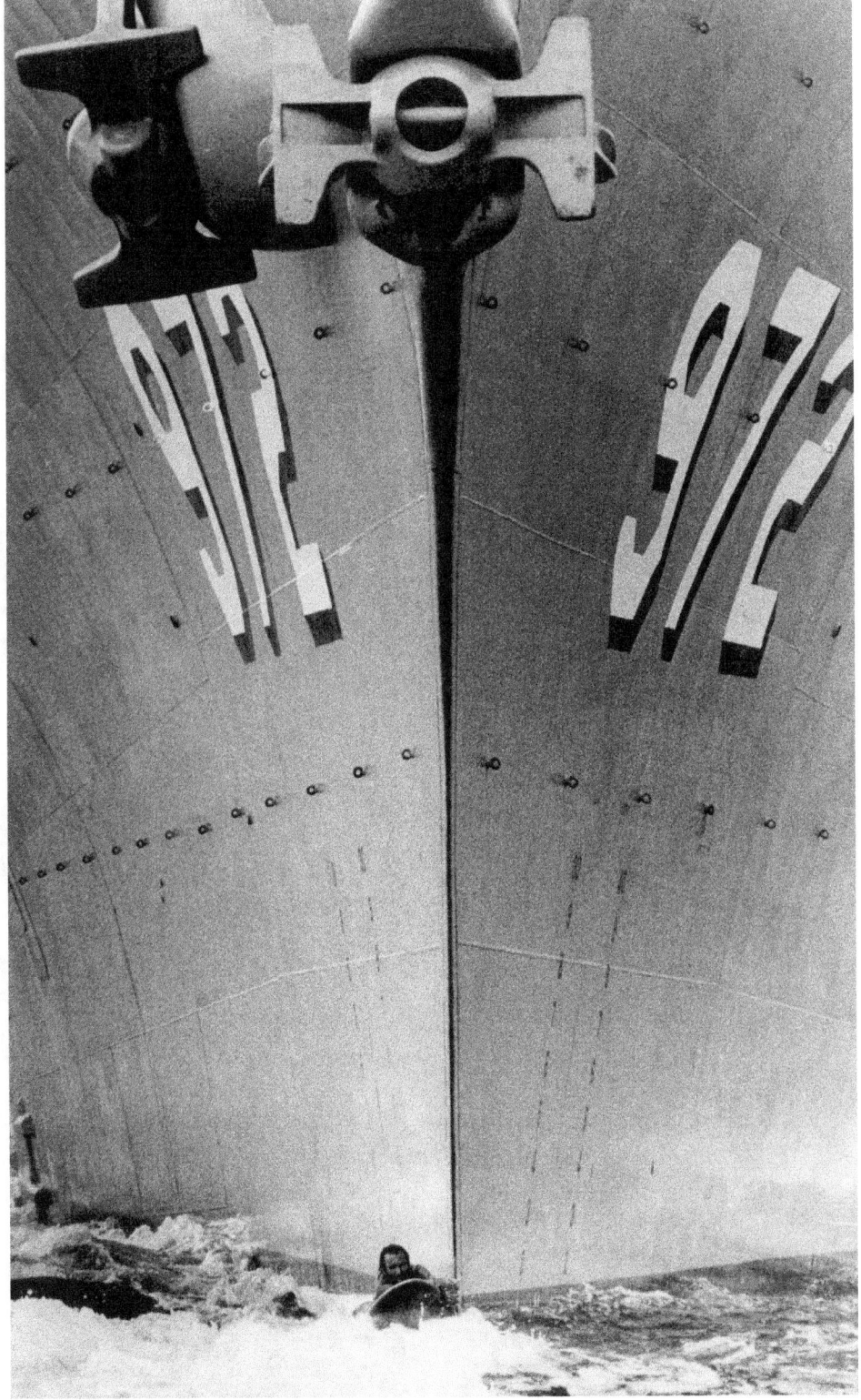

Latched on to the USS Oldendorf (top left)
The chase is on (bottom left)
Tug of War (top)
Arrested but 'Post Surf' euphoria (below)

CHAPTER 11
ELECTIONS
The Politics of Protest

verse 2 : Doesn't worry us if nations war, jet planes roar, buildings soar.
We're selling mush MORE than the year before, it doesn't worry us, you see.

verse 3 : Doesn't worry us if people die. We'll get by on nuclear pie.
We're on a radio-active high. Doesn't worry us you see.

verse 4 : Doesn't worry us about tribal lands, racial stands, nuclear bans.
We're all paid by the mining man. Doesn't worry us you see.

verse 5 : Doesn't worry us if people scream, poets dream, rebels scheme.
We're the stars of the silver screen. doesn't worry us you see.

verse 6 : 'nd it doesn't worry us if you all find out, start to shout, "Hey, let us out!"
We've scuttled the ship, and we've just bailed out. Doesn't worry us you see.

Google "Brendan Hanley Reverbnation" and you'll find over 110 of this prolific writer's songs.

Transcribed : Bruce McNicol

In Australia in the eighties, protesters evolved from greenies into greens and finally became The Greens, a significant political force for the future. The move into politics represented the maturation of the environment and social change movements.

Political success has traditionally been gauged by the winning of a seat, a fat salary and public acclaim. Green participants, like many voters, saw elections as an ideal opportunity to express frustration with mainstream politics and its environmental ethos of expediency, as well as to support specific issues and effectively utilise the electoral media frenzy. Calls for sustainable alternatives to economic rationalism, an end to the nuclear industry and a reduction in armaments spending gave the politically disenfranchised a new option in elections – a conscience vote. The Greens expressed the need to redefine humanity's role from controllers of the biosphere to that of stewards.

While the protest movement had traditionally existed outside of politics, many greens believed that we needed to be a part of the political process directly. In Tasmania, political activity began in 1972 when the 'United Tasmania Group' stood in the State election on a broad platform, but particularly in opposition to the flooding of Lake Pedder in Tasmania's south-west. The Tasmanian Greens entered State Parliament in 1983 in the person of Dr Bob Brown. By virtue of Tasmania's proportional representation electoral system, subsequent elections saw additional Greens elected. From 1989 to 1992, the ' Tasmanian Greens' five MPs held the balance of power in Tasmania's parliament and entered into an 'accord' that permitted Michael Field's Labor Party to govern.

In 1981 we ran a PEACE campaign for the NSW Upper House and gained 22,000 votes with Keith Suter as lead candidate. In 1984 The Greens supported the Nuclear Disarmament Party, which had high – profile musician Peter Garrett running for the Senate. The Greens also ran a low key campaign in the seat of Sydney. The NDP's near miss in the elections saw it implode on a national level. The following elections, in 1987, saw the NDP run Rob Woods as the lead candidate, but the campaign lacked the mass support and the media interest enjoyed by the Party in 1984. The Labor Government called a double dissolution of parliament. This meant that all senators were to stand for re-election rather than the usual half; instead of a 15 per cent quota, an elected senator only needed 7 per cent. Anything was possible.

During the election campaign, a surprise offer came to me from the Sydney Greens, a group which had formed as a political party in 1984, drawing its inspiration from the German Greens and from events in Tasmania. The offer put to me was to stand as a Green senate candidate in the coming federal elections. As I was a green activist and an anti-nuclear protester with a profile, it was felt that I would have something to offer the party (my warship image encouraged the view that I'd be a candidate who would 'stick to the vital issues'. The Greens offered me a platform by way of their four principles: social justice, ecological sustainability, peace and nonviolence, and grass roots democracy. These principles suited my brand of activism. I accepted the offer.

Little clarity emerged as to what was expected of me until I met up with a master of political antics, a fellow with a passion for creating dysfunction in society's political paradigm, Richard Gosden. Richard's axe to grind was the sewage issue and, in particular, ocean outfalls.

Our sole piece of political campaign equipment was a Sydney Morning Herald. In it, the 'Election Diary' section advertised the day's events and listed the campaign trail of major politicians. An early morning phone call from Richard decided our first action, which was to conveniently collide with a politician and the attendant media.

Our 'campaign' was launched at the Bondi Pavilion where the Prime Minister, Bob Hawke, and his Environment Minister, Barry Cohen, were due to present a programme in support of the arts community. As members of the audience we attempted to attract Hawke's attention, questioning his priorities in supporting the arts with a foul and stinking coastal environment over his shoulder. In response to the heckling, he offered to speak to us after the conclusion of the meeting. What we didn't know was that the offer was merely a method to shut us up; we took him at his word and quietened down.

Later we approached the PM but were intercepted by his security. Blocked by a thick wall of grey suits I saw Barry Cohen unattended. Up I walked and extended my hand. He shook it. "Hello, Mr Cohen, my name is Mr Cohen, Greens Senate candidate. You might say I'm the Cohen that's coming and you're the Cohen that's going." He looked startled. I thought at the time that it was my wonderful, off-the-cuff remark, but I later learnt that Cohen had, in fact, been privately informed by Hawke that after the election he would lose the Ministry. The press gathered like hunting dogs around their prey. In the political stakes I had nothing to lose, so I pressed on. The conversation moved to the issue of ocean pollution. "Can you imagine the Swiss defecating on the top of one of their most famous mountains?" I asked. Cohen was not amused. He answered, "The question of ocean pollution is a state issue. It is not the domain of the federal government." The story ran in the following day's media: "All at sea dodging dirty issues."

The next event was the much-heralded ALP launch at the Opera House. It was a Prime Ministerial passion to glide serenely across Sydney Harbour in the admiral's launch. Touted as his method of taking him a thousand miles from care, it seemed like an appropriate point to intercept the political system. I arrived early and hid under some bushes in the nearby Botanic Gardens. Playing out my superman fantasy, I surreptitiously donned a wetsuit and blew up my surf mat. Around my neck I strung a placard which read, 'STOP OCEAN POLLUTION'. Meanwhile, Richard chatted to the media present to find the PM's expected time of arrival. At a signal from my political adviser I moved out of the gardens, over the sandstone retaining wall and into the harbour. The nearest police boat was a mere five metres away. In the calm waters of the harbour and in the brilliant light of midday, it seemed impossible to slip into position unseen. However, I paddled the mat, slowly and quietly, at the rate that the police boat turned in the soft breeze, keeping the broad blue back towards me. He remained transfixed, looking across the harbour (perhaps he too was a thousand miles from care). From past experience in the harbour I knew it was difficult for boats to see an object at water level. I paddled to the Man of War steps at the Opera House and waited between the pylons. I presumed the small craft heading my way was the prime ministerial entourage.

Meanwhile, Richard was on the steps above me. The media were fifty to sixty strong. They were gathered in a hushed, awe-struck silence as if awaiting an event of grave importance. Richard later related: "At first, when you appeared, they simply ignored you. You didn't fit in with what they were expecting. Hawke was playing at royalty that day and the media were playing along."

I paddled for it. Twenty metres away, the pilot of the launch saw me and the craft stopped. My main worry was that it would circumnavigate me. The speed of such a boat compared to my clumsy surf mat could have made me 'miss the boat'. No such need to worry; Hawke and the crew presumed they were so important, gliding like Cleopatra across the waters, that there was no question of evasive action. They continued to the wharf, motoring straight towards me, so I grabbed onto the nose. The launch stopped again. It would not do for a politician to run a protester down. Sydney had the historical precedent of Premier Sir Robin Askin. In a car cavalcade in 1966 with US President Johnson, Askin, confronted by a group of anti-Vietnam protesters, instructed his driver to 'Run the bastards over!' That single line wrote him into the history books. Times and tolerances had changed, however. I attached myself to the bow and tried to engage Hawke in a conversation. He made no response, but a naval rating leaned over the edge with a boat hook and attempted to dislodge me. I, in return, pulled the probe and almost dislodged the seaman instead. He managed to push me aside and the launch headed for the wharf.

A second success! I had managed to infiltrate the Hawke media extravaganza. My image featured prominently on all the television news reports that evening. Photos, some on the front page, appeared in the evening and morning papers. The slogan I carried on my placard was prominent.

In stark contrast to the huge cost of Labor's launch, the Greens' campaign expenses could be broken down into $1.20 for my bus fare to town, $1.00 for a fruit juice for my political adviser (who arrived by push bike) and $1.00 for my placard. For a total of $3.20 we got complete media saturation. It had proved to be a highly successful action, launching the Greens into the mainstream of the political debate. The only down side to the event occurred when I dragged myself onto the wharf. Thoroughly pleased with myself, and expecting all to share in the amusement of such light-hearted political entertainment, I was surprised to find myself placed under arrest.

To follow up this striking success, Richard and I arrived at the venue of the Liberal Party launch a few days later. An advertisement in the morning's papers had invited the public of Australia to attend. Disguised as Liberal Party supporters with 'VOTE LIBERAL' stickers on our most presentable attire, we sat down next to a little old lady. She was keen to discuss the terrible state of the nation under Labor and the unions. We decided that a launch from that position could be fatal, so we moved once again. By this stage we'd attracted the attention of the security, so that when we took seats nearer the back of the auditorium, a burly individual stood directly behind me. After I was told this by Richard I was not game enough to look around. Surreptitiously I unrolled a sign beneath my seat which read 'GREENS NOT GREED' one side and 'LIBS' ENVIRONMENT Policy A DOWNER' (in reference to the then environmental spokesman, Alexander Downer) on the other.

My mind raced; my nerves were on the brink of chaos. Waiting for solo actions has always been excruciating for me. Richard, pleased to be on the sidelines, was calm. He leaned across and whispered, "Don't go yet!

Wait till he gets into his stride and the audience gets carried away with him. Do you want me to tell you when?" I just nodded. I sat with the sign concealed under my legs. It seemed like an eternity. Richard tapped me on the knee; I didn't look in his direction or behind me. I was told later that the guard made a great lunge, missed and then frantically radioed. I stepped up with a single-minded purpose: to place myself between John Howard and the media barrage that was filming him and steal the show. Any attempt to throw me out would be broadcast to the nation.

I hopped over media cameras strewn over the carpet to find myself directly in front of John Howard. We were separated only by a few balloons at the edge of the podium. Richard, who was close to the action but able to safely observe, said that large sections of the audience leapt to their feet and screamed abuse. Little old ladies with blue rinses shouted, "Throw the scum out!"

I was focused, oblivious to the noise at my back. It was just me and the leader of the Opposition. "What about the Franklin River?" I shouted.

"Will you dam it if you get into power?" Howard ignored my interjections, but he was affected: spit gathered at the corners of his mouth, sweat came to his brow. His Shadow Cabinet sat in the front row glaring at me. Senator Baume snarled in disgust and uttered an original creative line in keeping with a man of his intelligence: "Why don't you get a job?" My retort was, "Can't you see that I'm trying to do that right at this moment?" My sojourn out front was lasting much longer than expected. Howard stolidly continued, still ignoring my interjections. I was now completely relaxed.

The hard task, getting to the centre stage, was over. Finally after what seemed an interminably long time, I was grabbed from behind, fortunately by an official, and frog-marched up the hall.

One member of the audience jumped up from his seat, grabbed my placard, tore it up and stamped on the pieces in a frenzy (better it than me!). I might as well have been an assassin. The abuse and hate from such a group of law-abiding Liberal supporters was chilling. At the back of the hall I was delivered to the waiting arms of a blue uniform and comparative safety. A young cop trying to keep a straight face warned me that he would have to arrest me if I entered the premises again. I was happy to comply. An impromptu press conference was held in the foyer and we disappeared before the party faithful spilled out. Once again The Greens received media saturation.

So far the campaign, coming from nowhere and lacking finances, was proving remarkably successful. We had gate-crashed political parties and, with the 'leading lights' our targets, had created a media event each time. By now, we felt, my profile was sufficiently high to attempt an action using our own resources. Attracting the media without using a politician necessitated original theatre that the media could not resist.

It was decided (definitely not my idea) to make a splash on the sewage issue. Richard had a diabolical plan to put ocean pollution and myself on centre stage. To date the issue had failed to capture the imagination of the media and public; we intended to change that.

A press release stated that at 12 noon on Friday 3 July I would risk my life by climbing down the cliffs at Bondi and paddling out into the sewage outfall stream to collect samples of contaminated sea water. We blamed the then Attorney General, Lionel Bowen, whose seat was in Maroubra, for failing to force the Water Board to comply with national and international standards in line with the Commonwealth Sea Dumping Act, the London Dumping Convention, the UN Law of the Sea and the OECD Polluter Pays Principle. The statement concluded that we intended to deliver contaminated material and documents to Bowen's office. It was a tidy media package, though it was not likely to be the most pleasant job in my political career.

A representative group of Sydney's media assembled on the cliffs at Bondi on a cold winter's day. I was suitably clad from top to toe in wetsuit, gasmask and rubber dishwashing gloves. The impression was of an individual about to perform an act of bravado, verging on the foolhardy.

Actually I considered it less dangerous than swimming and diving under waves at Bondi Beach just around the headland. The stink and condition of the sewage stream itself would be little worse than surfing Bondi on an onshore day. I determined that I would not submerge my mouth, ears or eyes in the water and rationalised that once outside the sewage stream the water would wash the murk away in a matter of seconds.

I descended the cliff face to the quip of one of the reporters: "If you don't make it I guess we'll be seeing you in that great toilet bowl in the sky."

I jumped off the rocks, paddled into the stream, collected the samples and started on the long haul for Bondi Beach on a surfboard too small for the task. Due to the gasmask I was short of breath. A media helicopter hovered overhead, probably hoping for a shark attack to complete a sensational story. I reached the beach 20 minutes later, close to exhaustion, and gathered some young surfers to the final press conference on the beach. After that I had a long, cold decontamination shower and headed off to the Attorney General's office where a lone employee received the sample and uttered not a word in front of cameras and blazing lights.

Once again we received television, newspaper and radio coverage.

Following this success we consulted the BUGA UP founder, Bill Snow, who located for us a suitable billboard for campaign purposes. This was no mean feat. While the anti-tobacco billboard campaign had not achieved the 'final solution' regarding visual pollution, their impact had been sufficient to render ground level tobacco billboards a rarity in Sydney. A ground level billboard was necessary as Daphne Gollan, the number two candidate on the ticket, was keen to participate but felt herself to be a bit too old for acrobatics. The media was notified of an action without being given the exact location. We were moving into another arena. The public defacing of private property was a deliberate illegal act.

We travelled to a ground level billboard near Mascot airport. Out came the equipment – paint and brushes, buckets of glue and rollers. Bill had printed white on black posters reading 'CANCERLED DUE TO MASS DEATH IN OUR HUMAN FAMILY'. These were posted, with some artistic touches to complete the visual statement, onto a hard-drug advertisement, transforming it into a clever piece of anti-smoking artwork. We packed up and disappeared without being apprehended by police. Much of the media considered it too hot to run, but it worked with a few grabs on the television news that night.

With election day looming, the final action to draw attention to environmental and social welfare issues was to be a sleep-over in the rail section of the incomplete monorail in Sydney's central business district. The aim was to create political theatre to highlight the plight of homeless youth in Sydney. Current media reports stated that over 6,000 youths were homeless in the city every night; emergency accommodation catered for only 1,400. A protest against the misdirection of funds into a 40-million – dollar monorail link between Sydney's centre and the Darling Harbour casino site seemed appropriate.

Getting up onto the one-storey-high rail tracks was no problem, getting to sleep was another matter. Just as I had drifted off my name was called. A late night reporter from The Mirror wanted a picture. I was happy to oblige – without getting out of bed, of course. At dawn the reporter from The Telegraph woke me up for an interview.

Later in the morning, roused by peak hour traffic and feeling a bit the worse for wear, I climbed down and walked to court for an appearance on charges arising from the Prime Minister's launch. I decided to plead guilty and get it over with. In my defence I stated that certain forms of irreverent behaviour towards authority were healthy in society. It mustn't have been a particularly good day for the magistrate, either. The normally progressive arbiter of justice placed me on a $200 bond, to be on good behaviour for one year. He then ordered me to be locked up immediately until the bond was paid. I was carted off to the lockup out the back – an ignoble end to an otherwise successful political campaign, which netted The Greens 32,000 primary votes. Although we didn't achieve office,

Greens votes flowed on as preferences to the elected NDP candidate.

Participating greens considered the campaign a raging success.

After the Prime Minister and leader of the Opposition, The Greens were the most publicised political party in the elections. 'We had managed to kick – start the public debate on Sydney's ocean outfalls and place the environment firmly on the election agenda – something the major parties preferred to ignore. The campaign had been run on a shoestring with the only major costs incurred being for printing and phone calls. We had developed electoral media intervention to a fine art. We had beaten them at their own game.

Elections 1990

Crawling through the bush was not the formal manner of entrance to a National Environment Ministers' Summit. It was, however, the first campaign event of The Greens in the 1990 federal elections. The tactics we were prepared to use to gain public attention were as varied as the number of parties running for election. Although environmental and peace movements were fractured politically, attempts had been made to run one ticket. However, rivalries between former NDP senators prevented a coalition forming. It was now important that The Greens eclipse other groups and minimise the political splintering for future elections.

The aim of our first campaign event at North Head in Sydney was to gatecrash the Environment Summit, where Amory Lovens, a US expert on power generation efficiency was giving a speech. We were hunted down and apprehended by a bevy of police and special branch officers. They dumped us at the front gates just as Senator Richardson drove out. By force of habit I stood in front of his car, but there was no need; he had driven out to see us. He invited us to attend the conference if we promised to behave. On arrival I was interviewed by all assembled press – probably organised by Richo, with an eye to increasing the Green profile over the Democrats, which in the end would benefit Labor.

Inside the conference, Amory Lovens drew gasps of appreciation from his audience as he displayed energy-efficient products, dazzling Environment Ministers' eyes like a door-to-door salesman. The irony was that these products were already available in environmental circles. It took an American expert to make these Ministers take note.

As we had learned very effectively in 1987, sewage and politics have a certain affinity. After the North Head conference I went to South

Head on the other side of Sydney Harbour to buy a fish from a fisherman who cast his line directly above the sewage outfall. A sign prohibiting fishing at the top of the track was of no consequence to the band of twenty fishermen. The one fish I purchased cost $20; my attempts to bargain with the angler fell on deaf ears. He stated that he could get $8 a kilo at local restaurants, which preferred fresh fish direct from the ocean to those which went through the Fish Marketing Board.

I took my freshly caught, faeces-fattened fish to Parliament House with the intention of presenting it to the parliamentary chef and request he serve it as lunch to the Premier and the Environment and Agriculture Ministers. Fishing bans at the ocean outfalls had been secretly lifted in October the previous year, and even the Chairman of the Water Board had not been notified. The Department of Agriculture had independently made the decision, even though fish caught near the sewage outfalls were repeatedly found to be heavily contaminated with a range of toxic chemicals and metals. I appeared for the media assembled at the gates of Parliament with a waiter's napkin draped over one arm and the fish resplendent on a platter. A label tied to its tail identified the person intended to feast upon the dish. Unfortunately I was stopped by security and the hapless fish was left hanging on the fence outside.

The next action against ocean pollution was targeted at an industrial waste pipe from the Australian Lubricating Oil Refinery (ALOR), near Kurnell in Sydney. Toxic industrial waste spilled illegally from a broken pipe. The State Pollution Control Commission (SPCC) had issued a licence to pollute via this pipeline, specifying a submerged ocean outfall with supposedly stringent conditions, including limits on suspended solids, grease and oil, pH and temperature. However, these licence conditions allowed the expulsion of 2.2 million litres per day of industrial waste in dry weather (even more in wet weather), 20 tonnes per year of oil and grease and 40 tonnes per year of suspended solids.

The Greens campaign team – all three of us – convoyed to the outfall along a rough flooded track. The media brought up the rear. Picturesque heathland gave way to a vista of sandstone outcrops and ocean, marred only by an ugly effluent pipe. I contacted the plant manager by mobile phone and informed him of my intention to block the pipe, instructing him to hold the effluent flow to avoid equipment damage or worker danger. As the flow slowed I slipped a wooden disk horizontally in the pipe and secured hydraulic jacks;

the residual water forced the wood against the jammed jacks. With the release knobs cut off the jacks became permanently jammed. With an eye for overkill, a kitchen stool, stolen at breakfast that morning (my political adviser informs me that his standing morning coffee has since been a source of constant irritation), was jammed into the pipe and roped to nearby rocks.

We waited nervously for the next flush. ALORBS security and management appeared, adding to the high drama. The rush started; effluent squirted from the edges. Our plug was holding. We Greens quietly nodded to each other, like the ladies' auxiliary after a successful cake bake. The management was irate.

The satisfaction of a job well done was short lived. All of a sudden, at a point twenty metres upstream, the pipe burst like a Texas oil well. The spectre of vandalism charges crept across my mind, but the press loved it. New leaks spurted out all over the pipe. The gully was awash with toxic effluent pouring out like a river of death. The pipe, it was discovered, had previously been repaired with PVC tape. The media turned the heat on the management, who counter-attacked that I was a vandal. The accusation was quickly thrown back at the industrialists. The police arrived. After official inspections of the pipe, the threat of arrest faded. What was dubbed an 'industrial dispute' hit the major news networks that evening.

Our next opportunity for media attention was at a Malabar Sewage Works open day (fun for all the family). A press release announced to the media that I would slip into the plant unnoticed, head for the sedimentation tanks, enter on a surfboard, and risk my life surfing through the final screening process. The release read: "I want to show the people of Sydney that turds as big as a man can fit through Sydney's existing treatment system." The fact that one media crew turned up with an underwater camera for me to use was unnerving.

Premier Nick Greiner was scheduled to inspect the new (but still inappropriate) system that day. Meanwhile a mix of cornstarch, drinking chocolate and water in a poo-like paste completed my disguise. I appeared at the front gate on schedule, camouflaged in brown goo with toilet paper stuck over clothing, body and surfboard. I was stopped by the Water Board officer, Mr Chris Tweedie, with a mobile phone jammed firmly into my stomach. The media captured a fuming debate with Water Board employees against local residents, surfers and myself Mr Greiner arrived and drove through an irate picket line. The demonstration was considered a success. I retired, thankful to Tweedie and the police who barred me from the sedimentation tanks and a potentially unsavoury immersion.

While the Water Board continued the murk of public relations exercises, our demands were always clear: the Malabar plant needed immediate upgrading to full secondary treatment. Moreover, the Board needed to crack down on all industrial waste streams to the sewers. We demanded the introduction of a federal Clean Waters Action Legislation.

Next we decided to go 'window shopping' at ICI. The company produced carbon tetrachloride which erodes the ozone layer, yet capitalised on a market opportunity by manufacturing ultra-violet blockout to protect against skin cancer. ICI's net profits in 1990 were estimated to be $240 million.

Our first ICI site inspection was at the new car park. Signs prohibited puncturing the asphalt surface. Below the capping lay a mountain of intractable toxic waste, lined with plastic, on a shifting sand – dunal base over a rising water table. The toxic waste could only be disposed of if legislation to allow construction of a high-temperature incinerator was passed. This was the source of further controversy, as incompletely burnt toxics would pollute the atmosphere. As an action backdrop, the site was uninspiring. The main chimney stacks were too inaccessible, buried in the heart of the industrial complex, and the site of the 8,000 tons of hexachlorabenzine (HCB) in storage was inappropriate, being a low, inconspicuous shed which would lend itself to nothing more than a quick and anti-climactic arrest. This was not to belittle the terrible significance of the chemical which it housed. ICI was the only producer of HCB in Australia and recent studies through a Sydney doctor specialising in chronic fatigue syndrome have shown that the average Australian has a concentration of HCB 1,000 per cent higher than the average contamination in comparable US samples.

There it was. Never in my wildest imaginings would I have thought to have empathised with an industrial chimney, yet the perfect site for an eloquent environmental action stood before us. It towered over the plant, an arabesque minaret, elegant in its slenderness, a delicate-looking component of ICI's orchestra of industrial power. Smoke and flames issued forth intermittently. A ladder climbing the entire height would, I figured, facilitate the hanging of a twenty-metre banner. The chimney was a hundred metres inside the perimeter fence, a relatively easy access. Along the boundary where the media would be asked to gather, a market garden flourished on the border of this toxic wasteland – line after line of leafy greens for innocent consumption.

Our window shopping was at an end; ICI was an appropriate target and it was time to begin the real work. Richard prepared a detailed position paper, worked out the timing of the operation and liaised with the media.

I, meanwhile, procured steel cable able to withstand bolt cutters, a mobile phone, a two-way radio, padlocks and a Kryptonite cycle lock. The lock was for bolting my neck to the structure if police or workers broke through the web of cabling I intended to weave across the ladder access. With my kit including lunch, water and even a little pot to discreetly pee in, I felt thoroughly prepared. The only thing I didn't factor in was my fear of heights.

We held a press conference at the mouth of the Springvale Creek at Botany Bay. The creek, which runs through the ICI plant, was a designated site for migratory birds in an agreement between Japan and Australia.

When, under pressure from local environmentalists in May 1989, the State Pollution Control Commission tested the drain, a toxic mix of chlorinated solvents and HCB was found. At the press conference we unveiled our plan to occupy the chimney until the closure of the solvent plant and chlorine facility was negotiated. The former was producing HCB, which erodes the ozone layer; the latter was outdated and had leaked chlorine. Mercury had also been discharged down the sewer, contaminating the food chain.

We headed a media convoy to the chimney site. Twenty metres from the fence, near a service gate, I grabbed my pack, leapt out and headed towards a gate topped with barbed wire. My fear was that I would not be able to scale the gate, loaded as I was, but halfway up it swung open.

Feeling like a kid on a roundabout, I jumped down and trotted off across the field with a clear run to the tower.

Workers in the distance obviously didn't comprehend my mission.

They leaned on their rakes and stared. As I reached the tower my heart jumped. The trap door was six feet off the ground. I had to haul myself to the first platform, my arms shuddering under the load of the pack. The rest of the ascent was like climbing a ten-storey building straight up. Everything was in slow motion – the weight of the pack saw to that. At the last platform, before the chimney became too hot, I off-loaded, descended two levels and proceeded to weave the heavy cable in an impassable web across the ladder cage. With the cable locked I retreated upwards to my vantage point and with great difficulty hung the banner, which whipped in the strong wind. Security, police and management appeared. They radioed me and demanded that I return to ground, stating that they would not negotiate while I remained on the tower. I maintained my demand for an early closure of the solvent and chlorine plants and invited the management to join me for a summit meeting on site. They refused and continued negotiations with my ground crew.

Meanwhile, with the media list taped to the mobile, I conducted interviews with radio stations via phone (the heights one has to go to for media access during the election frenzy!). The wind affected the transmission of messages but added to the dramatic flavour of the chimney – top interviews. The police made a renewed demand that I come down, informing me that I was in a highly dangerous position and that they were not prepared to climb the tower. No-one actually told me that I was in danger of becoming a barbecued greenie if the tower had to burn off excess releases, as the chimney was a flare for the olefines plant. I was later informed that the tower was that height due to the size of the flame it emitted. The management had turned off the plant, otherwise I could have been incinerated. Ignorance was bliss as I huddled against the warm pipe awaiting the next move.

The minutes turned into hours as I continued interviews with radio stations and communicated to my support group below on the two-way radio. I was prepared for a long stay aloft, but a problem arose shortly after my ground crew informed me that major negotiations with company management were under way: the batteries of my two-way radio faded.

Reports were phoned through until the mobile phone also began to fade. All my support systems had collapsed. I suddenly felt very high and alone, bereft of my distractions, and became uncomfortably aware of this tall, skinny tower swaying with the growing intensity of the wind. From my vantage point, the red glow of the incineration process made the olefines plant look like two gigantic pop-up toasters. Drums of HCB were stacked to the roof of an open shed, while in the distance the toxic car park loomed high above the surrounding flat industrial area like a giant black bubble waiting to burst. With its chemical stench and shimmering emissions, the site looked like some evil empire in a science-fiction movie.

Without communication, the prospect of a lonely windswept night aloft was not a comforting one. In the distance my trusted friends, like little insects, started to ritualistically wave me down. Despite all the planning and available technology, the only communication that survived by the end of the day was sign language. I packed up and descended. Special Branch officers (whom I had met the week before at the Environment Ministers' conference) walked towards me. To my surprise, instead of arresting me they offered congratulations on a job well done before disappearing behind the LPG tanks, away from media eyes. My ground crew, exhausted by negotiations, announced the agreement to inspect the plant the following week. It was day's end, and with job completed we departed, surprisingly still free. Once again we had gained saturation media coverage.

As the elections drew nearer we anticipated that few opportunities were left to attract the media. For our next move we concocted a plan to confront Coca-Cola Amatil on their promotion of PET plastic bottles. We wanted to question their claim that the bottles were in fact recyclable. Our demands involved the reintroduction of refundable glass bottles (Container Deposit Legislation). Amatil's address in Macquarie Street was next to ICI House, so we arranged to meet at the latter, hoping to whet the media's appetite. We planned to enter the foyer at Amatil with detergent and buckets, dump a bagful of plastic bottles on the floor and proceed to wash up returnables. A simple message but, if adopted, one which would profoundly affect consumer and producer attitudes. We staged our event and phoned the management. They came down for a lengthy and at times heated discussion. The media, however, picked up on our commonsense argument.

Then it was up the road to Martin Place, where the Opposition Leader, Mr Peacock, was to address a lunchtime crowd. Conservationists had already gathered. A banner in defence of the South-East Forests was suspended between two abseilers, high above, on the walls of the Commonwealth Bank building. Various examples of Australian fauna cavorted brazenly amongst the crowd. Peacock arrived with a bevy of security personnel and stood facing the crowd with a two-and-a-half-metre – high stone wall behind him. Security positioned themselves in front, obviously ready to thwart any attempt to mar Peacock's personal meeting with the people. I stood at the bottom of the underground railway steps which rose up directly behind him.

The show was warming up when my political adviser, Richard, signalled to me. I launched myself up the steps, grabbed at the top of the wall and scrambled up. There was the Opposition Leader, with nothing between the two of us and gravity on my side. I jumped down amidst the crush of Liberal Party body heat. I was grabbed, but yelled, "Let me shake your hand, Andrew."

Political habit preceded caution. With a permanent media smile plastered across his face, he extended his hand. I grabbed it and didn't let go. A few pertinent questions on Liberal environmental policy drew his now famous reply, "I'll speak to you later."

The hasty interview ended as I was hustled away by Special Branch (again). A koala jumped on stage, South-East Forest banners unfurled in front. Peacock attempted to rev up the crowd but was howled down. He then sought a rapid exit, with protesters and media in hot pursuit. The Opposition Leader was visibly shaken by the intrusion of the 'rabble'. The event, which was high on the media agenda, was yet another shoestring success for The Greens.

Election time is the closest we come to a revolutionary change in this conservative culture dominated by power elites. Our overworked office staff at campaign headquarters worked at a fever pitch. We were not holding onto power like the established parties; rather, we were accessing it. We knew many agreed with our position and we felt that our dreams were only a vote away.

Andrew Garton had the unenviable role of office coordinator. This is how he saw the internal state of affairs at the time: "All the madness that the media captured would not have occurred without the support of a small campaign crew. Media coordination, preparation and distribution of media releases was a round-the-clock commitment. Not only were we fraught with sleep deprivation, exhaustion and accelerating demands, we were also up against the internal politics of The Greens themselves. On some occasions we despaired at the lack of trust and support from what we had thought were our own people.

"With a campaign to run and little time, we found ourselves under siege from those within The Greens who opted for establishing an egalitarian approach – a rotation of personnel to ensure that everyone got an opportunity to gain experience. Unfortunately this undermined our relationship with the media and public.

"Early in the campaign, news came that the Wilderness Society and the Australian Conservation Foundation had decided to support the Labor Party. This meant fielding votes from their extensive membership lists and media campaigns with resources that far exceeded ours. We were demoralised. Several members of these organisations protested publicly and a number resigned in support of The Greens.

"At the campaign office we were besieged with calls from the public asking us why 'we' had sided directly with the ALP. Some mistakenly saw the Wilderness Society and Australian Conservation Foundation alliance as representative of The Greens; they were concerned that their vote for us meant a vote for the Labor Party. Green supporters were looking for an alternative to the current political regimes and were sick of politicians who wore the same suits and smiles and spoke the same rhetoric, despite sitting on opposite sides of the fence. The public, it seemed, was inspired by the confrontational approach of our campaign. We represented their collective anger.

"We drafted a national Greens position on the liaison with the ALP and faxed it to other campaigning greens. The overall response was that the movement was being disenfranchised for political expediency. We were told that the peak groups were unfamiliar with many of The Greens' candidates. Many green bureaucrats were afraid that radical activists without connections would get elected. The executives of the peak groups made their decision without consulting their members, the majority of their staff and volunteers.

However, we had succeeded in placing the environment once again on the political agenda and captured media attention from the major political parties, who were keen to convince a gullible public that they had high-order environmental credentials. Most importantly, The Greens' campaign placed urban toxic issues on the agenda and notified industry that they would be subject to continued campaigns. Unlike 1987, the election was a half-senate one and we stood little chance of gaining a seat, but the Green primary vote doubled from the previous election to 64,000 in a theatrical and effective campaign.

During the 1991 New South Wales election campaign the odds were once again stacked against The Greens. Internal politics meant we had a rudimentary support system only. We had no significant financial backing: a campaign fund of $5,000 included the registration of candidates and the costs of printing. Despite alienation from many power brokers in the conservation movement and equally destructive sniping within The Greens, our vote-catching effectiveness was substantiated at that election. The continuing challenge was to nurture green politics, to realise the ideals of a growing number of disempowered members of the community.

This state election announced The Greens in New South Wales as serious contenders for those final seats which could mean the balance of power in the Legislative Council. At the federal level, Western Australian Green Senators, Dee Margetts and Christabel Chamarette, shocked the political establishment by coming from 'nowhere' to share the balance of power with the Democrats in the Senate.

The historical significance of this green political ascent lay in breaching the sacred cow of the 'two-party' system. With independents in the New South Wales Lower House vying for the balance of power and with elected Democrats and Greens 'knocking on the doors' of the Upper House, state political culture had been in the process of radical change and was able to provide an alternative power structure. State politics had entered a period of responsible government, forced upon the major players by the electorate. Through this maturation, the major parties were more attentive to the many issues that the Coalition and the ALP before them swept under the carpet.

The dry economic rationalists were under scrutiny from an electorate with more ethical values.

We turned away from the priority of 'political stunts' to elicit media interest. This presumption of sufficient political maturity, which would allow us to be recognised by the media on the issues and platforms we presented, fell flat on its face. Greens press releases piled high on every news desk but the media refused to show even the remotest interest. In hard economic times, environmentalism was judged out of vogue by the media and the agenda-setting major parties. A pall of journalistic censorship descended on election coverage, except for the presidential campaigning style of the then Premier, Nick Greiner. It seemed no success was to be gained with the mainstream media unless we backtracked to the formula of past campaigns.

So, we decided to stage a launch where The Greens would leave the ground. This did attract the media. A press conference was held in a park with the Waterloo incinerator as a backdrop. Resplendent in suit and tie and with Mark Berriman, our local candidate, similarly attired, the two of us outlined a Greens political strategy to the assembled media using the incinerator as an example of government ineptitude.

The Waterloo incinerator was fifteen years old. It was outdated technologically and was rapidly approaching its 'use by' date. The choice was either to close it down or upgrade the facility. The lack of available land-fill space was a major environmental headache for city authorities. Upgrading would mean a cost of $40 million to those councils using the facility. This option met with considerable opposition in surrounding areas. What was once primarily an urban industrial area was being transformed into a highly populated residential area. Carcinogenic dioxins (at levels 12 to 38 times those permitted by international standards) and furans, along with a cocktail of nitrogen oxide, hydrochloric acid and sulphur dioxide, were pumped into the atmosphere daily. The Greens opposed upgrading, as such incinerators did not always completely combust the toxic materials, despite the latest technologies. The problem would merely change from that of ground pollution to one of air pollution. Upgraded incineration ignored the problems associated with waste generation through society's habit of consumerism. The Greens favoured an integrated approach, incorporating reuse and recycling strategies with mandatory reduction in packaging. It all made good sense, but not to the media.

With our press conference concluded, I retired to a nearby van and changed into more casual gear. I then scaled a security fence, climbed the nearby tower, dropped a banner ('TOXIC VANDAL', recycled from the previous year's action against ICI) and returned over the fence unchallenged by security. The television and newspaper coverage ignored the besuited politicians and focused solely on the physical antics to satiate their daily appetite for sensationalism. The Greens message was kept at arms length in the media, felt to be beyond the pale of serious political contention. Despite considerable discussion and lobbying, the media refused to accept that The Greens were a challenge to the Reverend Fred Nile in the Upper House. I was given rudimentary instructions by an ABC 7:30 Report journalist to take myself to the western suburbs and go letterboxing.

Members of the Teachers' Federation decided to support Marie Bignold, a breakaway Call to Australia politician, to draw votes away from Fred Nile. A progressive union of teachers throughout the state was encouraged to vote for another fundamentalist Christian to defeat Fred Nile instead of supporting a progressive political group. The media and unions did not take The Greens seriously. Even if the Teachers' Federation had supported the Democrats we would have received a sufficient flow of preferences to cross the line in front of Nile.

How wrong these learned members of the media and progressive union movement were! The pre-election silence was broken by a cliff – hanger result. Like an episode of 'Yes Minister', the election campaign commenced after polling day with media focusing on the neck-and-neck race for last place. The Greens polled 105,000 primary votes for the Legislative Council, an increase of over 40,000 votes from the previous year's federal election. Fred Nile's Call to Australia Party vote dropped to 108,000 primaries. The issue of who would gain the last seat and balance of power received post-election media saturation. It took a month for the Electoral Commission to determine the victor.

The conservative pyrrhic victory, reliant on Nile's 'Balance of Prayer', was a tragedy for the Old Growth forests of New South Wales. The 150 votes in the seat of The Entrance, which decided who the Premier would be, gave no mandate to butcher forests, pristine water catchment areas and Wilderness.

Since the 1991 state elections The Greens have formally instituted a national organisation. Participatory democracy moves slowly, yet many regard the decision-making process to be a major issue. Steady progress towards an expanded and sound green political movement has continued in the post-election realisation that we were at last knocking on the doors of Parliament.

CHAPTER 12
SOUTH-EAST FORESTS
Rip Rip Woodchip

Early-morning trucks loaded with big timbers bound for the Eden chipmill on the south coast of New South Wales came to an abrupt stop. Directly in front; a vertical pole was secured in the middle of the road. Like a parody of an ancient forest giant, the top of the pole disappeared into the morning mist – an Indian rope trick of sorts. A voice called down from the shrouded heights. It was 1989 and the greenies were staging another blockade in defence of the South-East Forests.

The conservation battle had been waged for over twenty years in the South-East region. Local environmentalists had forced the Forestry Commission to reduce clearfelling areas from hundreds of hectares to smaller compartments. They also monitored the studies undertaken by the logging interests. A local conservationist secured a halt to work through successful court actions in 1987, 1988 and forced the Forestry Commission to prepare Environmental Impact Statements (EIS). However, corporate might, combined with Forestry Commission intransigence, held sway against objections from local conservation groups. The Commission claimed its practices were sustainable, but had no documentation to back up these claims.

The major focus for conservationists was the preservation of three areas: Coolungubra, Tantawangalo and Yowaka. They were all listed as National Estate Forests. In 1988 a renewal of export licences was granted by the federal ALP Government. The forests were to be chipped for seventeen years. The South-East Forest Alliance (SEFA) commenced peaceful resistance action in the disputed areas.

In January 1989 the Federal Government opposed all logging in the South-East National Estate Forests of New South Wales. Subsequently an agreement between Peter Cook, the then Federal Minister for Natural Resources, and Ian Causley, his New South Wales counterpart, approved the logging of 9 per cent of the area. The agreement was cosmetic: the Forestry Commission had originally intended to log only 13 per cent of the total area that year anyway. The public was hoodwinked. In reaction, the campaign broadened. Activist musicians formed a group called Coolangubra and the band toured the state to rally conservationists to action, with great success.

Woodchipping is the least economical use of timber as a resource. In 1989 90 per cent of the cut was used for chipping and only 10 per cent for sawlogs. The original justification for woodchipping in the South-East Forests was to utilise the sawlog waste as part of integrated forestry. The process, which turns Old Growth logs into Woodchips, is a perversion of the original industrial concept. Woodchip export profits are insignificant compared to the cost of importing sawn timber and paper products. Senator Cook in April 1988 said, 'Woodchipping is the lowest value, lowest effort way to export forest products. Relying on export sells short the resources on which our children will depend.' Similarly in 1989 Senator John Button called woodchipping 'a bastard of an industry'.

After the heady successes of the Nightcap and Franklin campaigns there had been a gap of several years since a full-scale forest action had been implemented. The New South Wales Labor government had been defeated and the Coalition was in power. With the Nationals in control of land-use portfolios, the timber industry found few obstacles in the way of its assault on Old Growth forests.

It was agreed that action was needed to promote the issues of woodchipping and damage to water catchment areas due to logging, but the potential for violence worried local supporters of our cause. Many were farmers who feared vandalism to machinery. It was a close-knit community; they knew the people in the forestry industry These farmers represented a broadening of community support for conservation.

The makeup of the participants meant a compromise had to be reached regarding the nature of action. The term nonviolent action still used the word 'violence' so a local farmer, Roland Breckwoldt, suggested 'peaceful resistance' as a more positive term. The public face presented at the Franklin campaign was the role model.

The basic rule was to act openly with police. Peaceful resistance under the guidance of nonviolence activist Rob Burrows became the accepted mode of action. This worked well when large numbers of inexperienced supporters were involved.

The South-East region was deeply divided. Understanding that the issue had to bite in the capital, activists Steve Berry and A.J. Brown linked up city and local networks. A base camp was set up in February 1989.

The first action took place at Egan Peaks State Forest. Activists slept in a logging coupe to wake up ready to confront police and workers in the morning. Protesters were arrested for trespassing, including the internationally profiled anti-nuclear physician Dr Helen Caldicott. With this celebrity arrest the campaign was launched.

A debate arose shortly afterwards regarding the removal of survey marker tapes from Wog Way, a controversial road through the magnificent Coolungubra Wilderness. Removal of tape from the trees was considered a violation of Forestry Commission property. Burrows suggested telling authorities we were going to remove the tape and act upon our words in a mass action.

The Sydney Wilderness Society office and the South-East base camp were visited by Special Branch police with the stated intention of making ground rules for a better relationship easier. When told that a thousand people were going to remove the survey tapes, Special Branch officers got uncomfortable. Organisers therefore promised to ring them before the action. SEFA's confidence and cooperativeness was unnerving for the police.

At Coolungubra the police demarcated an arbitrary line between legal areas and those which would incur trespass penalties. Protesters saw it as an opportunity for mass action. They crossed the line and marched along restricted roads to the logging coupe, tying pink ribbons to all large trees imitating the Forestry Commission's practice of denoting habitat trees for protection. The mass action worked; protesters outnumbered police ten to one and each cop could only arrest one person at a time. Arrests that Sunday totalled forty-two.

Peaceful resistance activists and police both saw benefit in observing a peaceful process of mutual cooperation and openness. Cops in charge gave information to the organisers, who in turn felt they were winning over the law enforcers with their convincing arguments and high – order manners. No secrets were kept from the police. It is a matter of conjecture as to which side benefited the most.

Celebrity actions played a pivotal role in increasing the public profile of the campaign. The musician Sting arrived on site with a group of Amazonian Indian chiefs. These Kayapo warriors, minus lip plates and traditional garb, still made a powerful impact as they stood in silent protest for the forests. On a worldwide tour to save their forest homelands, they added with their presence an air of legitimacy to the campaign, linking Australian forests to the global implications of destruction.

Designer Jenny Kee also came to the forest and was arrested several times. She motivated young people to participate in art actions. These visual invocations and artistic statements all made powerful media images.

The chipmill was an ideal focus for action. Not a pretty sight, the woodchip mountains were an eloquent statement of an industrial reduction of the exceptional. We walked down the road in front of a truck loaded with a single Old Growth log. It nudged us as we walked with our backs against the bullbar. Out of the crowd came a clean and neat protester of the peaceful resistance mold who shouted at us (not angrily I might add, but to overcome the noise of the roaring beast behind), "Get off the road!

You're being violent to that truck!" Arm in arm with my partner Carol, being shunted down the road, our minds were joined in memory of past days of action in circumstances not dissimilar but far more dangerous. We were determined not to be removed by a peaceful resistance activist of two weeks' standing.

Breaking the rules of any society can at times be a wonderfully liberating act. It is a fine balance, indeed, between group rule and pioneering individual action. This balance is rarely found, although sometimes touched upon inadvertently when working under pressure in actions. The South-East forest campaign faltered on this point.

From my experience I believed we had to push beyond the boundaries of what was acceptable to create appropriate conditions of pressure on the authorities. Originally, those in charge had requested that everyone gather on the side of the road to the mill. My idea was to encourage people to take a more militant stance. Hence the meeting took place on the road. This caused a considerable backup of logging trucks. The peaceful resistance organisers at first refused to be involved and acted in a codified, unimaginative manner. They decided what to do and ignored what was really happening. The events of that day were to be a microcosm of the campaign: if fluidity had been allowed, the campaign could have been a greater success.

As the campaign dragged on, the police budget for Operation Redgum – the code name given to the police mobilisation – escalated. In response, mass action as a tactic became strained, and the frequency and size of the campaign diminished.

Attitudes hardened. `One day, a pair of devices nicknamed 'wog wogs' (steel tubes with internal locks which closed when an arm was inserted) were cemented in the road and seven protesters were locked into the devices at dawn. Such an action was a radical departure from the accepted code of peaceful resistance and was a forerunner of tactics to be used in later campaigns. At this point in time, however, it was a controversial action and the subject of much debate.

It was in the Coolungubra campaign that the use of tripods as blockading equipment was pioneered. These consisted of three long poles lashed together in a pyramid shape with a sitting area at the lashed point on which one or more activists would perch. On finding one such device straddling the road, the loggers and police decided to lift the installation and move it off the road. Unable to do so properly, they spilt its human contents. David Burgess crashed to the ground. Fortunately a bush broke the major impact of his fall. He was

PM launch launches Green campaign '87
(Sydney Morning Herald)

Centre stage with Howard – Election '87
(Sydney Morning Herald)

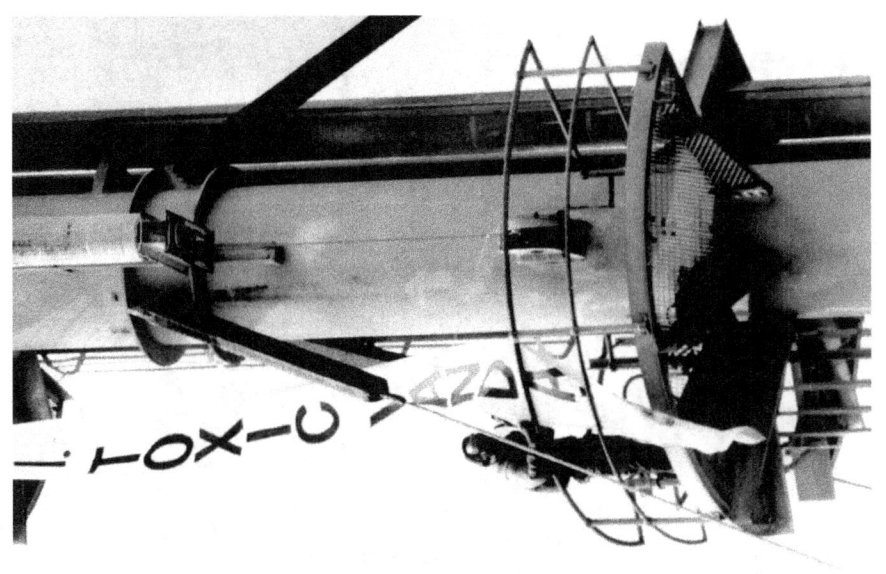

ICI heights – Election '87
(Sydney Morning Herald)

Green campaign BUGA UP

Chaelundi – Front line totem
(Tony Grant)

Chaelundi – Bush team erects the Star of David
(Tony Grant)

Chaelundi – Concrete fortress
(Tony Grant)

Chaelundi – Atop a tripod
(Sydney Morning Herald)

Chaelundi – PJ takes protest to the limit (Tony Grant)

South-East Forest defence

arrested and hospitalised but was released the following day. This event was filmed and repeatedly shown on television, causing the police image to suffer as a consequence. A gap opened in the previously cordial relationship between SEFA and the cops; these were not the tactics espoused by the authorities on either side.

Starsky, another protester, was perched seven metres up another tripod. A cherry picker was brought in to deal with him. Having had a considerable record of conservation arrests by this time, he attempted to escape through the trees. He fell, causing serious head injuries which put him in intensive care for two weeks. The point was rammed home that it was a police responsibility to minimise danger to the protesters.

Small actions continued. The June long weekend of 1990 was billed as a major event. Support numbers flowed in. The number of protesters grew enormously and a party atmosphere prevailed. Bega town hall, the venue for bands and speakers, was rife with Forestry Workers who, because of the peaceful resistance formula, were allowed to be part of the consensus decision-making process.

Later a massive action meeting was held on the road to the chipmill. A decision had to be made: either occupy the mill, or go to the forest. Excitement and confusion reigned. There were 2,500 people gathered and 1,000 were prepared to be arrested. The decision, made by a small number of organisers against the advice of the on-the-ground activists, was to go to the forest. Most participants were from the city, so trees had more appeal than an industrial site. The 2,500 people left the mill road and headed for the forest. Truckies effectively blockaded them. By the time they reached the forest it was 4 pm – too late for media deadlines. In a deft public relations initiative, the Forestry Commission opened Coolungubra for the day and offered guided tours for protesters and media alike. A day which could have effectively moved public opinion and pressured politicians was lost.

The construction of tree platforms continued in the forests for over a year. It was a stunning effort by those who stayed on after the crowd dwindled and the safety of numbers disappeared. People took shifts. A crew of experienced abseilers constructed platforms from boards and seatbelt webbing. These hardened souls tied seatbelts on like nappies to scamper up trees and literally run down them when the job was completed. They interconnected occupied trees with fencing wire. Thus interlocked, no tree could be safely removed and the compartment saved. Their 'living areas' were extraordinary.

By setting up in the crown of old eucalypts, they succeeded in stopping work in that logging coupe.

The whole operation was done with great danger to the occupants, perched thirty metres high in the canopy. If any attached branch or crown were to break off in a high wind (for which the South-East forests were renowned), disaster would result. Far too high for cherry pickers, the treetop activists were left as sentinels over a small patch of protected forest. Their perches swayed in often abominable conditions. Between trees, ropes and pulleys were set up to transport gear. If one ran out of toothpaste, for example, it would be trolleyed through the treetops. Under windy conditions it was impossible to communicate by voice and only the ropes permitted the sending of messages.

When a fourteen kilometre road was being bulldozed through Coolangubra, a team walked this distance through the bush to put a dunny door (the only thing available, at short notice, that resembled a platform) up a tree in the path of the dozer. It worked. At dawn, a protester named Marion locked her neck to the dozer with a Kryptonite bike lock. Several pairs of boltcutters later, the cops called for an anglegrinder. She was freed by 3 pm. The dozer left, not to return for fourteen months.

The scope of action considered nonviolent was extremely narrow.

Treesits, according to some, were unacceptable, as they did not involve everyone and secrets were kept from the police and the Forestry Commission. Peaceful resistance activists wanted a revolution without stepping outside the bounds of society. A spiritual movement had degenerated into a religion where bigotry abounded and the means were the ends.

Opponents to peaceful resistance adherents saw treesitting as a spiritual connection with nature. The longest aloft was a woman named Cathy Campbell. She maintained her position for fifty-six days in a huge monkey gum. It was the largest tree for kilometres. This was highly effective campaigning; one person could prevent the felling of a large area.

Andrew Baker, another activist, staged a hunger strike up a tree platform. This attracted media as a genuine and moving interest story. However, Wilderness Society operatives were furious. They saw it as the ploy of a young, egotistical activist, an action which diverted their media plans. From my perspective, the answer was to ride with such an action rather than control or oppose a gift offered from an unexpected quarter. Andrew was staging his protest for the right reason and was being extremely effective in drawing the media to a new angle. This style was deemed by SEFA to be too extreme to support.

As the campaign progressed, frustration set in. Activists stormed the chipmill, occupied it and chained themselves to the conveyor. Without backup from the city conservation groups, these were seen to be desperate acts by a minority.

On another day in the Coolungubra Wilderness, contractors were working when stopped by a crew of greenies in front of their dozer. Three protesters chained themselves on. Another two stood with their arms around the hydraulics on the dozer in a gentle embrace, their hands clasped.

"Supaglued them together," announced one cheeky greenie. "Gonna have to go to Bega to pick up some acetone."

"Not on your life!" was the emphatic reply from the dozer operators. Bega was a four-hour round trip. Instead, they got out the tool kit and dismantled the hydraulic arm, a task which took several hours. Just as they finished, the greenies, who had omitted to tell them that the glue wore off over time, let go and escaped into the bush.

Actions continued without the crowds but with audacious regularity. Local farmers, timid at the beginning of the campaign, threw caution to the winds when their water catchment was threatened by the Tantawangalo logging.

At early morning muster the sound of last-minute checking of harnesses and the snuffling of horses signalled a group strong in their element. Like a band of bushrangers, the farmers were going to ride against the logging operators. All dressed in Drizabones, they headed out through a gate, broken open the night before by an action organiser. At a point in the road stood a line of police and Forestry officials. Ten riders refused to move off the road, so police drove their four wheel drive into the group. The horses didn't kick each other or panic; rather, they leaned against the police vehicle. The push and shove of horse against machine held up work for several hours. Eventually the authorities cornered the horse riders and work recommenced. Still the riders were determined to stop the work. As one they charged past the police and into the operating area. Angry at their intrusion, the driver of a trackscavator swung the bucket at them. A huge, yellow, mechanical monster snapped at the riders as they galloped into the logging coupe. Work stopped. The police attempted to control the riders.

However, as one, they wheeled their mounts around and bolted off to another coupe.

A local farmer had warned the police not to pull anyone off a horse because, if it panicked and the rider's foot was stuck in the stirrup, the rider could be dragged along the ground and killed. Nevertheless, a young cop attempted to pull a woman off a horse. This same farmer yelled, "I warned you! Ride 'em down, ride 'em down!" He rode straight at the cop. The barrel of the horse's chest knocked the officer to the ground. After that the police didn't attempt to remove anyone else from the horses.

The riders' actions were not within the prescribed guidelines of peaceful resistance but were a spontaneous expression of protest. It was powerful theatre which resonated with the strength of the movement, and appropriate reaction in keeping with the progression of the campaign.

In lobbying politicians, SEFA was willing to compromise early to please all parties. It showed itself to be a toothless tiger, seeking agreement instead of keeping to the bottom line in negotiations. The group so convinced itself of the efficacy of nonviolent action that it believed in it as a campaign goal rather than seeing it as a vehicle to the end of saving Old Growth forests. SEFA thought it would win the political battle by making the compromise instead of making a strong stand and intimidating the politicians. It continued to trust the system. Eventually, it was offered mere crumbs.

The conviction displayed on the ground was not demonstrated at a political level. Old hands in Sydney, who were used to working from positions of little power, didn't act confidently, unaware of the support in the community. In early 1990, in a Herald-Saulwick poll, 87 per cent of the public surveyed in New South Wales said saving trees was more important than loggers' jobs.

In its early stages the South-East Forest campaign had the potential for great success, but the death knell for the campaign was internal politics. The struggle against authority and vested interest was sometimes energising, but when that struggle became primarily internal it led quickly to activist burnout.

The base camp lasted for over two years. While efficient at the start, by the end it was aimlessly anti-establishment. It was not an appropriate working environment in which to conduct a campaign. Early voluntary arrests squandered the people resources. It was an intensive campaign for all involved, particularly those on the ground. After 1,200 arrests and some significant media attention, conservationists were offered 60,000 hectares of national park. Most of this was forest unsuitable as a timber resource anyway. Other concessions to SEFA had been old national park or flora reserve areas. Only 6,000 hectares was removed from production forest. It was a political and industrial rort. The public was placated, but the political reality was that the industrial dominance was maintained.

CHAPTER 13
CHAELUNDI
Wild Forest Spirit

The Chaelundi blockade, in defence of Old Growth forests, occurred a decade after the early rainforest struggles of Terania and Nightcap in northern New South Wales. The green movement was supported by an emerging global awareness of the need to protect our diminishing natural ecosystems and maintain biodiversity. Equally as significant was the strong backlash from the industry, using jobs as the cudgel to gain the high moral ground. The political influence held by the greens in the era of the Franklin River campaign had since been eroded. The conservation of Old Growth forests was ignored at the 1991 New South Wales elections, despite our campaigning attempts. On the ground, the North East Forest Alliance moved on site. This campaign was characterised by a degree of sophistication and tactical response that only a decade of forest action could produce.

In the northeast of New South Wales lies a 7,000 hectare expanse of Old Growth forest – the Chaelundi State Forest. Surveys in the late 1980s revealed that Chaelundi supported nationally significant population densities of Old Growth dependent fauna. It was found to have the highest population densities of arboreal (tree-living) marsupials in Australia and correspondingly high population densities of owls, ground mammals, tiger quolls and a number of rare and endangered species.

In March 1990 the North East Forest Alliance (NEFA) established a blockade to stop the Forestry Commission of New South Wales illegally roading and logging an area of Old Growth forest. An injunction to restrain the Commission was obtained from the Land and Environment Court. On 4 July 1990 Justice Cripps issued a judgment which noted an undertaking not to proceed with roading and logging in the Pine Creek catchment of Chaelundi State Forest. The Forestry Commission was directed to prepare an environmental impact statement (EIS) for the area and the work proposed.

Thirteen arrests were made before the injunction was obtained. These were later vindicated when those appealing had their convictions dismissed in the Grafton District Court. NEFA won on the grounds that the Forestry Commission had closed the forest to facilitate an unlawful act.

In November 1990 the Forestry Commission submitted its environmental impact statement. Submissions by NEFA and other conservation organisations exposed problems with it, forcing the Commission to undertake additional studies. As expected, the poor quality of the report failed to reveal the significance of the area, which totalled 561 hectares. The Forestry Commission decided to proceed with logging anyway.

Chaelundi represented the re-emergence of the radical activist. Demonstrators took on the authorities on their own terms with a set of matured tactics and outrageous theatre of the environment. This cultural phenomenon related directly back to the Terania protests over a decade before and gave rise to a new generation of young, alternative environmental activists. Chaelundi spawned this new generation, just as Terania had years before. These actions included a number of original campaigners. It provided a formula – the art of protest combined with scientific and legal action – to rock the New South Wales government.

The election result of 25 May 1991 was disastrous for the environment. New South Wales was condemned to another three years of Coalition rule with the National Party holding all the land use portfolios. Our failure to highlight forests as an election issue was disappointing to the conservation movement but did not deter activists on the ground.

In July 1991, after four months of on-site monitoring by conservationists, the Forestry Commission publicly announced its intention to extend the road through the State Forest in preparation for logging. An air of disbelief pervaded the on-site camp. Many felt the loggers would not proceed, as the post-election Greiner government was teetering on the brink of disaster with impending court challenges to the election results in The Entrance and Maitland.

Information trickled in that local police had been rostered to Chaelundi for two weeks and would meet to plan their assault on our protest contingent. We established camps in hidden bush sites along Broadmeadow Road in readiness. A number of devices were to be used to obstruct the police. Concrete pipe 'totem poles' underwent last-minute fine-tuning (viewing holes were broken into the sides) in readiness for the protester who would be chained to an underground base. Others set up bush-pole tripods to maintain themselves aloft. While most were confident, others with experience saw the shortcomings of our defences against the onslaught of an efficient paramilitary force backed up by loggers and heavy equipment. Our hope lay in media coverage and public reaction in concert with a successful court case. The formula had worked before, but there was never any guarantee. If we could survive long enough at Chaelundi and get sufficient public focus we would embarrass the Greiner government into positive action.

The Chaelundi blockade represented a dynamic combination of old guard green activists, locals and new protesters with the keenness of youth. Included in the latter group were the 'punks for the forests' a wonderfully rare breed of wild young men and women, outrageous to the extreme, who shocked everyone, from police to protesters. Wild and often drunk, they surprised all with their outlandish humour and bravery. Under the rough exterior of rags and skull earrings, nose rings, boots and beer were some of the finest people I had encountered (when they were sober).

Late one night as we returned to the camp from Grafton, we passed a wreck of a car. A black anarchist flag poked out of a broken window, and inside could be seen several wrecks of punks. They were written off dead drunk. With the night to be spent by the side of the road, the only mode of appropriate action was to get thoroughly plastered. We wondered if it was worth taking them into camp so late at night. Their car was undoubtedly in a shocking condition – ideally suited for sacrifice under an advancing cavalcade of heavy machinery. My fantasies ran riot: a disabled vehicle with black flags flying from broken windows, punks chained underneath (wild and decidedly unfree), that should hold up the inevitable advance.

Feeling that drunks being towed would be as bad as drunks driving, the unenviable job of taking the wheel of the ear fell upon Jonno. Minus windscreen, he was towed behind my vehicle on an extremely dusty road, head wrapped like a Bedouin and sunglasses ready for a desert storm.

Fifteen kilometres later we arrived at the blockade site, punks hanging out of the windows screaming obscenities and spewing stale lager over their vehicle as it headed to its final moment of glory. They got straight into trashing/constructing a punk section of the blockade by digging out under the vehicle. Our sympathies went out to the cop who would have to extract that crew from its hole.

The following day was coloured by the impact of our new arrivals. Anarchy ruled. The cops approached me in their inimical search to discover the real enemy in the 'community' One said that the rest of the people were OK, but could I control the punks? Having spent many a year with long hair and beard being the pariah of the authorities, I looked the cop in the eye and said to him, "Give me four days with them in the forest and they'll be our crack troops." The cop walked off shaking his head.

The next morning the police convoy snaked down the access road in the pre-dawn light. The first obstacle it encountered was a roadblock comprised of locked and abandoned cars, parked at angles and extending for a quarter of a kilometre. The time taken to identify owners and clear the traffic allowed other activists to take up their positions.

After the cars were voluntarily cleared, the next sight to greet police was Benny Zable, that familiar masked figure in black, up a pole in the middle of the road with his decade-old message, 'CONSUME, BE SILENT, DIE', emblazoned on his garments. The police moved in with a dozer.

Standing in the bucket, they were elevated within reach of this icon of Australian protest. They cut the chains from him and led him to the paddy wagon.

Up the road, due to our inefficiency, pipes had been taken over by police and workers. Someone drove past like Paul Revere on a motorbike, screaming "the police are coming", only to find that police were already there. Three cops and a forestry worker sat atop the pipes to prevent anyone from jumping inside. The situation was critical. The pipes were located at a strategic position: a deep cutting lay to the lower side of the road and a steep embankment rose above it. Six people went into a huddle; they moved toward the pipe. Someone pulled the clip off a cop's gun holster. This earned the person an assault charge but allowed others to dislodge the worker who was lying on a pipe with his copious belly covering the hole.

Our people jumped into the pipes.

Back at the main point of confrontation, work abruptly stopped when Ned, a NEFA coordinator, bolted through police lines and successfully locked himself onto the step of a grader. While the police awaited the rescue squad, Ned gave an interview (Kryptonite lock around his neck) over the two-way radio to an ABC morning show. The only indication of his anxiety was the nervous tapping of one leg in rough time to the rapid fire of his interview. Ned was eventually cut free by the rescue squad and joined Benny in the back of the paddy wagon.

The bulldozer laboured up the hill to our first serious fortification, a six-metre-high tripod planted across the road with three people aloft.

Others were positioned inside cement pipes. Morning was passing and the police juggernaut had advanced 200 metres. Now began the arduous task of taking people down safely. Those in pipes were dug out using hand tools and the bucket of the front-end loader.

After the initial obstructions, the dozer moved on, scraping protest art accumulated during the months of waiting. One protester, Scottish John, dived under the dozer from the rear while it was backing up. The crowd let out a collective scream. The dozer driver stopped, obviously shaken. John attempted to chain himself to the undercarriage. The police struggled in the churned-up earth to remove him. He was unable to manipulate the lock into position but held on underneath so tenaciously that they had to dig a trench by hand to gain access to him. More precious time was gained, but John was charged with obstruction and three counts of resisting arrest.

The 'Bart pipe' was the next stop for the forces of law and order.

This obstruction was so named because one pipe had a life-sized painting of the cartoon character Bart Simpson with the caption 'FUCK OFF LOGGERS!' emblazoned on it. The question of who would have to jump into the Bart pipe when the time of reckoning came was the subject of many an idle campfire chat.

A large fire burned in front of Bart's visage, which shimmered through the smoke and flame. A tripod was positioned so that machinery could not get to the vertical pipes without dealing with it first. The night before, a concrete slab had been poured with chains embedded into it.

These chains were then connected to pipes on the ground a metre above. Two horizontal pipes were butted together, and two activists crawled into them and were joined at the neck with chains. The chain from the slab was then inserted through the join of the pipe and locked around their waists, pinning each participant to the ground.

A group of protesters stood back to witness the effectiveness of this defence against rescue squad expertise and police muscle. The cops dug by hand until they reached the chains. They cut them away from their mooring with bolt cutters and then prised open the pipes. Flo screamed in pain as the chain around her neck tightened. Communication was through a hole broken in the pipe. Flo looked (and sounded) like a modern-day Ned Kelly wearing an oversized helmet. As the police applied greater pressure to the pipes, hence their necks, Flo screamed, "Stop, you bastards, I'm pregnant." The cops stopped and had a rethink. The bulldozer was then brought in to dig out each pipe meticulously (if it's possible for a bulldozer to be sensitive, that was it!).

The police then turned their attention and considerable anger towards the tripod, but didn't succeed in bluffing the sitters down from their perch. At 3 pm I joked to Inspector Beck, "You have to give us one win in a day of loss." He laughed and grunted an agreement. Satisfied that his forces had done enough to damage our defences for the day he called an end to work. The cops had broken through but for us Bart had held. The police had a long journey back to Grafton. They dozed up a pile of dirt to bury the parallel pipes.

That night we erected the tripod at the first blockade site once again. A sleepy crew was gathered for a tripod-mounting quorum (the number of people it takes to erect six-metre-high hardwood bush poles lashed together without the said poles getting out of hand and dispatching one of the work crew). After several aborted attempts under the beams of car headlights, the tripod was finally erected. In the shadowy light the results were impressive. One protester spent the night aloft while two slept below, determined not to be caught out again. The next day the police proceeded to our first installation with specialist equipment – a cherry picker. Despite the euphoria of the previous night's construction work, our defences looked inconsequential and primitive against that long arm of technology. Ned and Andrew, the two sitters, were pulled out of the tripod. Once down they took off their shoes and danced around one of the tripod legs in readiness to scamper up again. Police swooped and detained them on a suspected breach of the peace.

The new equipment moved on slowly but relentlessly to Bart, where the bulldozer excavated the defences. The cherry picker then moved into position and plucked the person from the second tripod. It was effective, but still time-consuming. The cops withdrew for lunch, but two remained to guard equipment a hundred metres away.

We erected banners to hide the site where the tripod had been felled. Some of us stood in an act of theatrical defiance and waved flags while we warned our partners as to where the police were looking.

Fortunately, they were wholly absorbed in protecting the machinery. We brought out poles which had been hidden in the bush and erected another tripod right under their noses. A protester was atop the construction before they noticed.

In a state of agitation not conducive to post-lunch digestion, the police had to clear the tripod. This time it was difficult, because the legs were in front of the pipes. Just a slight modification of our design meant that the cherry picker had to extend fully in an attempt to reach the sitter. Several police lifted one front leg of the tripod to the side, allowing the picker to get close enough to the apex.

Meanwhile Gavin, resplendent in black leotard and rainbow flag, danced gracefully onto the bucket of the dozer. He kept dancing (horizontally) as three cops carried him to the paddy wagon. The poor lad had not intended to be incarcerated or for that to be the end of the dance. Expecting to go to the toilet during some interlude, Gavin found himself busting to have a pee and be free. His gaoler must have sensed the seriousness of the problem and let the prisoner out to relieve himself As the cop reopened the wagon to put Gavin back, the prisoner decided to abscond and present himself for action further up the track.

Off he bolted. The police, caught flat-footed, went bush after him.

Gavin was long gone in the shrubbery. Later, remorseful at such a transgression and having heard that after his escapade no-one was allowed to pee if incarcerated, he decided to surrender in the public's (or at least their private parts') interest. Fearing an escape charge, he approached Inspector Hocking, who asked him to wait on the bank for Beck. The two inspectors talked at length, about what Gavin could not hear; perhaps they were appreciating the wildlife? Gavin recounts: "I sat on the bank all day and still they did nothing. So what could I do? I joined the blockade on the road."

The police, in a bad mood from our lunchtime resurrection strategy, arrested four women who stood on the road in a stance of defiance. They were treated so roughly that their husbands and friends ran to their aid. In the ensuing confrontation nine people were taken.

When the dozer was a few metres behind Scottish John and coming up fast, he knelt in genuflection before a bizarre altar of branches poking out like timber rays – an upturned buttress root like a work of art. Two policemen, seeing but not comprehending this strange individual's act of devotion as he crouched on hands and knees with a large bunch of burning incense in one hand, ran to him and with one on either side lifted him out of harm's way. During this 'rescue' John maintained his prayer position. I ran past, thinking, "Bloody inappropriate hippies." Later I heard his side of the story. He had left a 'wee joint' in the front section of the altar and on a whim had gone down to scoop up his prize before the dozer swept it to oblivion. It was in one of his hands when the police lifted him off the road and left him neatly on the sideline. I have since decided to take that man seriously, in a fashion.

We kept up a trot as police rode 'shotgun' on the lead dozer. They jumped off to clear the road of small obstacles, behaving like a friendly crew of garbos on the job. They believed they had our measure. Their expressions changed as they topped the final hill, revealing Feral Camp, our last line of defence. This site was chosen because at this point the road passed through a magnificent section of Old Growth rainforest. The tripods stretched high towards the dark green canopy. Smoke from fires below wrapped around installations and trees alike. People moved along the structures in a relaxed fashion, despite the fact that they balanced on narrow poles high above ground. Below, drums throbbed out deep rhythms as people moved in and out of nearby camps nestled in the rainforest. Two distinct cultures moved towards an inevitable clash.

This site was our strongest, yet the police had now gained a high degree of expertise. They had even constructed a small tripod in an attempt to work out how we erected them. We needed something new. As the dozer drew near, there it was: a tripod-bipod combination like a five-legged animal. Two people were perched atop the tripod and one on the tripod at the other end of a six metre horizontal pole. The far end was out of reach of the cherry picker while the front tripod could not be dismantled until the person at the rear was safely removed. Like a move in chess, we had them in check.

The police moved in on the two at the front. PJ, an archetypal feral forest-dweller and a tai chi expert, moved out from the relative security of the rear end and balanced in the middle, tightrope walking for the forest. All eyes were glued to a man, his arms outstretched, bouncing on a flexible horizontal pole six metres in the air. He maintained his balance and equanimity as the police closed in, PJ moving like a cat ahead of their every move.

Unable to capture PJ, they turned their attention to more vulnerable quarry and set about capturing the others. In a stunning action, PJ then ran and leapt onto the arm of the cherry picker, six metres off the ground, and ran to the machine's elbow. He turned and stood with arms outstretched.

There was a collective gasp from the crowd. The police action stopped dead: they could not move their machine, as PJ stood on the fulcrum of the machine's extension arm. When he moved under the arm it really looked like checkmate. The rescue police in the basket stood there, unable to do anything. There was a cacophony of shouting as everyone on the ground yelled different advice at once. Then PJ made a wrong move. Climbing back on top of the arm of the picker, he ran past the police in the basket to get back to his original position on the crossbeam. The police grabbed him and clamped the cuffs to one of his ankles. PJ was nonplussed. He did not immediately realise that he was trapped. However, once they began applying pressure so the cuff tightened, it became an excruciating torture. PJ took it to its limit. At one point, obviously mastering his own pain threshold, he hung upside down, suspended by the cuff around his ankle. Eventually he could withstand it no more and allowed the police to haul him into the basket. When the cherry picker delivered him to the ground he was roughly dragged off to the waiting prison van and thrown inside headfirst. The next obstacle to the police advancement appeared. Helmut, buried up to his neck in the earth and anchored by chains below, represented a shift of position, tempo and temperament on the part of the protesters. The patience Helmut demonstrated was admirable. He gave the police no cause for frustration or aggression, chatting convivially as they dug him out by hand. The patient digging stretched into hours. Police and protesters alike had been stunned by the previous action, and each side relaxed as the police dug resolutely away at what they believed to be fortifications underneath Helmut. It was only when they eventually dug him out that the truth was revealed: the lower fortifications were a bluff. The most volatile day of action so far wound down with a passive act. The police removed Helmut, pulled down the tripod and quit for the day. Everyone was near exhaustion, but the task of rebuilding the blockades went late into the night.

The next day saw the arrival of Steve Tripp and Ian Mortimer, two street musicians from Sydney and Gerry Bradley, a Nightcap campaign veteran. They revelled in their role as lead act for the day. The banjos and the bush bass appeared, and song and dance had police and protester tapping to the music. The site took on a carnival atmosphere while police continued to clear the road.

The previous night's constructions held the police at the Bart pipes (again) for two hours. When they broke through, the pipes were not occupied. In a last-minute scramble people jumped into them. A number of patriotic souls found themselves inside concrete sarcophagi when they had intended playing guitar and singing in the fresh air.

"One minute I was singing, the next minute I was breathless from running and was crouched inside a concrete pipe," recalled Wendy Falkner. "Police milled around. I started to shiver with cold; I was unprepared.

Suddenly a friendly face appeared above and Ian handed down a shawl, water and sultanas." We had many people down pipes and were unclear of their physical condition. The police maintained an air of nonchalance, saying, "They can come out if they're suffering so much." They checked the pipe occupants and returned disconcerted. The ambulance officer was sent over to check, then I was called over.

"One of those chaps has his head down in the pipes and is not responding," an officer said. "You'd better go over and have a look." I climbed onto the pipe and peered down at Helmut (yes, him again!), then called his name. No response. I pulled his hair to get his head up, then whispered, "It's Ian, they let me come over." Slowly a cement dust – begrimed but smiling face looked up at me. He was OK but groaned and pretended to be in a quietly insane state in an attempt to soften the police. His ploy worked: we were allowed to take food and supplies to everyone in the pipes.

The dozer went for Wendy's pipe. "I had to stuff a shawl in the viewing hole to stop the diesel fumes," she related. "Not the place to be, considering my doctor's advice that I was allergic to petrochemicals. They tried to lift me out, but being so small I wedged myself deep. Those huge police couldn't get leverage to remove my seven-and-a-half-stone bulk.

They then dug the pipe out with me still inside choking on fumes. They were busy above for half an hour, then tied chains around the pipe and tipped it. The base was still covered so I snuggled deeper into the dirt. Again they tried to pull me out from the top of the pipe – a policewoman crawled most of the way in to get me, but I stuck it out. Finally they pulled the pipe right out and forced me into the hole itself. I pretended to be half unconscious. Ambulance men were summoned, my pulse was taken and four police were instructed to carry me to the paddy wagon. As I was carried off I made a peace sign to reassure friends that I was OK after one – and-a-half hours of semi-subterranean action. My police bearers laid me out in the sun next to the ambulance for half an hour before placing me in the paddy wagon."

By lunch we had surprisingly few defences left. I discussed the matter with Jonno. The crew up the last tripod were few and inexperienced. We agreed that I should bolster our last defence.

When the police broke for lunch I climbed up. Timber was hoisted up and lashed to the frame to create more obstacles. We called for more people to join us on the perch. Our two punks, Rory and Simon, tried to climb the rope, but due to all-too-frequent inebriation were unable. One young girl, Melanie, tried and made it. I asked her how old she was. "Fourteen," she responded.

Who was I to say who should stay or go? "We won't be going easily when the police move in," I said, sounding as old as a Humphrey Bogart line. "This is our last line of defence."

We continued to build our defences and discussed tactics to avoid the handcuff. Some confidence seeped into the group as we worked on a scrum routine six metres up.

Police lunch ended. Sergeant Jones came directly below and yelled, "I bet you a six-pack you're on the front page of the Herald tomorrow." (A Herald photographer and reporter were on site).

"No bet! That goes without saying!" I yelled back, then added, "I bet you a six-pack I'm still here when you knock off work tonight!" ('Big mouth,' I thought.)

"You're on!" replied the sergeant, and walked off to his rescue squad mates preparing to do the dirty work.

Two men ensconced in the bucket moved robotically toward us.

G'days were exchanged as the rescue cop began to dismantle our defences. The lashings were easily cut with a knife, but valuable time ticked by as each piece of wood was lowered. They moved in on their first target. The tripod swayed in a scramble of hands and feet. We struggled to avoid capture. With five people aloft, the construction was extremely unstable. We held onto each other, as there was little else. Once the cuff was snapped onto the ankle of one of us, we all stopped the struggle. Fear was replaced by the grimace of pain. The cop was able to reel him in as if catching a fish. With one protester dispatched, the mechanical arm returned and the struggle continued. I sat at the back, pulling the cops' hands away from those in front. The next activist was cuffed and hauled in after a brave struggle.

The bucket returned; Melanie was the target. She gamely fought the police off until the cuff was locked to her ankle. She stood up, quivering like a trapped and frightened animal. In a flat monotone her capturer said, "Give up, you can't get away It's impossible to escape." As he said this he tightened the grip of the cuff. She resisted. He stepped down on the rope.

Like the far-off roaring of a football crowd, I heard the frenzied voices of those below, but the sound was dim and distant to my ears.

The cop spoke to me: "Tell her to let go. She can't escape." "That's her decision," I replied.

He pressed harder on the rope. Melanie collapsed under the pain and fell into the bucket.

Released from the intensity of the situation atop the tripod, the outrage of the crowd below broke over me like a wave. With only two of us left, the bucket of the cherry picker approached. I expected them to go for Tamara, my last companion, presuming I would be left until last. I had been counting on room to move.

They came for me. Arms attempted to pin me down. I moved around the other side of the uprights. Screams sounded from below and at the same moment I was grabbed from behind by a cop on a ladder (it may well have been our ladder, such was police ingenuity). I pulled away but had less room to move and lacked the nimbleness of PJ. They grabbed the arms of my thick jacket. I tried to wriggle free but another cop got me around the neck. The cuff of authority bit into my wrist. Now it was me he was talking to: "It's no use struggling, you might as well save yourself unnecessary pain." I looked into his eyes and said, "Just doing your job, aren't you."

He stepped on the retaining rope harder. I slid my wrist around in the cuff so that the metal edge was cutting into the soft muscle of my forearm instead of the bone. "Come into the basket, it's no use," he said. By way of saying I wouldn't give in, I wrenched my arm up with all my might to send him off balance. I crashed in agony headfirst into the bucket.

Sergeant Jones won the bet. I watched through the bars of the prison van as police dismantled and cut up the tripod. Behind them a fire raged. All who were free stood beyond the fire on the roadway. Forty people, as one, grew from the shimmering heat of the fire. They rocked from side to side, singing, "We shall not, we shall not be moved…"

The police packed up and retired for the day. We suffered an inhumane trip to Grafton in a packed van as choking dust poured in where rear doorseals were missing. Those who remained shared their feelings quietly by the fire. They assimilated the day's events in readiness to build for the next day. It was up to those left behind to prepare for the confrontation to follow.

The next day the Rainforest Information Centre (RIC) van was deemed ready for sacrifice due to its excessive exhaust emissions. A hole had been dug to accommodate two protesters. The van was positioned over it and the wheels removed, lowering the vehicle over the volunteers. They then locked themselves onto the chassis. A tripod-bipod was erected over the van. The police had to dig for an hour to gain access to those underneath and finally bring in the 'jaws of life' (high-powered hydraulic metal cutters). Chains and locks were cut, but they still couldn't remove the people. Extra police were called over and the van was rolled onto its side to reveal two young men curled up in a foetal position. They were removed and the van was bulldozed into the bush. The long arm of the law then stuck a defect sticker on the windscreen.

At the next installation, Andy was perched at the more inaccessible end. Inspector Beck attempted to monster him from ground level with threats of resisting arrest and cajolings at "It'll be much easier if you come down now, son." "You've got to be joking," Andy replied. He was confident and had a Kryptonite lock around his thigh and the pole for good measure. A stalemate occurred. To add to the staleness, Andy felt the call of nature. He brazenly unzipped and without a word of warning urinated from up high. I am not saying that he deliberately aimed for the police, but the men in blue had to dash for shelter when there was not a cloud in the sky. The police retired at midday. It was rumoured a football match was pending on TV that night.

For the weekend that followed we worked day and night. Tripods went back up. Holes were dug. We excavated those filled in by the police for reuse. A huge hollow log was rolled into position on the roadway with the words 'TUNNEL OF LOVE' painted on it. The natural pipe was large enough to accommodate two people joined together by chain and locks. Our most spectacular innovation was the 'Star of David'. It was a construction made from six poles lashed together in the shape of a star and mounted horizontally on a single bush pole ten metres high, tied down with fencing wire and anchored by star pickets. By our reckoning it was beyond the reach of the cherry picker. That installation was a monumental effort by the whole camp, with the assistance of four-wheel drives.

With the start of the new working week, a police nightmare loomed: a wrecked car with black anarchist flags flying and a crew of snarling punks chained inside and underneath with a half-consumed flagon of port on the bonnet – not a pretty sight for the rescue squad. It took the police over an hour to clear that mob. They went peacefully but not quietly. What the police didn't know was that they were young idealists, reflecting in dress and demeanour an abhorrence of the establishment and its destructive ways.

Next, the police convoy moved to our main defence, the Star of David. The hushed silence was broken only by the whirr of the cherry picker motor as the arm slowly ascended in pursuit of its quarry perched atop the star. Closer and closer, the arm finally reached its maximum extension several feet below Sage, our star volunteer. A loud cheer filled the air. We who had done the calculations nodded gleefully to one another and avoided eye contact with police. We thought we had their measure for the day.

The picker came back down. Lengthy discussions ensued, then up it went again. A truck with log-loading callipers was moved in below and the bucket of the picker was lashed to the vertical pole. The callipers grabbed the pole a metre from the base. Still we wondered what their intentions were. Then out came the vital weapon, the chainsaw. They secured the pole and chainsawed the bottom metre off. Lowering the pole a metre, they cut it off again, repeating the process section by section. Regardless of the regular accusations of industrial sabotage made against forest demonstrators, it had not occurred to any of our group to drive nails into the post to prevent the use of chainsaws. At the end of the day, police ingenuity was congratulated. Early the following morning the call went out across the camp that the Green Grannies had arrived. For everyone weary of the confrontation it was support from another realm. A wave of excitement rippled through the bush as the message rang out: 'The Green Grannies are here!' People appeared like shy young animals from the forest as the minibus pulled up. Obviously they were here to help, but what would they think of the young ferals?

In the words of Marianne Loyd Smith, the organiser, "We sat down on our plastic chairs across the road; I guess you could call it a sit-in. What affected the older women more than any interaction with the authorities were the young women from the feral communities who presented their babies to us as if to say, I want you as part of my social structure, as part of my tribe. We took the children into our arms and unconditionally accepted the mothers. It felt like a concept from the past, lacking in today's society: people of all ages coming together, sharing a mutual belief and purpose."

These older women took on the role of real matriarchs. They were the protectors, stepping into that youthful, potentially dangerous environment, alleviating the intensity with the authority of their age and demeanour. They did not criticise the young people for their lifestyles but acknowledged their commitment to the future.

The police arrived, faced with a dozen grannies seated in the middle of the road on chairs (some with knitting on their laps). They went into a huddle. After the necessary communication of each side's intention, the police moved in, placed the grannies under arrest and escorted them to the waiting paddy wagons. Off they rode to the cheers of the young. The police used their discretion; a few miles down the road they stopped and released the grannies, who rejoined their minibus for the journey home.

The next day's theme was people in the cement culvert. Twelve people were tied together. Some were inside the tunnel, others sat on top of the pipe with their feet dangling through a hole. A small person was needed to go in and chain them all up, so a rehearsal was undertaken in the middle of the night. The greenie designed for the job was Zac (aged twelve) from Pilar Valley. Rio Grieves (eight years old) also decided to do his bit to help the forest, so he pushed dirt out of the pipe for twenty minutes so it would be in good condition for protesters the next morning. He was given a coat to wear, as it was bitterly cold, but it was hard work for a kid wearing a man – size greatcoat. Other children also gathered chains and locks for their mothers' actions.

The next morning Zac went at it for real. "I was a bit nervous," he said. "I had a really big torch and dropped it. I had to get past Lou, who was pretty big, and I was a bit worried that I wouldn't be able to get out again."

When the cops arrived they found us staging a mass sit-down on the road. Not having enough prison trucks to deal with the entire crowd, they opted to go around by a back road and attack the top installations. The 'tunnel of love' with its two occupants chained together presented the first obstacle. Unable to remove the protesters they opted to roll the tree out of the way, with the occupants still inside. Next was a complex installation, an accumulation of tripods stretched over the road. Ten people moved along its many branches; two fires raged behind. This was our final position. Fate came to our rescue when the cherry picker slid off the side of the embankment – to a spontaneous chorus of cheers.

With this information, John Corkill, who was in Sydney working on the legal challenge, took action. He was able to prove that police were causing environmental damage when attempting to arrest demonstrators.

The communication with John by phone via radio meant that he had powerful media opportunities, with the receipt of up-to-the-minute information. In return, we received legal and media updates in the bush.

Our resources were dissipated. Two small workcrews had laboured late into the night to rebuild defences front scratch. By 2 am a huge tripod had been constructed at the original 'Bart' site. Its size and position compensated for our now low numbers and equipment which had been confiscated. The other obstacle was the 'web of life' a construction which in our bold fantasies was to consist of a camouflage net pulled taut and suspended horizontally from trees some eight metres above the ground and reinforced around the perimeter with fencing wire. We struggled for five hours and came up with something more akin to a massive marble bag, but it was impressive nonetheless. The officer in charge of police rescue gave the design a six out of ten, his first compliment for the duration of the entire action.

The police contemplated our 'web'. They first cornered Toohey, tangled him in the netting and dragged him into the cherry picker. The second person, Nick from Greenpeace, shook the net in an attempt to stop police tangling it up and scampered to the other end as they lunged for him. When they tied up the corners of the camouflage net it made the field of potential escape increasingly smaller. Nick scrambled to the other side of the net and started to bounce up and down. The police restricted his ability to manoeuvre and captured their prey like a slow-moving spider after an insect in its web.

All our defences had now been broken. Dispirited, we watched from the sidelines as the police swept debris to the side of the road. The forest was then officially closed to the public by John Murray, the district forester.

Some protesters, myself amongst them, decentralised to camps outside the restricted area. Others stayed inside. Our numbers did not diminish, but the forest closure meant we had to run and hide both day and night to avoid capture. What we needed now was an action which would both stop work and raise morale.

That night, five ton of rocks was loaded onto a flat-bed truck. We backed the truck up to a log bridge at Misty Creek on the south access road and dumped the load. The truck was hidden and timber, branches and bark were piled over the rocks. Lighting the pile we gathered around, warmed ourselves and waited. First to arrive were forestry personnel, who waited a reasonable distance away. Then a lone cop arrived. He radioed out then stood beside us, warming himself by the fire. Such was the pleasure in the warmth we did not discuss the fact that the fire was on road base over a wooden bridge on a major access road.

As the flames were leaping five metres in the air Inspector Beck arrived. Previous contact had taught us that it did not take a bonfire to light this cop's rather short fuse. Beck was not impressed. Workers arrived and clearing started in earnest. Things were going well enough for them until they cleared the wood to find a glowing rock wall over a metre high. With sweat pouring off them, they ignored our protestations and threw the hot rocks into the surrounding bush. (The media stories the next day were damning, prompting the suggestion of a police investigation into the incident.)

Meanwhile, with a synchronicity which adequately replaced our malfunctioning radio systems (some explained it as 'Mother Earth attunement', the camp to the north moved into action, blocking the Dalmorton Bridge. PJ related, "We started work after the late night shift change. As the cops were on patrol we worked without lights. We spent hours chucking rocks and firewood up onto the bridge. We lit the fire at 4 am. Police arrived at 6 am and took an hour to clear the bridge. They later installed a generator and floodlights. A grader was halted by protesters and a woman locked herself onto it."

The police worked hard at Dalmorton Bridge to remove the obstruction, then drove to Feral Camp and on to Misty Creek to deal with our burning bridge. Meanwhile, those at Feral Camp locked themselves onto the dozer.

In the courts a final decision was fast approaching as to the fate of Chaelundi.

In the forest our objective was to select three habitable trees on the path of the logging road to prevent further destruction of Old Growth.

Activities also continued in the restricted area. We put out a call for tree sitters. After dark, with little preparation time, Owen, who had just arrived on his first forest action, volunteered with no idea of what lay ahead. "To live in a tree twenty-five metres above ground in an Old Growth forest sounded like heaven to me," Owen later said.

The workparty consisted of twenty people. Our resident tree surgeon selected and scaled the mammoth eucalypts to secure shackles, ropes and pulleys. We worked all night, breaking only every forty minutes as the police patrol drove by.

With daybreak fast approaching, two sitters scrambled up the trees. One had managed to make his tree platform from canvas and branches; Owen had to make do with a hammock for a home. He remembers, "Against a pre-dawn sky I wormed my way into my hammock, hoping my knots were strong. Suspended like a giant cocoon twenty-five metres up, I fell asleep with the rising warmth of a new day."

Police and forestry workers clocked in to discover two people blocking their workpath. The height of their perches made the cherry picker useless. One cop demanded that they descend, arguing, "The forest is closed." Owen's reply was, "Forests don't close. 'All you birds, koalas, snakes – forest is closed! Everybody out!'" At that point the frustrated cop threatened to shoot Owen, then huffed and puffed and stormed away.

"Two days passed with magnificent views on the edge of the abyss.

Behind was life in all its splendour. On the other side was machinery voices, commotion, strategy, progress, destruction, lives and jobs," Owen recalled.

The authorities finally made their move, inching the bulldozer between the two occupied trees and pouring fumes into the faces of those atop. The machine disappeared into the ancient forest and could be heard ripping into the Old Growth vegetation. The police and forestry workers were smug, but for those in the canopy it was a day of intense sadness.

The police were determined to arrest the tree dwellers. That night it was so bitterly cold, the police huddled close to a roaring fire. The prospect of an enforced night in the wild, baby-sitting two fools in trees, must have got the better of them, for they passed their shift harassing the two protesters. Verbal abuse through a loudhailer was interspersed with the four-wheel drive siren every fifteen minutes. A chainsaw was pulled out and revved for an interminable period, then the police radio was set upon them at full volume and static. Next came another novel torture; their vehicle was backed up and a revolving spotlight switched on. At shift change their parting words were, "I don't think they'll be going anywhere. They seem to be asleep. Not a stir all night."

The new shift of police checked the protesters every twenty minutes, poking their heads out of the car window and shining a torch up. Between inspections Owen organised the ropes and stuffed gear in the hammock as a decoy. His objective was a quick descent and run. After a short sleep to warm himself up he was ready "I peered below, the fire was dying," he related. It was unlikely the police would be outside in the freezing conditions. All was quiet except a creaking and hollow whistling from the trees, like rigging on an old ship. I rolled up my bedding and dropped it into ferns. Going down the rope my hands burnt on the inside and stung with cold on the outside. Halfway down my fingers locked with cramp and I slid the rest of the way. I swung on top of the police van. On the return swing I jumped to the ground. A splintering sound ricocheted through the night as I landed on a dry branch, but the cops slept on. I ran into the forest, clutching my gear, and fell onto my bedding. Sleep came fast. I emerged briefly from sleep as torch beams shone through the foliage. I knew they wouldn't find me in the undergrowth., Morning saw Owen at camp for breakfast.

Despite police controls, seventy greenies stormed back into the forest. Declaring the forest open in defiance of police was an important propaganda victory.

Our efforts in the forest were an integral part of the overall strategy. It was imperative that the blockade continue in a forceful manner. We were not alone. During this period we were in daily contact with John Corkill, our legal and political activist in the Sydney offices of our barrister Tim Robertson. The case was being assembled at a remarkable pace, with all – night sessions. It was not unusual for John to stand on the eighth floor office opposite Parliament House and call Terry and Izzie Placing at the radio outpost to be patched direct to the forest. "Macquarie Street calling Feral Camp. Do you copy? Over." John's was not the typical phone call from the upper echelons of the legal fraternity in Sydney, but for John this communication was critical to the success of the legal and political campaign.

On 25 September a telephone report came through. "Guess what, mate, we've just stopped them cold in the court," said John, expecting effusive congratulations. Instead Ned replied, "We stopped them in the forest today, too." We had out-manoeuvred the Forestry Commission in the forest, the media and in court. Judge Stein had ruled that forestry activities would disturb endangered species and ordered that work be halted in the Chaelundi State Forest. We told the police it was all over; they didn't believe us. While we partied, a vehicle arrived from Dorrigo to confirm to the police what we had told them hours before. (It was acknowledged later in our Freedom of Information requests that the Forest Products Association complained that the greenies had better radio communications than the Forestry Commission or police.)

As a result of the win the Liberal government, distorting the court's judgment, claimed that all forestry, farming and even the airlines would grind to a halt. They filed an appeal. In the New South Wales Court of Appeal the Forestry Commission's appeal was refused and Justice Stein's decision was unanimously upheld. Tim Moore, the Minister for the Environment, brought out a regulation which overturned the court's decision and exempted most activities involving the destruction of protected species.

Parliament attacked Premier Nick Greiner over the issue. Terry Metherell resigned from the party, citing the Liberals, lack of environmental credentials. He voted with the Opposition to overturn the regulation put forward by Moore. The Endangered Fauna Interim Protection Bill was presented by the Opposition. It was the first time a Bill had been introduced by the Opposition and passed through Parliament to become law.

Ultimately Tim Moore and Nick Greiner lost their positions in Parliament. Chaelundi almost brought down the government. Legally it set an historic precedent on the issue of endangered species.

CHAPTER 14
KILLIE KRANKE
Forestry Credibility Slides

Forest activists, under the banner of the North-East Forest Alliance (NEFA), buoyed by the successes at Chaelundi the previous year embarked on a new campaign at Killie Kranke.

The Killie Kranke forest is at the headwaters of the Bellinger, Nambucca and Kalang Rivers in northern New South Wales. Bellingen is the nearest town, fifty kilometres away by dirt road and in the same region as the Chaelundi State Forest.

The issues were Old Growth forest protection, the logging of steep slopes in the pristine water catchment and the resultant massive degradation of water supplies downstream. This all added up to one overwhelming problem: soil erosion. The disputed areas, or 'compartments' were within the New England Wilderness area and had been promised for inclusion in the North-East National Park as early as 1973.

The activists arrived under the guise of a Chaelundi reunion. It was a small but now determined group, prepared to defend the environment with all its experience and the growing tribal cohesion from the Chaelundi victory. The authorities were well aware of the costs – financially, logistically and politically – in having a repeat of the previous year's protests. Activists were potential long-term participants with an ability to hold up work indefinitely. The Forestry Commission refused to accept that there was any problem with soil erosion on the slopes. Yet the evidence to the contrary was substantial. Forest activists took photographic records and decided to prosecute the Commission for soil pollution. Experts were called in and the Soil Conservation Service (SCS) notified.

Solicitors for NEFA had written to the Environmental Protection Authority (EPA) stating that there had been a breach of the Clean Waters Act. This was accompanied by our consultants' reports. Dr John McGarity was quoted in The Sydney Morning Herald citing that it was the worst case

of logging practice and resultant soil erosion he had ever seen. Phillip Pells, an international geo-engineer, likened the logging of Killie Kranke to a Third World operation. The EPA was requested to prosecute; instead, it issued a licence to pollute. The case against the Forestry Commission went to a local court and they received a maximum fine of $10,000 – a mere slap on the wrist.

The Forestry Commission had insisted on a secrecy clause with the SCS regarding the investigation. Information later gained through the Freedom of Information Act found that the Commission had breached the Act in so many instances that it prompted the SCS to completely re-write conditions for logging.

It was the failure of this legal action that fired conservationists to initiate the protest at Killie Kranke. Using the direct action formula we intended to barricade the sole access road to the area. We began constructing tripods, which soon developed into an elevated campsite. Old pipes, left behind from careless forestry work of the past, were found and used as receptacles for chained protesters (the pipes were smaller in diameter than those used at Chaelundi, so the job of pipe 'divers' had to be left to those with Twiggy-like figures). A huge logging cable as thick as a wrist was strung across the road for what became known as the 'wild women's witchy weaving' fortification, a cross between a camouflage net and a tank trap.

Due to work on steep slopes of up to 44 degrees, a gradient far in excess of SCS guidelines for logging, a new strategy imported from successful forest actions in the United States was brought into play. This was a cantilever, a single pole fixed horizontally across the road and extending some five metres over an abyss – an effective new device to obstruct machinery access along the road. A suitable location was found with a steep, rubble-strewn slope. One crew went hunting for a suitable bush pole while another set to work with a crowbar, chipping away at the rock wall on the uphill side of the road to create a slot in which to fix one end of the pole. Once staked and secured horizontally, it was a simple blockade structure. The addition of an activist balancing on its end created another element. Perched fifteen metres above the rocky slope, the balance artist experienced magnificent views of the Wilderness.

We had now trapped a bulldozer six kilometres inside our defences.

The dozer was sitting in a devastated logging area. It was the worst site that many of us with years of experience had ever witnessed. A tripod with protester atop soon locked up the dozer, with one tripod leg placed between the machine's body and blade.

When we first inspected the area we had found a brush box, estimated to be a thousand years old and marked by the Forestry Commission as a seed tree. On our second inspection a few days later it had been cut down. It was a deliberate, provocative act of vandalism.

NEFA's local opposition were members of a prolific family of hillbilly loggers who had ruled over Thora Valley for generations and had been known to beat up greenies in the local Bellingen pub. They were rumoured to be intending to descend on the camp at an unknown time and clean us up.

With the blockade in place, the waiting game began. The first arrival at the blockade site was the owner of the Thora sawmill. We questioned him as to whether it was true he had sold out to Japanese interests. He merely swore at us. When he and the police later inspected our installations, the police seemed mostly interested in maintaining a sense of calm. The blockade held.

The next request from the cops was to allow Forestry Commission and SCS officials to inspect the logging sites – something we were glad to permit. Still, we were not prepared to dismantle the blockade to allow them through.

We had two vehicles inside the 'quarantined' area. I was asked to drive the officials in one. Instead of our slick four-wheel drive, I was relegated the old Holden station wagon: mistake number one. I turned the car around before the police arrived so they would be less likely to notice the muffler, sounding like a jet at liftoff, when executing a three-point turn on the narrow track. Such smug forethought instantly evaporated at the sight of the tailgate with gaping holes of cancerous rust staring at the rapidly approaching official entourage. A few of us stepped in front; our welcoming smiles and well-positioned rears hid the tail of our forest transport vehicle. The policeman, eyeing the four-wheel drive, moved towards it, but the car was full to overflowing with a fleshy abundance of Forestry Commission officials and workers. I had to flag him down: 'Over here, Officer.'

"I thought this was a four-wheel drive track," was the first thing he uttered between my attempts to extol the limousine qualities of the old Holden. "It is," I answered as we cruised over some slippery sections with a steep drop. I noticed him eyeing some owl feathers hanging from the rear – vision mirror and what looked suspiciously like a marijuana stash box sitting on the dashboard (I checked it at the first opportunity to find it empty but with a discouraging smell). And when he stared across at the speedo for an inordinately long time I was sure it was not my speed that interested him but the rather large, plastic heart stuck to the gauge in question.

When the officials returned grim-faced from the site inspection, their only comment to our questions was 'no comment'. We felt vindicated in our stance.

After their departure, rain set in. A number of us had to appear in court the next day as witnesses over a Chaelundi matter. I was glad for the excuse to leave. As we made to go, I looked back at the camp, observing everyone huddled around the campfire under a bamboo and tarpaulin construction that looked like a giant living room in the middle of the forest. Wet clothes and sleeping bags hung from the rafters to dry. Dinner bubbled away flavoured by the occasional drip from a sleeping bag, and the kettle whistled, constantly supplying hot drinks to the protesters jammed together like bees in a hive.

Our intended escape was abruptly curtailed. Trevor Pike, a local conservationist, arrived and told us that the loggers had decided to blockade us in. With a hot shower becoming a fading reality, a few of us decided to investigate. They were an ugly crew of angry men, some thirty in number. With four-wheel drives across the road they stated: "No-one is passing through in cars."

"Congratulations on upping the ante in the blockade stakes," I said. "We've radioed the media about your action." They were not amused.

When asked who they represented it took some time in coming; eventually they admitted that they were acting at the behest of the National Farmers' Federation. I thanked them for their active participation in the ongoing theatre of the situation. Obviously unable to appreciate the subtlety of my conversation, they took offence. Their leader cautioned me and insulted me with the usual 'dole bludger' line.

A young boy standing next to me chimed in: "You're wrecking the forest that is as much mine as yours." At first they were taken aback by his eloquence, then they snarled, "Shut up and have some respect."

"I could put in as hard a day's work as anyone here," I interjected. One surly fellow stepped forward. Obviously a man of few words,

and closely resembling the outhouses of yesteryear with a neck unnervingly the same thickness as his head, he scowled at me and said, I'd watch what I was saying if I was you."

To that a greenie responded, "Is that a threat?"

The logger replied, "You can take it any way you like."

It was all becoming too much like a B grade movie. We retreated and left our mate Jonno with a radio on the hill, sniffing danger like a rat after cheese.

There was agitation in the camp: people didn't realise the power that we, as a group, exerted. Two carloads of women and children attempted to exit, but the loggers would not permit them to pass. The police arrived and, sensing the mood of the loggers, defused the situation. They persuaded them to let parents and children through their blockade. The loggers had stirred up the issue just as it was beginning to fade in the media. The following day the headlines ran, 'LOGGERS ARMED WITH CHAINSAWS BLOCKADE CONSERVATIONISTS.'

Realising that their tactics had backfired, the loggers retreated to discuss matters. They came back agreeing to end their blockade if two members of their group would be allowed entry to record on video their 'hostaged' bulldozer. They then negotiated for the return of the bulldozer on the condition that they would not bring it back into the forest without giving NEFA prior notification. Getting the bulldozer out involved some organisation, as the only environmentally sound method of removing it was through the existing series of blockades.

Many of us were attached to the idea that the bulldozer was locked up and under the control of greenies. Others saw it as an ideal opportunity to get the dozer out of the forest, which was our aim all along. It was decided, after lengthy debate, to allow the dozer out by a back way. We believed the loggers' claim that there was an existing track which could be used. The dozer driver and a police officer as escort were ferried to the captive machine. We removed the tripod and watched the dozer slowly crawl out. Conditions were very wet, but when we suggested that the vehicle might get bogged the driver was adamant that there would be no problem.

He and the young cop riding shotgun were destined for a long, cold and wet night. The dozer bogged down ten kilometres from base, forcing its occupants to walk out. Another dozer was driven in the next day to rescue it, but being smaller it was unsuccessful. Urgent messages were relayed over our CB radios that a mess was being made on the steep slopes of the site, so a group of us went to investigate. Loggers and greenies worked hand in hand to free the bogged equipment. Environmental disaster was combined with a diplomatic victory of sorts.

Overall at Killie Kranke we had achieved a win. Locals who had been a law unto themselves in the region had been successfully challenged and the notion that reckless environmental practices would be tolerated, vaporised. The Soil Conservation Service's powers were significantly expanded, giving the organisation greater control over the Forestry Commission. NEFA was proven to be correct once again in its assessment of logging practices, and the industry had been given notice by the radical conservation movement that no operation would escape our scrutiny. We would act in a forceful manner on the ground, in the courts and politically in the call for accountability over the excessive powers of the Forestry Commission.

The success at Killie Kranke was a resounding victory for NEFA, but the win was not without environmental costs. A Conservation and Land Management (CaLM) report found that 88,000 tons of soil had eroded from the site. The report stated that one truck working a forty-hour week would take seven months to transport an equivalent load of soil from the site.

The outcome of Killie Kranke empowered the SCS to prosecute. It was an enormous black mark against the Forestry Commission, and it raised NEFA's credibility to discover these breaches. The police played a conciliatory role because it was clear the blockade was justified. Green action won the day.

CHAPTER 15
DUCKS AND BATS
Defending the High Fliers

Driving into Rockhampton from the south the most outstanding roadside feature is the Big Bull, which proudly states: 'WELCOME TO THE BEEF CAPITAL OF AUSTRALIA'. In the late eighties Queensland was still the heartland of the National Party, and Rockhampton the headquarters of the Cattlemen's Union.

A desperate call for help from a group of locals had sent us north to Mount Etna, a cone-shaped limestone mountain formed from an ancient coral reef. Over millions of years, water dissolved the soft rock to form an intricate system of caves. To industry it meant cement, development and jobs; a cement processing plant was nearby. To conservationists, and cavers from the Speleological Society, it represented a unique aspect of the web of life, a series of beautiful underground labyrinths in the most cavernous limestone area in Australia.

A colony of rare carnivorous ghost bats with a 70 centimetre wingspan depended on the caves, and 80 per cent of Australia's little bent – wing bat population used Bat Cleft, a cave with unique temperature – controlling features, as their maternity cave. For over twenty years conservation groups had fought to stop the scarring of the mountain.

Thanks to their efforts, quarrying had been directed away from the known cavernous areas and the central section containing Bat Cleft had so far been protected.

In December 1987 Queensland Cement had started to quarry the main mountain. In the presence of the media, local conservationists filled in drill holes prepared for blasting. Speleological Society members started provisioning caves for a blockade. The following year Queensland Cement called a media conference to announce the imminent destruction of Speaking Tube and Elephant Hole caves.

Only two locals were able to blockade at short notice; they set off to occupy caves within an hour of the announcement. An emergency call went out. We responded. Within a few days, 80 people were in camp undergoing training in rope techniques and caving. Blasting of the mountain ceased.

Lights were set up by the company so they could keep an eye on us, and security guards patrolled a 20 hectare area of the mountain.

Our aim was to maintain a presence in the caves to prevent the cement company from blasting. Small crews of two and three entered and lived in the caves for a week at a time. Ample food and water was already stashed in caches. Defecation was done with deft aim into a plastic bag, which was tied and placed in a sealed tin. This, along with a urination bottle, was carried out at the end of a week's shift. This routine lent a new perspective to the concept of looking after your own shit. 'Wet Ones' (moisturised cleaning tissues) were a fragile thread in the maintenance of comfort and sanity. The cave environment was so sensitive that not even breadcrumbs could be left on the floor, as fungus would develop in the humidicrib atmosphere.

Around midnight one night early on in the campaign I accompanied Jonno on a run to check on the current cave dwellers. I also wanted to take a look at the living conditions, as I was next in line for a shift. We had to run a gauntlet of flood-lighting and security guards – hard work, as we couldn't use our torches for fear of being spotted. Razor-sharp limestone formations glowed ghostlike in the night. It was difficult to keep up with Jonno, despite the fact that he was somewhat inebriated and was carrying a pack loaded with supplies, mainly recharged batteries. He worked best under those conditions. We scrambled around a scree slope and came to a small hole hidden in the rock formations and rainforest growth. The crack, indistinguishable from a thousand other crevices, opened into a small antechamber. We crawled on all fours to a ledge.

Forty feet below, the pale glow of candlelight lit up a scene from another world. Soft voices talked slowly, oblivious of our presence. It seemed a week in chambers far beneath the surface of the earth had slowed them down. We gave a gentle call so as not to shock them. Powerful torches shone up like searchlights from the depths. A conversation ensued, but it was unclear and at odds; we were even thinking at a different pace. We tied gear to ropes and lowered it down, bade them farewell and headed once again to the surface. Before we had even left, they were deeply immersed once again in conversation in their subterranean world. We worked our way around the shadow line of the arc lights and headed back to camp for the night.

When the time arrived for my shift I climbed the mountain, wondering what a week in the dark left to my own devices would do to my psyche. Once inside I settled down on a ledge. Ages of water flow had smoothed the floor to resemble a wave of rock. The roof just a metre above, curved in the same shape as the floor. It was a time-smoothed room. In the centre, one narrow column stood like an altar to some ancient deity. Time lost its relevance; an occasional bat flashed around the circle of light cast by the candle. With the lack of stimuli, the ancient rock sculpture of my retreat led me to another world, bringing to me a feeling of profound fullness I had never experienced before.

I left my isolated retreat after some 72 hours – measuring time by days was inappropriate. Leaving the shelter of my grotto I joined the other cave dwellers and went exploring the underground depths. Like creatures of the underworld, we had lost interest in the sun and sky outside. We went deeper, squeezing along ochre-coloured canyons that plunged to the darkness below. At Speaking Tube, which gave the cave its name, people could talk as though standing next to each other, when in fact they were separated by a 60-metre shaft.

We trotted along pathways with stalactites that looked like teeth in the jaws of a dragon. Spiky cave coral glowed orange in the torchlight. It was an exhilarating dark world of ancient rock sculpture; the mountain was a huge limestone pyramid overlaying a foundation of crystal. I reflected on how many of this earth's sacred places end up as crystals adorning the altars of New Age meditators.

We expected an intrusion by police or security at any time. Our familiarity with the caves meant we would not be easily removed; it would be a struggle in the underworld. Besides, if they caught us, how would they remove us? We thought we had it all worked out. Unfortunately we were soon to discover that they had their own plans. At the end of my week-long shift I emerged and was blinded by the setting sun in an alien world. After the security and joy of life in the dark depths, the sky was hostile. I waited till night before I climbed down the mountain back to the camp.

Confrontation continued, with growing media coverage turning public opinion against the miners. Queensland Cement slowly withdrew security. By June 1988, the blockade was at a low level but successful. After 46 days, the first blockade finished with no arrests and no blasting. The company agreed not to go into the mountain until conservation groups had prepared a report on the natural values of Mount Etna.

By November, intense lobbying had failed to convince either the National Party government or the mining company that quarrying should cease. Concerns about blasting on the mountain resulted in a vigil being established. Despite this, senior staff of Queensland Cement went in under the cover of darkness and blasted the entrance of Speaking Tube Cave.

Though the beauty of this cave was destroyed, luckily its importance to the ghost bats as a warm roost was not. The following day, the second round of blockades began – both on the surface and underground. Arrests started immediately. We settled in for a long confrontation, feeling confident of keeping people in the caves to prevent blasting. The company retaliated by lowering a high-pitched alarm siren into one of the main chambers. For those inside, the continuous noise was debilitating. They attempted to destroy it with rocks but it was positioned inaccessibly high in the cave roof.

Two locals, Joe Vavryn and Andrew March, were forced to give up. Both suffered ear damage as a result of the company's tactics. Our supply depot in the cave was discovered and removed and the cave entrance was filled in by a bulldozer. They upgraded surveillance to prevent our re-entry. We were defeated.

Elephant Hole and Speaking Tube caves were destroyed. The direct action employed by conservationists and concerned locals had delayed this act of vandalism for a year. The efforts of protesters also succeeded in highlighting the importance of Mount Etna, most of which is now a national park. The campaign drew attention to the decrepit anti – environmental views of the Queensland National Party. Spanning the demise of Joh Bjelke Petersen, then Mike Ahern, the Mount Etna campaign was the major Queensland conservation issue in the run-up to the state elections, which the Nationals lost disastrously under Russell Cooper. It assisted the demise of the National Party era in Queensland.

The year following the blockades centred on court action. Due to lack of funds, legal action under the Fauna Conservation Act failed. In 1989 the company blew the main chamber in Speaking Tube Cave in a wanton act of vandalism. Realising the negative implications of mass arrests, the authorities contained the last round of protests by simply detaining people at the mine site and then letting them go. That, at least, was the rule for locals. Outsiders were not treated so leniently. One person arrested and charged under the Vagrancy Gaming and other Offences Act for being on site without lawful excuse argued, under the Fauna Conservation Act, that he was there to protect the bats. He used a curious precedent to win his case: that of a Mount Isa man found in bed with two nurses on hospital grounds who was charged under the same Act. The defendant claimed he was in the nurses, quarters for intercourse, which was lawful. His case was dismissed.

On a wider level it was argued by conservationists that the processing plant at Mount Etna should close on economic grounds due to the out-of-date and inefficient style of production. The plant produced 150,000 tonnes of clinker (cement raw material) per annum. Tiny by international standards, it was the second smallest cement plant in Australia. One hundred and twenty kilometres south of Rockhampton a modern, efficient cement plant was situated. It was fed by a slurry pipeline from a massive open-cut mine. This large-scale, efficient plant indicated the future direction of the cement industry in Queensland.

Four years after Speaking Tube was destroyed, Queensland Cement announced the end of cement production in Rockhampton and the closure of the plant.

Rehabilitation has been under way in the buffer zones and is being negotiated on the eastern scarred surface of the mountain. Conservation groups are attempting to set into place rehabilitation procedures that will become a blueprint for all mine sites in Queensland.

Animal rights violations were not restricted to Queensland. The commencement of the 1990 duck shooting season in New South Wales attracted hundreds of not-so-sharp shooters. Fortunately for the wildlife it also attracted hundreds of conservationists bent on thwarting the shooters' so-called 'sport'. One hunting site where ducks and the odd protester were shot was at Lake Cowal, a wetland in the state's mid-western region.

An assorted contingent of animal rights activists, animal lovers and greenies had descended in groups of hire buses in the dead of night, like some off-beat tourist operation. After a short sleep disturbed by late arrivals, we had been woken by the drone of motor boats carrying shooters out in the pre-dawn darkness. It was the beginning of the day's sport.

As protesters assembled in the first light of day a volley of gunshots could be heard in the distance. Barely able to recognise each other in the receding darkness, we wondered aloud about the shooters' ability to distinguish legal game from those on the endangered species lists. We convoyed to our launching area and unloaded. Canoes and kayaks slid quietly into the shallows. These craft were appropriate for the task at hand as they were able to move quickly over distances, rescuing injured birds left by the hunters to suffer a slow and agonising death. Inflatable zodiacs from the Peace Squadron motored out to serve as a backup, but these often ran into trouble in the shallows.

Most people waded into the water with hand-held nets and old pillowcases to wrap the birds in a degree of comfort on the way to the vet. These medical volunteers set up a rudimentary 'field hospital' onshore, which consisted of a tent and an operating table. Medications included tape for splinting broken wings and injections to treat the victims for shock or to put them out of their misery if the injuries were too great.

A group of some 200 people waded, kayaked and boated out to a cacophony of shotgun blasts exploding near and far around a superb inland wetland system, its normal tranquillity metamorphosed into a battle scene. Protesters were recognisable by their rainbow colours and bright craft. We were under instructions from our organisers to be as visible as possible.

This was a different type of greenie action from any I'd been in before: the opposition used live ammunition.

Duck shooters were invariably dressed in the full regalia of jungle greens and flak jackets, lurking in the shadows (from the ducks, one can only presume), silent and invisible save for the give-away bulge of green where corpulence spilt out beyond protective vegetation. Many of them looked like misplaced Mexican bandidos with their huge belts, studded with the brass-tipped shotgun cartridges, strapped across their bellies.

It was the same every time: a Wobbly formation of creatures in slow flight would appear and wend its way down a corridor of death. Shotguns blasted from every direction. One or two victims would fall like wet rags. If the first series of shots missed the birds, they would be blasted out of the air further down the line. It was a lucky duck indeed that took flight and lived.

Those birds fortunate enough to be killed outright bobbed lifelessly in the water. If the walk was deemed to be too far for the shooter they were often just left. Sometimes the prey was not even noticed in the hunter's zeal to go for the next formation. Wounded animals flapped frantically in a circle if one wing was broken, soon to be dispatched by a casual one – handed swinging wring of the neck. Other injured animals hid in the shadows, half submerged, to die an agonisingly slow death from wounds – or, later still, from lead poisoning. Lead pollution in the wetland environment is an aspect of this sport which is often overlooked. Metal leaches into the wetland from shotgun pellets and certain species ingest them, thinking they are stones, only to suffer a long and painful death from poisoning.

Ducks, a gentle species, spend a portion of their lives in the tranquillity of wetlands. They seasonally inhabit these oases in the hot degraded farming lands of the western plains of New South Wales. These timid creatures' only defence when unable to fly, due to broken wings and bleeding gunshot wounds, is to dive and swim. When captured, unlike other animals in danger, they do not even attempt to bite their captors to protect themselves. They are the soft side of nature, and it is this appealing quality that makes them sought after by humans as domestic pets. This type of sentiment was far from the minds of the hunters, however, as they stood with guns in hand, waiting for the next passing target.

The rescue team's task was to gather injured and dead birds discarded by the hunters and take them to a vet for treatment and/or identification. This goal was intended to be achieved without antagonising the hunters; we were not to rescue birds that they were retrieving. However, this often turned out to be an unrealistic expectation on the part of the organisers. A number of protesters sided zealously with the ducks, and inevitably incidents occurred. Fortunately, in a race between a wading hunter and a kayaker armed with a pillow case, an activist could slip out of reach with the duck tucked safely away.

Police were present at the protest, but they remained onshore while the water became a scene of confrontation, the site of a cultural clash between two opposing groups with vastly differing points of view. When communication occurred (rather than the pointless abuse which can be a hallmark of such occasions), the two sides agreed to differ. It was made clear that the shooters would defend their right to continue their 'sport', just as we would continue our campaigning.

In what went on to become an annual tradition, dead birds were laid in a line on the footpath outside Parliament House a few days later for the attention of the media and public. Included in this gruesome display was always a large number of endangered species.

When the ALP gained power in New South Wales in March 1995 the issue of preventing the annual duck slaughter was championed on the floor of Parliament by the Democrat MLC, Richard Jones. He was supported by myself of The Greens, other minor parties and the ALR. The Game Birds Protection Act passed through the House with great opposition from the Shooters Party, the Call to Australia Party and the National Party. As a result of this significant victory, the annual duck shoot is now banned in New South Wales.

CHAPTER 16
OCEAN OUTFALLS
The Politics of Poo

Coffs Harbour on the mid north coast of New South Wales was expanding rapidly. To facilitate development, the local council in 1991 proposed to build an ocean outfall at Emerald Beach, a sleepy village at the northern end of the shire. The issue had been a festering sore since 1983, at which time two other outfall sites had been proposed but rejected. A Commission of Inquiry decision moved the outfall to Emerald Beach. The village awoke to the pending desecration of their 'dream by the sea' and a wave of anger ran through the community. Led by a local councillor, Alph Williams, the solid citizenry of beachside suburbia took to the dunes and the headland in defiance, radically reshaping local history by fighting for their environment.

The council wanted to lay a sewerage pipe to the headland, blast the rocks and pump sewage effluent into the sea, disregarding the fact that not only was it an area of unparalleled beauty but that a marine reserve lay just offshore. On one side of the headland was a little bay with safe swimming for children, and to the south a magnificent surf beach.

In the stylised media controversy which followed, reactionary politicians and interest groups presenting themselves as the pillars of the establishment vilified those opposed to the ocean outfall proposal as 'extremists'. This further inflamed the protesters – people who, in fact, might better have fitted the description of pillars of the establishment. The social revolution, facilitated by environmental concern, took on a new dimension.

The Emerald Beach residents' revolt was a far cry from the radical alternatives' protest at Terania more than a decade before, but the anger, sense of betrayal and indignation were exactly the same. Anti-establishment attitudes were transferring like a political wildfire. While such stirrings were still occurring only in small pockets of the community, the effects were reaching across the entire mosaic of Australian culture.

The story of Emerald Beach began with the forest confrontation at Chaelundi. High in the mountains, a small band of people fought for the forest against the power of the state and were successful. Like the streams of the highland being defended, we were mostly young, wild and full of effervescence. During this tumultuous period the Green Grannies had come to Chaelundi and were arrested in support of their 'children'. They then returned home to the coast where, like a river on the lowland ending its journey, they bestowed another power – the strength and majesty of society's respectable citizenry.

Both young and old, Emerald Beach residents were part of the 'mainstream'. In most cases they had not questioned authority before. They emerged as a community cohesive, coherent and angry. With the wild youths of the forest, they stood on their beach to confront the bulldozers. Grace Bartram, author and local resident, had been one of the Green Grannies at Chaelundi. She attended the first confrontation at the beach. A dozer started, so Grace stood in front. She called to the driver, "Hey, can you see me? Don't run over me." A policeman approached and demanded that she move. When she refused, he said that he would have to arrest her, to which she replied, "I haven't got time to be arrested today, I've got to get home to look after my grandchild." She backed off and others stepped forward in her place.

For three weeks the locals held their ground against the authorities. One morning the local protesters arrived at the beach to find tripods had been erected. The forest contingent had arrived to give support. At first, many of the locals did not want to be associated with the hippies, but Grace and others cautioned them to observe how the newcomers acted. "Do you know how to make a tripod?" she said. "Do you know how to stand up to the police? Watch these people and see how they are and don't judge them by what you've read in the papers."

These young people, often rejected by their parents' generation, were part of a sub-culture with its own sense of belonging. Regardless of how they looked, they had come to fight for a beach in which they had no investment but their ideals. They were quickly adopted, loved and protected by Emerald Beach residents. Forming the front line of defence, they were backed up by the majority of locals, many of whom rushed to the site in the morning, avoided arrest, went to work and rushed back in the afternoon to join the protest.

"A number of protesters were old returned soldiers coming along with their walking sticks," recalled Grace. "One old man nailed a sign to a tree giving his war history in the Royal Navy and saying he came to the freedom of Australia to raise his children."

Early on in the campaign the police were sympathetic, but either at the command of someone high up in the force, or as a result of a political directive, the police later came in with riot tactics. With the memory of Chaelundi, the cops believed their own propaganda. Protesters were pigeonholed as hardcore radicals, even though most of them walked out of their back doors to the action site.

Significant mass action combined with a stronger blockade of tripods caused the authorities to overreact. One day the riot squad stormed the blockade site before dawn wearing balaclavas and carrying machetes. Protesters had been expecting police at some time and had put defensive installations in place. Radio contact functioned between the front line and a communications base located in a nearby house. The police scanner was on: the commander's voice was heard. With this, the telephone tree (a coordinated community phone network) was activated. People drove around the village honking their car horns. Protesters were mobilised, and the police only managed to get one tripod down.

Two days later the police announced they would arrest protesters under a section called 'watch and beset', a union-breaking law used during the Great Depression. Rather than having one's arrest recorded as a misdemeanour, this was a criminal charge. Any public servant could lose his or her job with such a conviction. The police also used the criminal charges of 'inciting unlawful assembly' and 'unlawful assembly'. During October 1991, 250 people were arrested. This represented 20 per cent of the population of Emerald Beach.

Eventually fifty police were on site. Green Grannies, war veterans and a councillor supported the actions each day at the front line.

Mainstream locals carried the torch of rebellion in their minds and hearts. It became their norm, the real purpose in their lives. A group of residents, meanwhile, went to Sydney in a chartered bus to lobby politicians and access media.

There were older people who, with their beach under threat, were forced by circumstances to protect the land. It was a volatile mixture for change.

After three months of confrontation, Christmas 1991 arrived, and with it the council decision to approve work on the headland. All the older people came to the front line. First the women, then the men, fought desperately.

Any time a police car drove through Emerald Beach there were catcalls from the houses of erstwhile law-abiding citizens. For the police it was like downtown Los Angeles. "There are only two places where this would happen in the suburbs of Australia," said Alderman Alph Williams. "Redfern and Emerald Beach." The small seaside town went from being the suburb with the least arrests in the Coffs Harbour shire to the suburb with the most arrests in Australia. The vast majority of people previously hadn't had so much as a parking ticket. For the first time in their lives they saw the inequality of the law.

Intimidation was a tactic used widely by police. Many people backed off in fear. One resident, a middle class housewife, was threatened with the removal of her child to a welfare agency if she continued to participate. Another was charged with seven counts of resisting arrest because seven police touched him. A fourteen-year-old boy had been arrested for breaching the peace, assaulting a police officer, two counts of resisting arrest, offensive language and 'watch and beset'. When asked if he had resisted arrest he replied, "Well, sort of, I was up a tripod and they knocked it down."

JR, sixty-four years old, was born in Poland and came to Australia after World War II as a refugee. He spoke of his treatment at the protest. "We were victimised, arrested, handcuffs were placed on my wrists, so tight they lacerated my skin," he said. "I lost my glasses. I felt harassed . . . it was totally unjustifiable to treat us like that. I was arrested for incitement and resisting arrest and wasn't allowed to look for my spectacles. We were not criminals. We were people standing up for our rights."

RF, also sixty-four and a grandmother with three grandchildren, had never experienced anything like this before, even though she belonged to the Wilderness Society and had walked against the Vietnam War. She was arrested along with twenty-five other women who sat together in front of a bulldozer. Four policemen picked her up and told her to leave the site and stay away. "So of course I came back," she said. "I sat down again and we sang protest songs. We weren't inciting others to come and join us, but next thing there was a hand on my shoulder and a policeman told me to go with him. I didn't resist, nor did my sister who was sitting next to me. We were taken to the police station, fingerprinted and photographed with a number in front of us. I felt like a real criminal." RF was charged under the criminal act with 'incitement to unlawful assembly'. She was told she'd be charged under unlawful assembly, but on the charge sheet she found the police had added incitement.

Outstripping even the dawn raid, the most controversial police action was the introduction of riot dogs. The event was pivotal; it had the effect of hardening the resolve of residents in the face of the authorities' hypocrisy. At a meeting I jokingly suggested we form our own dog squad – a line of blue rinse ladies with their white poodles (preferably female) on pink leads to stand nose to nose with the police German shepherds. The group broke up with laughter.

Grace related the events which followed. "It became increasingly obvious that decisions of police action were being directed from up high," she said. "I was outraged that police could be ordered to bring in the dogs against peaceful citizens of a small community. I walked fast through police lines, glaring at any policeman who stood in my way. I found a group of gold-braided officers and asked who was in charge. One stepped forward."

"Why have you brought in the police dogs?" I asked. "It's normal," he replied.

"It's not normal to use police dogs against ordinary civilians," I retorted.

"It wasn't our idea," he said in a softer tone. "Who gave the orders?"

"I can't tell you that. It was someone high up." "How high?"

"About as high as you can go."

"I thanked him for his honesty. Another officer stepped forward and said, "Well, I can tell you something else. Those dogs are going to stay right where they are, in their vehicle. They can send in the dogs but they can't make us take them out."

In *The Canberra* Times the police denied both the balaclava-clad raid and use of dogs.

It was difficult for the police, as they couldn't separate themselves from the type of people they were opposing. One local chained herself painfully to a police rescue vehicle. The process of being removed caused even more pain, and she noticed that the rescue vehicle driver had tears running down his cheeks.

People left the site one day to support an arrestee who refused bail on the grounds that police treatment was an invasion of her civil liberties. We rallied outside the police station then marched to the council chambers 400 strong. Entering the main foyer, we staged a sit down. The crowd sang 'Advance Australia Fair' with rarely witnessed emotion. There I sat in what for me was a normal situation, surrounded by a crowd sitting on the floor, but most were at least twenty years my senior, with eyes gleaming and some in tears as they sang. One sprightly old chap offered me a hand up.

A monumental blockade in the sandhills confronted the police and workers, so they bypassed the blockade and started digging pipes in at the headland as a final act of domination. This backfired when a Land and Environment Court injunction to stop work was successful: the headland work was deemed illegal.

Aboriginal artefacts were found during the headland excavation. As the site of the Gumbaingeri creation myth, it is of great significance. The local Aboriginal Lands Council undertook to investigate the find.

Emerald Beach suburban barbecues continued as the close-knit community raised funds and stayed informed in case of possible future action. Their defiance had been cemented. People moderately concerned about the ocean outfall had become incensed with police brutality. Under parliamentary privilege, National Party politicians attacked locals, calling them anarchists and liars. Many of the locals had been National Party voters and felt deeply betrayed.

Shock tactics are often effective and can take many forms. The deployment of one unlikely stratagem took place in front of an assembled group of Emerald Beach citizenry: I announced that we needed a giant turd for the campaign. My intention was to spark up some enthusiasm. As I mouthed the words, I had a sinking feeling that a softer-sell option on the concept might have been more appropriate.

My idea was to create a symbol which would make the general population mention the unmentionable and look collectively at an issue most preferred to ignore. While flush toilet systems deliver maximum cleanliness and discretion at the personal end (no pun intended), they account for maximum filth in our rivers and oceans. A giant turd would provide high-order theatre of the environment. As a large three – dimensional, movable, interactive sculpture, it would be both thought – provoking and out there on the road: art of the environment, in the environment, social comment for the people.

For many a year, members of Stop the Ocean Pollution had dreamt of an ultimate symbol to embody our concerns. The task had seemed too onerous until police brutality at Emerald Beach prompted a continuing strategy to keep the ocean outfall issue alive. We needed a constructive, long-term focus to let the authorities know that they could not continue to pollute the ocean without community opposition. Hence the birth of the Big Poo, the more 'user-friendly' title the sculpture came to adopt, inside a garage in the hills behind Coffs Harbour. Mostly inside, to be accurate, as its enormity had part of it protruding two metres from the garage doors.

Bamboo was collected, split and bound together as a light frame construction. Chicken wire was then laid on top to give it form. Old bed sheets, donated by the Emerald Beach community, were saturated with a concrete sealant and laid over as a skin. Sam, the architect of the operation, claimed that the next layer would make it bounce like a football. It was a rubberised paint, very definitely shit brown. An entertaining workshop ensued, well endowed with anal humour.

There was much debate in the community during the construction phase as to the efficacy of such an object. Fear of association with the Big Poo prompted a group of local residents to take off to Sydney to visit Parliament House and lobby politicians on the issue of ocean effluent.

Meanwhile, construction continued, and the myth of its dimensions grew with it. When it was finished, I asked to borrow the product for an impending action over the Ballina sewage outfall issue. The Big Poo, however, was in demand for a surf contest, a fashion parade and as an ongoing roadside display. There was serious opposition to its removal from the Emerald Beach area for even a short period of time, as its popularity was growing to the extent that some locals were becoming possessive. I was annoyed at the thought of such an edifice only entertaining the local crew, many of whom had originally been opposed to its construction.

I decided, therefore, to steal the turd (with the full intention of returning it, of course). I headed off to Emerald Beach, timing my arrival for the midnight hour. There it was, sitting quietly, lit by the pale glow of nearby street lights. Not a soul on the street and, luckily, all of the overabundant local dogs (capable of doing their own rather large volume of little ones everywhere) locked up for the night. I hitched the Poo's trailer to my van and motored slowly out of town.

Upon turning onto the Pacific Highway I contemplated police questioning as to the nature of my load. Such an unwieldy charge atop a boat trailer gave no guarantee of remaining secured between Coffs Harbour and Byron Bay, with only yours truly struggling in the middle of the night to load it back on. Its long-distance transport had never been attempted before. Much had been made of its fantastic length (almost requiring an escort with a flashing light), but its formidable girth here deserves a mention to give an indication of the magnitude of the job at hand. At its centre point the turd was two metres wide and almost as high. Musing upon these things, stealing the Big Poo seemed at that moment a stupid thing to be doing. My other major worry was that the local residents would report it stolen to police. (In fact, fearing it had been taken by their pro-outfall opponents, they had been about to do so when the story broke.)

Now in possession of the famous faeces, there was nothing to do but go into action. Effective media angles had been going through my mind ever since I had instigated the construction. In fact, I had a diabolical plan to make this giant turd an icon of the sewage issue and a considerable pain in the arse to all people hell-bent on continuing to collectively defecate in our ocean. It was a personal vendetta, a surfer's revenge. First step was to design an event and alert the media. The following press release was issued:

BYRON GREENS: PRESS RELEASE 5TH JANUARY 1992
ALTERNATIVE SEWAGE STRATEGY FOR BALLINA
SHIRE THE BALLINA LAUNCH OF THE BIG POO
(EXTRAORDINARY EXCREMENT)

In keeping with the much-heralded Australian sentiment of immortalising that which represents the achievements of our industry and culture (Big Banana, Big Prawn, Big Pineapple, Big Cow etc), the Big Poo has been created and a festive event will launch it in Ballina Shire to celebrate Ballina's claim to the title of beach sewage capital of the north coast (in close competition with Coffs Harbour). This will be the last public showing of the artwork before it heads south to be a central attraction at Manly's Sewage Festival on the Australia Day Weekend. Ballina will be offered the option of hosting the Big Poo permanently in the future with negotiations under way for a site at Lennox Head Reserve overlooking our internationally famous surfing beaches.

Once the Big Poo is in motion, like nature itself, it will be unstoppable, so be there: 1 pm.

Venue 1 The Big Prawn, Ballina, for Press Conference. Venue 2 Assembly outside Ballina Shire Council

Chambers, street theatre and offerings to Council.

Venue 3 Photographic opportunity with the parking of the Effluent Edifice against the scenic backdrop of the sewage outfall at Skennars Head (next point south of Lennox Head.)

"This action is but one event in a programme for a state – wide and national Clean Water Action Party (CWAP) to include all ocean, riverine and waterway pollution issues. In the case of the proposed outfall upgrading at Lennox Head, the Ballina Council has a clear choice. It can either have a full and open public inquiry or an ongoing public shit-fight to be dogged in its every polluting move by local public interest and environment groups," Ian Cohen said.

In prior discussions with Ballina Shire president Keith Johnson on the proposed upgrading of the Lennox outfall, I had threatened to 'go big'. Obviously he had no idea what I had in mind.

The launch appropriately commenced at the Big Prawn, Ballina. Two mermaids officiated. Speeches and the distribution of turdingtons (appropriately shaped lamingtons created at the local bakery) for those present to savour. The media was in abundance and thoroughly enjoyed the fare. The protest then cavalcaded, with media in tow, to the Ballina Council Chambers. We parked as discreetly as possible, considering we were towing an eight-metre monster.

Turd untied, we gathered twenty bearers and headed for the council chambers, hoping our plans were so beyond the expectations of council staff that they could not anticipate our next move. We were right: as turd bearers rounded the corner, the automatic doors opened and in we went ... almost.

The Big Poo shuddered to a halt, firmly wedging itself into that orifice where councillors come and go and where all important decisions are made for the benefit of the shire. We thought it appropriate. The council ranger did not agree and called me over for a conference, demanding its removal. I encouraged him to inspect the blockage.

"Do you have something for council constipation?" I asked. "Yes, I'm calling the police if you don't remove it immediately," he stated in his most threatening tone. I pulled a long face, trying to conceal my pleasure; police would be the icing on the cake to a well-orchestrated media event. He made his call. Meanwhile, the music played and turdingtons continued to be passed around the crowd.

The police arrived, rather bemused. Used to being the meat in the sandwich, what was presented to them here was altogether a different thing. When asked to remove the obstruction I stated that I didn't think it possible but would take the idea to the assembled anti-outfall protesters. Seeing that we were in the council chambers, I put it to those assembled, "I would like to put a motion that we take the motion to the ocean." The response was a resounding 'No'.

Police amusement was wearing thin and the media appeared satiated, so it was decided that the police might assist in moving this solidly wedged object of grand proportions. They entered by the rear and gathered around the front of the offensive intrusion. To the shouts of 'Police push!' and 'Police press!' the remainder pulled from the outside and together we dislodged the Poo from the doorway. Assured that we had completed our business at the Council, the police left without making any arrests. All parties were relieved.

The Big Poo was then returned to its hapless owners at Emerald Beach through a major rainstorm and several hundred kilometres of bouncing highway Needless to say, it was a mere shadow of its former self, sunken and saturated. Its main builder, Sam, mused that he would allow it to dry out, climb inside and build a few supports so that it would be an even better and more robust model. It was just as well he did.

The next major event for the Big Poo was its starring role at the Manly Sewage Festival. With a group of Emerald Beach locals it was decided to take the giant turd on a grand tour. Having found the visit to the Big Prawn so exhilarating, all of the relevant 'Big' spots on route to Sydney would be visited. So it was the Big Banana at Coffs Harbour, followed by the Big Oyster at Taree and the mock-Ayers Rock at Leyland Brothers' World at Karuah. Our proudest moment, of course, was driving the Big Poo over the Harbour Bridge – a moving cultural experience. However it was probably the visit to Bondi Beach, the original scandal spot in Sydney's ocean pollution history where surfers have contended with effluent for generations (hence the famous

'Bondi Cigar'), that had members of the entourage stop for a moment of quiet reflection.

The festival at Manly was a gala event with the Big Poo leading the beach parade. As one of the speakers I took the opportunity to announce plans to deliver the Big Poo to Parliament House the following day. A serious request was made for Poo bearers.

The next day we gathered on the grass in the Domain. Our presence there seemed inoffensive enough until the council rangers sauntered up and informed us that the article lying there was likely to kill the grass. We explained that it was not the real thing and promised that it would be on the move very soon. With enough helpers having arrived we headed for Parliament House. Outside the Mitchell Library we took a break while Richard Gosden, my former political adviser, cased the front gates. Upon returning he informed us that they were unlocked. Entering Parliament House, an action beyond our wildest dreams, was looking like a real possibility.

Along Macquarie Street we struggled. As we came to the parliamentary fence I stepped ahead, leaned down and easily flipped the latch, allowing the gates to swing open. The Poo went in with great momentum, crossing the front courtyard and ascending the parliamentary steps. Its gargantuan brown nose pointed directly at the hallowed front doors of Parliament House. Unfortunately (or perhaps fortunately), a group of dignitaries stood gathered at the top of the steps. Those of us at the front yelled to stop. The mobile motion ground to a halt, but not before it bowled over one of the assembled group of Upper House Parliamentarians and 'Queen's minders' charged with overseeing Her Majesty's upcoming visit to Parliament House. Interestingly, one of the subjects they were discussing was the special soundproofing of the parliamentary-designated royal lavatory, should it be required on the occasion.

The Poo was laid down to rest on the front steps. In fact, it covered all of them. After innumerable actions over the years, for the first time we had managed to breach the front fence of Parliament – carrying an eight metre-long symbolic excrement! The point was made to the assembled media that the Big Poo was delivered as the ultimate organic material to fertilise the barren minds of the politicians. As a theatrical battering ram, the Big Poo had broken through the great Australian apathy syndrome.

Two years after the stop work at Emerald Beach some residents dug up the pipes on the headland. The police arrived as the exhumers were having a coffee break. The legality of the original pipe laying was disputed; police said they would check with their legal department. They retired and did not return.

The diggers received admonishments from other locals disappointed at being excluded from the last act of community defiance. The pipes were presented back to council. The action hit the local news. The mayor stated that it proved beyond doubt the residents were anarchists. Suburban vigilance was the revolutionary act which transformed a quiet coastal village into a model of citizen participation for social change. It was widely acknowledged in the community that the outfall would not proceed.

On Sunday 21 February 1993, 2,500 outfall opponents formed a human chain from beach to beach over Look At Me Now Headland. Grace recalls, "All ages were there, from babes in arms to people in their seventies and eighties. The vast blue ocean, surf creaming up long lonely beaches, the green bare headland with flags and banners flying and that amazing chain, linked warm hand to hand, claimed the headland for posterity."

In 1995 the ALP was elected to government with a promise of no more ocean outfalls.

CHAPTER 17
PARLIAMENT TO PACIFIC
Wilderness Experience

Since 1988, with the National Party controlling the landuse portfolios in the Coalition government, the environmental movement had been under a pall of oppression. It was agreed in the green movement that 1995 would be the last election for the Old Growth forests. Coastal development was running rampant in New South Wales and the environment was being viewed as a resource of the state. Defeat to the Reverend Fred Nile at the previous state election in 1991 and his resultant 'Balance of Prayer' which gave a priority to conservative and moral issues, was a bitter dose for The Greens. Every time I heard of another disagreeable direction that the government had taken, my heart sank, realising that if I had been more effective, The Greens could have held the balance of power.

It was time that this defender of many causes became focussed: I decided to stand for pre-selection. On a personal level, I was staring at the prospect of the first serious job ever undertaken. The Greens, despite (and in some cases in spite of) my significant profile, were not guaranteed to vote me into the number one position. It was the members from my local area, combined with others I had worked with over the years, whose support saw me win preselection in March 1994 with a convincing majority one year out from the election date.

The Greens set about organising a campaign that combined activist skills with a serious determination to win a seat. Transport and grassroots advertising had to be attended to. My old red truck received a facelift – bright forest green, of course. 'VOTE GREEN' emblazoned the vehicle, including roof lettering one metre by four, just in ease helicopters and high risers took an interest. It was hoped that more than the birds would notice it.

Our campaign gained strong support from Dr Bob Brown. As the highest profile Green in Australia, it was indeed a boost to have Bob along on a twenty-four-stop twelve-day tour throughout the state. As we burnt up the miles in a talking roadshow, expected redneck hostility did not materialise. Bob lent legitimacy to our campaign. His style and hilarious stories kept both audiences and the rest of the roadshow enthralled. In my position as support speaker I learnt a lot from the man. He started every talk by saying how good it was to be back in the town and went on to tell an anecdotal story about his past experiences in the vicinity. With his father having been a country cop in New South Wales, Bob was the consummate grassroots campaigner. In addition, T-shirts, badges and stickers were spread far and wide in an action launch to our campaign. We saturated country media.

The election date had been set with a four-year fixed term. This was part of the charter of agreement between the independents and the government in its previous term. We therefore had adequate lead time to build electoral momentum.

It was a summer of protests at coastal sites under threat. The signs were clear: each community was outraged at the treatment their favourite area of coast was receiving under a strongly pro-development government. Our mobile team met with residents. Demonstrations were followed by a swim with the locals. It was a heady mix of community action for a party which prided itself on its grassroots connections. We knew that this type of outrage would not dissipate in the months leading up to the elections.

Once in Sydney it was difficult to get mainstream media attention without resorting to mediawise stunts. We trod a fine line, wanting to access the media yet appear as a party serious enough to be voted into a parliamentary position. The northern New South Wales greenies did it again: they appeared in a five-tonne hired truck with two gigantic tallowwood stumps mounted on the table top. Hence another roadshow circuited the state, with special attention paid to Sydney suburban shopping complexes. The major parties had never been so on the nose; it was clear that people were looking for an alternative. Whether we were that alternative remained to be seen.

Sensing this voter disenchantment with the major parties, an unprecedented number of smaller parties had registered to contest the Legislative Council. In the 1991 election The Greens and the Democrats were the only small parties on the progressive side of the spectrum. This time we shared the protest vote with many others, including the No Aircraft Noise Party (NAN), the Daylight Saving Extension Party (DSEP) and A Better Future for our Children (BFFC), which would split our vote. Old political rivalries meant that NAN preferences went to others before The Greens. Everyone was starting to get a little nervous.

The Greens rented an office at the edge of Sydney's central business district. Our landlord, George, blending his superstitious past with a supportive modernity, insisted that all who rented his premises moved on to bigger and better things. The prospect of this didn't look likely when our media releases were met with little response.

Despite the close call of the last election, we were unable to get coverage. It was decided we had nothing to lose by crashing a political party in the time-honoured Green campaign fashion. Premier Fahey, along with Clean Up Australia patron, Ian Kiernan, was due to launch a campaign at the Balmoral

Clubhouse. Merve Murchie, the local Green candidate, my political adviser, Jan Barham, and myself slipped inside along with the media. It was a small, cramped space, with Fahey only a couple of metres away in front of the cameras. He gave his speech, expanding upon government efforts to clean up roadside litter and asserting that recent devastating brushfires were a blessing in disguise, for they exposed debris, thus allowing it to be picked up in the clean-up campaign.

I arose and stepped forward, saying, "I really can't sit here and listen to this hypocrisy." I challenged his ridiculous position for launching such a campaign when the very beach in front of the clubhouse was unfit to swim in, due to pollution. Fahey's government was doing nothing about the most serious health problem facing Sydney's harbourside beaches.

I had confronted many political leaders in similar style before. From Hawke to Howard to Peacock, all had reacted differently, but none had ever stood and stared at me like a stunned mullet before. After publicly challenging him for an inordinately long time, I realised that this man would be incapable of decisive leadership. Allowing me to finish my diatribe, Fahey simply asked me who I was. It was another perfect opportunity in front of the assembled media. 'Ian Cohen, Greens' candidate for the Upper House,' I answered. In reply, all he managed to say was, "That explains it," and the fouled media conference ended with a dull thud.

Outside, my media conference was disrupted by a more vocal Liberal supporter, but the damage had already been done. The Green campaign hit the media in a small but significant manner, and Fahey the Incredulous took a nose-dive in some people's estimation. Buoyed by this political success, we decided on a corporate raid to highlight what was for me a local issue and at the same time heighten the profile of the political campaign. The St George Bank annual shareholders' meeting was due to be held in a venue in Sydney's Darling Harbour. Several parcels of land near Byron Bay had been taken up in receivership by St George. The degradation of the land through tree clearing and inappropriate fire regimes, and their desire to flog it off, made a mockery of its advertising campaign. St George promoted itself as the good neighbour. To their misfortune I was their neighbour and they refused to answer my calls. Under their management, a fire policy was implemented, with regular burnoffs severely impacting on the environmental values of the property. I attempted to enter the meeting with a proxy but was refused admittance. Another Green, Jan McCulloch, a bona fide shareholder, took my place and managed to stand up and state our case. Meanwhile, I broke Darling Harbour rules by displaying a large banner ('SAVE BROKEN HEAD') and by distributing material on the land in question – for which I received coverage from John Macleay in the business section of *The Australian* with a picture of considerable dimensions. The media exposure was welcomed. St George has since sold the land with the stated aim of avoiding any further confrontation with environmentalists.

Old professional campaigners like printer, Colin Charlton, pumped out the propaganda. Posters blossomed all over the city and spread with supporters as they travelled across the state. Our best break came with a *Sun Herald* article, by Frank Walker, which hit with a controversial angle about Labor and The Greens in a secret political deal. This was followed by Matt Peacock, an experienced and well-respected radio journalist, who requested to travel with us on the campaign and record a behind-the-scenes story to come out after the elections. He seemed genuinely surprised when we refused to take him. Eventually he agreed to run the material focussing on our major campaign issue, the forests, on the Sunday prior to election day. He had himself a deal, and we had ourselves a passenger in the campaign vehicle as we hit far-flung places, from universities to the Timber Workers' Union offices. The radio programme set off a recognition in media circles that The Greens were indeed heading towards a place in parliament and the balance of power.

Election day thundered toward us. The Greens worked around the clock to distribute material and allocate booth workers. By election night's end we looked as if we were heading towards 4 per cent and were strongly tipped for victory. The celebrations went late into the night. Only the following day did we fully realise that we would have to wait the best part of a month for the complicated counting process to be completed.

Theories abounded as to the likelihood of other small parties with better preference deals sliding past The Greens in the count. Memories of the 1991 'Battle between Heaven and Earth', in which I narrowly lost to Fred Nile, flooded in. I existed in a world of grey indecision, unable to declare victory, just hoping. The days turned to weeks and the conspiratorial theories of being beaten on preferences grew stronger. As the hiatus became accepted, I disappeared to my north coast home and gave up worrying. The Greens galloped away in the polling and the message came through that I was elected number fifteen out of twenty-one seats – a major victory.

I had crashed through. This alternative protester greenie ratbag was now a parliamentarian. The Greens had come of age. We had mounted a campaign, dealt with the ALP to gain agreement on forest reform in exchange for our support, and had come through with our assertion that we would be significant players in New South Wales.

At many past events I had been outside the fence of parliament, protesting. Now I had burst through that big oak door into the dark recesses of another world, I was on the inside for the ultimate Wilderness experience. This greenie – sorry, I. Cohen MLC – tiptoed down the corridors of power. Behind every closed door lurked dangerous creatures plotting unknown schemes, appearing from the shadows with striped suits, gleaming yellow smiles and figures of grand corpulence, or with bouffant hairdos and power dresses, all so friendly, wishing to help the rather odd newcomer. Almost respectable, but where was the tie? One day I found myself alone in the lifts with three Nationals. No communication, none of the civil g'days of the ALP or the reasonable hullos of the Liberals. One involuntarily sniffed in disgust. The great unwashed had arrived in the fortress of privilege.

The controversial M2 motorway was high on the green agenda. The failure of the new government to act, despite pre-election promises, was not helped by the intransigence of the Minister for Roads. The destruction of remnant urban bushland and significant Aboriginal sites, combined with the total disregard for local communities desperately affected by the onslaught of a road to nowhere, facilitated my decision to make my first speech in parliament on the matter. This introduction speech is the only opportunity in a parliamentarian's career that he or she is permitted the courtesy of speaking without interruption. It was an opportunity taken up with relish. With friends interested in the issue, we worked all night to prepare my speech, which was later described by the leader of the Opposition in the Upper House as scurrilous and likely to bring New South Wales into disrepute for business investment.

I found myself experiencing an entirely different aspect of political life one day soon afterwards. A boat trip on Sydney Harbour with parliamentarians from the new multi-racial South Africa was a pivotal event in the first session. Inspired by the South African contingent and having just heard that the French were going to recommence nuclear testing in the South Pacific, Labor MLC Franca Arena and I decided that we had to act on the issue as parliamentarians. Our idea was to get a boat and set sail for Moruroa. Franca was delightfully spontaneous. For me, such a protest action was a way of life, but I wasn't quite sure how it fitted in to my new role. A letter was sent to New South Wales parliamentarians inviting them to join us on the venture. The response was overwhelming: politicians of all persuasions were enthusiastic. It was agreed that an organisation be formed – Parliamentarians for a Nuclear Weapons-Free Pacific. Letters were dispatched to other states, as well as to the Federal Parliament and international politicians. The response was equally positive: politicians from all over the world wished to join us. All we needed was a suitable vessel, something capable of carrying over one hundred parliamentarians to the test zone.

Here I was, a protester-politician, gearing up for the biggest protest I had ever been involved in. The support for our cause was a reflection of the effectiveness of activists who had persevered with the issue over a decade ago, who were abused and marginalised by mainstream society.

Now the issue permeated all levels so that few in the community were prepared to speak out in favour of French nuclear testing.

The hunt around the Pacific rim was on; agents as far afield as the west coast of the United States were notified. Details of possible vessels came faxing in from all corners of the world. With lengthy and involved discussions we negotiated a ship which looked appropriate on video.

As if being in parliament wasn't enough for my first year, in the winter recess I had to take a crash course on the details of ocean-going ships. The federal government, slow to act at first and more interested in their own initiatives, eventually offered our organisation over $200,000 on the condition that the ship sail under an Australian or New Zealand flag. That narrowed the field of search considerably, almost to the point of impossibility. We dispatched a member of parliament with naval experience to New Zealand on a mission to inspect several potential vessels. One New Zealand ship was reported to look like an inner city doss house, so that possibility was scrapped.

Franca, myself and our staff were working around the clock. With senior politicians supporting our initiative, we held a press conference and announced that a suitable vessel had been procured. The die was cast. We didn't identify the vessel, but it appeared capable of doing the job in comfort, but by no means in luxury.

Calls flooded in at all hours with inquiries ranging from details of the expected schedule and costs per passenger, to whether facilities for a hair drier (indispensable equipment on the high seas) were available. A major sticking point remained. Was it Australian flagged? Could it be registered such? The negotiations became an unending nightmare. A number of maritime organisations warned us to steer clear of the vessel. Meanwhile, the requests for berths continued to pour in, with twenty from Japan, including one for the Japanese finance minister. The Australian government had no alternative vessel available at such short notice. Any reasonably large ship was booked up for months ahead, if not years.

The boat lease arrangements began to falter. The international sharks of charter operations were circling. Across the Pacific, shipping agents had been informed of our short-term desperate bid to deliver a boat to Papeete, Tahiti's capital, by 2 September. This was to make a deadline for the first of the planned tests, and also fit in with the schedules of many politicians, whose time was limited by other obligations. This was no simple greenie action we were organising. The world media pressed us for information.

Desperate times were indeed upon us, but still we didn't have a boat. A German broker had an ex-Soviet luxury liner moored in Vladivostok ready to go. We did our sailing-time calculations and let that one pass. Then came what seemed like a breakthrough: a large ocean cat was due in Sydney and its booking had been cancelled. We could inspect it in our own harbour. It was our last chance, one which seemed too good to be true and it was. After lengthy phone calls to Germany it became apparent that we had been outbidden by a German consortium. On one call a suspicion flashed into my mind: "Were they media?" I asked. The affirmative reply, with apologies that it was a commercial decision, summed up the absurdity of this Moruroa regatta. The German media had beaten us in a bid for a ship which would travel thousands of miles in the South Pacific to film the international brigade of parliamentarians who wouldn't be there!

The press conference room felt decidedly like the Colosseum. It was packed. Some noted right-wing media luminaries were present, ready to attack as we entered to announce that we had failed to procure a suitable ship and would be returning the moneys held in trust, including fares. We could not accept the Federal Government's financial support. Despite our lack of a ship, we declared we would still go to Papeete to protest as an international contingent of parliamentarians.

A campaign to boycott French products was launched. The effect was moderate, Australia having only a relatively small market for French products. Our information was sent to Japan where, coincidentally, or perhaps prompted by international actions such as Australia's, the Japanese embarked on a strident boycott campaign.

The buildup against nuclear testing continued, with the failure to secure a ship fading into the background. The thirty Australian parliamentarians flew out from Sydney airport amidst a blaze of media. Upon arrival in Papeete we were greeted by a hungry international media contingent. Australian politicians played a significant role in the marches and forums in Papeete. We met with the French ambassador in Tahiti and delivered thousands of petitions. Meetings were also held with indigenous anti-nuclear and pro-independence activists. Parliamentarians for a Nuclear

Weapons-Free World was formed at a traditional Polynesian meeting place by the ocean, with Australian Senator, Bruce Childs, and independence leader Oscar Temaru elected to head the organisation. The international spotlight was on French Polynesia.

Meanwhile we waited for the promised arrival of a privately organised ship to transport politicians to Moruroa, some 1150 kilometres away. Greenpeace offered me a place on their boat but I was uneasy, paranoid actually. Knowing I would be seasick, I imagined I could cope on a larger ship, but the thought of a thirty-metre motorised sailboat did not assuage my growing fears. I attended a Greenpeace meeting, where operatives spoke of the appalling treatment the French had meted out to Greenpeace captives. The room was crowded – even that made me claustrophobic. I had to retreat outside after I listened to a report of people packed into tiny cabins in high seas. This was an adventure I didn't need. I convinced myself that to go with Greenpeace would be to desert my companions, with whom I had agreed we would go on this one together. Yet Greenpeace had submitted an immigration application for me only. For them it was me or no-one. Brent Hindstrop, a Danish Red/Green parliamentarian, and Richard Jones, another New South Wales parliamentarian, were magnanimous in their support.

After much internal panic (fortunately not too many people noticed) I decided to cast my lot with Greenpeace, knowing I would curse if a luxury liner full of parliamentarians sailed past on the high seas. It was not to be so. In a comedy of errors the long-searched-for ship arrived in port and left in the other direction a few days later with only one Australian politician aboard – a fitting end to the saga of shipping charters in the South Pacific.

Yet again, with media fanfare, we boarded two launches to deliver us to our Greenpeace vessel, which was avoiding French territory. The last word in interviews with the Australian media was that the French government had announced that anyone entering the twelve-mile zone around Moruroa would be gaoled for twelve months and receive a fine of $150,000. It was something to contemplate. With my trademark surfboard on deck, and supportive cheers from the media, the launches set off. I felt like a kid involuntarily off to boarding school. We boated past glorious beaches and surfers frolicking in clean tubes at the edge of the reef. I was heading out to the unknown – to the ocean to be sick, to the military to be abused, to gaol...

We boarded the yacht and I was immediately sick overboard. I looked into the hold where I was supposed to sleep. It was dark and dank; the smell of the pervading damp and the last cargo mingled with the odours of the toilet. I was immediately sick again. This was shaping up to be the greenest campaign of my career. I carried my gear into the hold but couldn't get my seasickness patches out, because to bend over and concentrate made me violently ill again. It was into the toilet this time to throw up. Job done I hung onto the pipes trying to work out the plumbing.

Back on deck I lay down, the boat swaying under me, and began to feel faint, but I couldn't imagine facing the hold again; claustrophobia competed with my nausea for my undivided attention. The yacht motored on. Sickness made me drowsy but I couldn't stay lying down as the deck was awash with the rolling ocean. Someone told me to look at the horizon to ease my sickness. "Five days looking at the horizon," I thought.

I could hardly stand up. There was nowhere to rest except down in the hold. I descended to my designated bunk, into my private nightmare. Sliding into a bed space the size of a coffin, I lay in the half-light, sipping water to avoid dehydration. Occasionally I rallied to look for seasickness medication but collapsed with my head in a spin from the effort. I escaped only in sleep, waking in clammy realisation of my prison-like surroundings. One pitch black 3 am I awoke (I hadn't managed to find the light switch in my delirium) and had nothing to do but contemplate my fate. I had a job, the acclaim of my community and plenty of work to do at home. I had been elected in part to help defend New South Wales' Old Growth forests; the legislation was coming up next session in ten days' time. If I didn't make it back I would be letting green supporters down across the state, not to mention those wonderful forests to be lost forever.

If I were locked away for a year, technically I'd lose my job for being absent. If I were fined $150,000 and declared bankrupt, that would be another reason to lose my job. The other Australian on board, Senator Tom Wheelwright (who wasn't sick once – which says something about the right wing of the ALP), was absolutely confident that his government would bail him out. All I could think of was the fact that there were many in the major political parties who would not be upset to see me redirected, compliments of the French government. My internal debate about entering the twelve-mile exclusion zone reduced to the fundamental position that despite massive global protest, the

French still intended to detonate nuclear bombs in a South Pacific paradise. Why would they be inclined to treat anyone reasonably?

I must have recovered, my mental turmoil overtaking my gastric disturbance as my prime object of obsession. I emerged on deck to the crackle of the satellite phone and ongoing 'mushi! mushi!' from the Japanese, 'pronto! pronto!' from the Italians and 'hullo! hullo!' from the English speakers. Repeated incessantly it became the international linguistic joke of the voyage. We drew together as a group.

We stopped for an international news broadcast. With the shimmering blue of the ocean, a clear sky and warm breeze caressing our faces, we listened to the announcement of the first detonation on Moruroa. Until that point, in the back of our minds, somewhere in our hearts, we thought we could stop it. All those anti-nuclear campaigns flashed through my mind: a picturesque beach destroyed by sandmining for radioactive products, the nuclear-armed ships in Australian ports, uranium mines in our vast and beautiful deserts. So many times I had felt powerless in the face of world events. Now, millions of people relied on our little venture to fly the flag, to say 'no'. Blue sea and blue sky stretched out ahead, unchanged but now so different. The little boat continued on course, without deviation, didn't miss a beat as we sailed into the eye of the global nuclear storm.

APPENDIX 1
ALL THE WAY WITH NVA –
CO-WRITTEN WITH FELICITY RUBY

The debate on nonviolent action (NVA) is ongoing throughout the environmental/social change movement. In every action, large or small, discussion would arise as to how activists as a group will represent themselves to the society at large and, equally importantly, what philosophical position is to be taken in order to allow participants, actions to be a reflection of their ideals. In a sense we are prisoners of conscience with an acute need to work within the framework of our own ideals, both in terms of our goals and the means by which we pursue those goals; hence the incessant, passionate debate.

The green agenda includes continuing experimentation with concepts which translate into modes of action. A general consensus in the Australian political context is for nonviolence in political action. However, problems arise with the varied interpretations of such action and in defining what is acceptable behaviour.

As practised at the Franklin River and South-East Forest campaigns, NVA represented a strict set of rules to guarantee maximum safety for those involved. Any action which did not accord with all the basic principles was referred to as 'direct action'. The term direct action was not acceptable to many, who felt it indicated some departure from nonviolence. Such activists felt that they, in fact, had a more flexible and realistic framework in which to work. To these proponents of what is perhaps more appropriately called 'nonviolent direct action', the strict school of thought was regarded as 'orthodox NVA'.

For these activists, training in NVA has all too rarely been about channelling the dynamic fires of social change and too often about organising and taming the cheeky sparkle of indignation. This, despite the fact that the very survival of the planet hangs on the fine thread of human endeavour.

Sections of the green movement have turned their understanding of non-violence into rigid forms. Orthodox NVA can stifle creative energy, disregard the strength in diversity and brand its critics as 'violent', but adhering to specific structures, processes and theories can be problematic; codes of openness and cooperation with the authorities make any secretive action out of bounds, instantly outlawing the actions of groups such as Greenpeace and the Peace Squadron. The mass participatory, nonviolence theories of Gandhi and Martin Luther King cannot always be plucked out of an historical context and applied to today's circumstances.

The practice of consensus employed by orthodox NVA activists can actually duplicate existing power relations, albeit in a hidden way, unless the group is small and has a uniformity of views. The essential factor in any revolutionary thinking is empowering people to make decisions for themselves. In this, orthodox NVA fails, for it merely replaces old structures with new. If one pays lip service to ideas of consensus, one cannot implement definite ideas to make diverse groups of people work together.

Groups and individuals are being disempowered by organisational and bureaucratic processes which mimic patterns existing in the mainstream society.

We are witnessing developments not dissimilar to the counter – cultural explosion of the 1960s and early 1970s. What arose as a pioneering spirit degenerated in a few short years to become the victim of dilution and exploitation. The environmental movement, on the crest of a wave in the early 1980s, had captured the imagination of the public, spreading the word with evangelical zeal. It had caught government and industry off guard.

Since then, vested interest groups are reasserting their power; consumerism is merely given the gloss of environmental consciousness.

Many people use the environmental/social change movement as a career path or a vehicle for expressing other personal agendas. The dance of the pioneering spirit is inevitably taken over by bureaucratic personalities who, by their very nature, seek to gain control. This destroys the essence of revolution in the process and society ends up with another means of control. Such a process is occurring in parts of the movement in Australia today.

At Middle Head in 1980 the NVA debate was unconscious and not labelled as a specific doctrine. Similarly, actions at Terania Creek in 1979 and Nightcap in 1982 were pioneering experiences. Both forest events drew on local people moved by a passionate desire to defend rainforests. Training was not even thought of, and the areas of action were accessible to all. The more experienced activists dealt with the potential problems positively and dynamically. It was the role of protesters using nonviolent direct action to stay one step ahead of potential violence and turn it towards creative action, channelling raw energy instead of sitting back at the camp to block or negate those sometimes unwieldy personalities and desires. Instead of a system to control blockading initiative and enthusiasm, it was cooperative decision making on site which forged dynamic action; in short, it was training in action. This dovetailed with political lobbying, which resulted in a major victory in defence of rainforests.

Activists can learn more than just rules and regulations if predetermined concepts of appropriate political behaviour do not stand in their way. They can learn to deal with authority structures by seeking to understand how and why they work. This implies an understanding which sees human, social and political relations as multi-dimensional and changing, and thus unable to be accurately predetermined for each and every action. The practice of orthodox NVA training fails in that it refuses to cater for the unexpected and aims for the safe option of stereotyped behaviour. It teaches passivity and acceptance of rules, producing compliant, productive adherents to the doctrine.

In 1982, members of the Tasmanian Wilderness Society were sent to observe the Nightcap action. These agents did not make their official presence known. Judgments were not made by observing actions in the forest but by witnessing the dynamics of the base camp, which was dominated by the loony fringe who did not participate in campaigning, were often drunk and violent and disrupted the camp. Fearful of this problem, organisers of the Tasmanian blockade considered cancelling the Franklin action. A compulsory (orthodox) NVA training programme and strict control in determining who went upriver was both a reaction to the Nightcap campaign and a reflection of the extreme conservatism of the Tasmanian Wilderness Society. This became a means of control at the Franklin.

On the positive side, the training process was of great assistance to those needing skills, confidence and a key to deal with potentially violent situations. For many, gaol was a new and daunting experience; the bonding that occurred during training helped create the support needed to deal with confronting situations.

However, hierarchy soon took a stranglehold and a cult arose around orthodox NVA, beginning with the NVA training initiation process. This process acted in many cases as a block to the free flow of communication and action. For those who had only a week to donate of their time in defence of the Wilderness, most of it was spent training, despite the fact that the upriver blockade site was often starved of numbers.

Well-intentioned rules took on an air of absurdity. Once, two qualified scout masters, on holidays from teaching and obviously well equipped and bush wise, offered their skills to gather information for a proposed action in the forest. Their offer was blocked due to a lack of NVA training. Such a rigid structure negated individual responsibility, failed to recognise personal ability and presumed that only a codified set of rules would create the ability to deal with all situations. While the Tasmanian Wilderness campaign was highly successful, orthodox NVA alone was not responsible for the win. A concerted national effort and the significant contribution made by people based at the upriver camp – people who were effective but were not necessarily practising orthodox NVA – were also of importance.

There is a growing acceptance by authority structures in our society of citizens' rights of expression. This is an essential step towards an ethical and sustainable future. Orthodox NVA lays claim to nurturing such a growth process with the police. However, such trust can become a manipulative advantage for authorities.

Experienced activists often have a politically astute analysis and past experience of the 'unpleasantness' of police. Their reaction to such experiences is not acknowledged as a valid perspective on authority. The trust in the inherent 'niceness' of police conversely means that blame is placed on the victims of police violence if they 'don't handle' the police correctly. The police will often pay lip service to the values of environmentalism and human rights, but when their own authority is attacked they can revert. The often misguided trust of police goes hand in hand with rigidity in orthodox NVA training. Such training lays down a set of rules which dictate how to behave. However, a more evolving and fluid process of training would equip protesters to deal with situations in a creative, and still nonviolent, manner.

Groups and individuals can be disempowered by organisational structure, which limits a movement that would otherwise have the potential to challenge the establishment. If both police and orthodox NVA practitioners value social rules and regulations, their tactics peacefully co – exist – and no real change takes place. By minimising the differences between police and protesters and making the relationship between the two a priority, attention is distracted from the issue. A penchant for structure makes orthodox NVA the issue rather than the process. It dictates that one can go so far, get so much, but that the line is drawn and it is clearly within the bounds of 'reasonable behaviour' as defined by the authorities.

Orthodox NVA proponents are actually undertaking a police role, guarding the value systems of the establishment and at the same time controlling potentially revolutionary elements.

Orthodox NVA activists take a simplistic view, blaming 'consumerism' for global ills. This is an irresponsible view considering the overt complicity of government and corporate enterprises in environmental devastation. Rainforest destruction is not just an issue about trees, it is a manifestation of the interconnected web of economic, social and political atrocities currently inflicted upon the earth. Environmental organisations, which on the one hand present radical solutions and on the other fail to challenge the status quo, are at best ineffective because they merely parallel the government's stand and at worst disempower the ill-informed.

The understanding of issues comes with continuing debate. When a theory translates into a mass movement it can become a dogma. This packaging simplifies its complexity. It assumes that people cannot understand the nuances of the broader philosophy thus disseminating a rigid set of ideas. This leads to a limited form of radicalism which is either blindly adopted or rejected. Reactionary forces either radical or conservative will not further any cause.

In a truly revolutionary movement a society can grow from the unexpected, evolve from processes rather than try to control them.

Participants in change must accept that the movement cannot unfold exactly as pre-planned. Respect for the diversity of ideas and actions of individuals is what makes the movement powerful.

APPENDIX 2
GROUND RULES FOR GREEN RADICALS

It is inspiring to recognise the increasing number of people who choose to make environmental and social change efforts part of their lifestyles and that so many undertake to play a proactive role against injustice in its many forms. This book is a series of stories contributing to a great and timely movement to help heal the planet. Yet to portray the efforts of one small group alone is insufficient; everyone has a role to play. This appendix explains the groundwork involved in organising for change and includes anecdotal sections which, it is hoped, will allow a deeper understanding of these types of events in the Australian context. From such awareness will come the recognition that we all can empower ourselves to act. My hope is that the information provided here will encourage people to embark on their own projects, to save the world through liberation from powerlessness.

For those already involved, this appendix is a reminder that as we stumble along, attempting to bring our dreams for a better world into reality, we must be aware of the danger of personal burnout and recognise that there are other like-minded people ready to support us and our ideals.

Perhaps the most important issue is this: we must maintain the ability to laugh, particularly at ourselves.

Most of the successful campaigns in Australia have been the result of a multi-dimensional approach. In what should be a symbiotic relationship, each element of a campaign relies on the cooperation and smooth functioning of other 'departments' to survive. A group of people protesting environmental destruction or social injustice will have their efforts fall on deaf ears unless supported by fundraising teams, political lobbyists and media savvy activists. Conversely, organisations seeking to wield power on an issue can be exposed as 'paper tigers' without the support of those on the ground to back up demands.

A creative change of roles by various players also assists success. An organisation that has participants both in the office and in the field, with a practical understanding on all levels, will create the most formidable campaign.

Familiarity with the various functions is a definite asset. Working with the different sections, knowing people, their problems, hopes and fears at all stages, is a bonus not often achieved in major campaigns. Despite the political success of the Franklin campaign, the protest failed in this practical respect. Friction between grassroots movements and the green bureaucracy dogged its operations from start to finish. This resulted in bad relationships and a negative legacy for future cooperation.

In contrast to this, a successful formula for people's actions was created in the various protests in northern New South Wales. With an interesting mix of flexibility and sharing, it grew out of a movement that was to give great respect to those on the front line. From Terania onward it was truly a people-power campaign. The North East Forest Alliance likewise acted successfully in support of forest blockades, accepting the role of leadership without taking the power. Their emphasis was on community action.

Much of the following is based on a paper prepared by Samantha Potts and Aiden Rieketts of the Big Scrub Environment Centre in Lismore. It highlights some of the activities that can be undertaken for the local and global environment.

FORM AN ACTION GROUP

Establish a clearly recognisable action group with defined goals and objectives. A group can provide invaluable support and can develop ideas to create an innovative and effective campaign. Simple things like nominating spokespersons and creating a letterhead will give a professional and organised demeanour to activities. There must be a postal and phone contact for all public statements and leaflets.

Just as a picture is worth a thousand words, a clever acronym can be a decisive tool in the struggle for public recognition. Stop the Ocean Pollution (STOP) and People Opposed to Outfalls (POO) can justifiably claim great success in mobilising the population on the sewage issue in

New South Wales. From small beginnings, organisations can become recognised in the wider community. Thus some greenies have become The Greens, a formidable political organisation at a local, national and international level.

Tactics should be approached with an eye for diversity. Investigate all angles and place events in sequence. If there are too many to put in place at once, keep one tactic in reserve. Above all, don't fall into the trap of allowing your tactics to compete with one another. Consider actions as cooperative steps towards the shared goal. In too many instances various parts of the movement compete to achieve goals 'their way'.

At times, the temptation is great to name a new organisation to reflect the radical and fiery ideals of those pioneering a campaign.

However, it is easy to become stuck with an odious label just as the movement is gaining wider social acceptance. Notable historical backfirings have gone beyond the simple failure of a group achieving their goals and resulted in a backlash that could have been avoided.

A case in point was the Tooheys Forest Liberation Army on the Griffith University campus, Queensland, in the early 1980s. The aim of this group was to save forested areas on campus from being carved up for building extensions and car parks. Members of the Army, took to kidnapping other students and the occasional onside staff member. They were not averse to bursting into lectures armed with toy machine guns and wearing balaclavas; death threats were jestingly made and the university was awash with propaganda. This attracted the attention of Special Branch and ASIO. With the campus being intended for use as a residential village during the 1982 Commonwealth Games, the threat to security was taken seriously. Investigations led to a pair of imposing plainclothes police knocking on the door of a very middle class home one evening. Startled parents were questioned as to the political activities and associations of their son – an action not conducive to congenial familial relationships. As a final blow to the fun war, the 'Army' failed to stop the demolition of their forest.

The formation of an action group need not depend upon the gathering of a safe number of people. If the issue is urgent, chances must be taken. Organisations can be formed as a skeleton crew behind a name and encouraged to jump in at the deep end. If the cause is just it will resonate with sections of the community and the group will grow. Often the initial 'splash' of media will aid credibility and draw inexperienced and unconfident people together into a successful working group.

The Australian 'cultural cringe' extends to a lack of recognition of our environmental heritage. In every debate it is vital to convince would-be supporters of an ecosystem's value and rarity If for instance, a patch of local forest has been a favourite spot for locals to visit, broadcasting the threat to it in the media can quickly legitimise the forest's importance.

In our society, symbols are of great importance. My rule of thumb has been: the more radical the aims and methods of the group, the more conservative the name. For example, the Broken Head Protection Committee was formed by myself and another local surfer in a desperate move to kick-start a campaign against a tourist resort that was pretending to be an educational institution, the Cape Byron International Academy (the resort was not even at Cape Byron but was located next to the Broken Head Nature Reserve, which it intended to utilise). In a four-year campaign we combined education with theatre and the threat of court and direct action.

When the developers decided to sponsor a professional surfing contest, we threatened to paddle out and disrupt it. The sponsors withdrew in a storm of media controversy. The thought of disrupting a professional, international competition, with thousands of spectators, was daunting. We stood our ground, and surprisingly enough the media went our way

THINK GLOBALLY ACT LOCALLY

Success is not measured just by heroics splashed across the media but by concerted, unending action at the local level.

Local issues are often some of the hardest. In my home town of Byron Bay, radioactive tailings remained as the residue of beach sandmining. In protest against this I formed the Byron Radiation Information Centre – yours truly with a Geiger counter. Greg Tollis and myself plotted the many areas of radiation in the town. Sites included the hospital, a school, an old people's home and private residences. I was not the first to raise the alarm, but I recklessly promoted it in the local media. (My most notable venture into journalistic hyperbole followed the discovery of radiation under the local girl guides' hall; the press release was entitled 'BROWNIES FRY'.) My truck had become a rolling billboard. On the front doors were large radiation symbols with the caption 'BYRON SHIRE RESIDENT – RADIOACTIVE'. I regularly parked my vehicle outside local real estate offices. Government action was soon forthcoming: the State Health Department called a public meeting and a cleanup of contaminated areas was undertaken.

As Byron's tourist potential grew, the major issue became coastal development. The presumption of legitimacy through land ownership and money had been pervasive. When land adjacent to an Aboriginal women's sacred site was auctioned at Surfers Paradise, members of the Broken Head Protection Committee attended and, amidst ridicule from the white shoe brigade, let potential buyers know that they were purchasing a political and environmental issue. No-one made a bid on that land and we provoked a significant storm in the local media.

While Byron entrepreneurs attempted to extract profits from our local environments, a bigger shark circled our town, attracted by its international profile as a tourist Mecca. Club Med represented a significant upgrading of the town's tourist industry. The pro-development lobby preached economic benefit with religious fervour. The opposition, initially led by local environmentalists, grew to include others from the local community. The network broadened and the Byron Shire Businesses for the Future (BSBF) group was formed, creating a more substantial opponent to Club Med. The council granted approval for Club Med. The BSBF had a significant win in the Land and Environment Court which ruled that a fauna impact statement (FIS) was necessary. Club Med has complied with the court's decision and has produced an FIS, which led to the discovery of additional endangered species.

Rallies sparked media interest across the nation. Our main stumbling block was a reactionary majority on council; absurd in their ineptitude, they highlighted the need for electoral action. The community organised to regain a progressive majority at the next council elections. Byron Shire in the local government elections in September 1995 saw a new council elected. The Greens now had an elected councillor in the shire, Richard Staples, and there is a majority of progressive thinkers holding the balance of power.

INCORPORATION

It is not always necessary or desirable to incorporate an action group, but it can be of assistance to larger groups with premises, employees and tax-deductible bank accounts.

On the down side, incorporation can lock a group into a bureaucratic framework which mirrors the power structures and institutions being opposed. People-power stands in contrast to both bureaucracy and corporate culture. The latter generally involves a transfer of decision – making power away from individuals towards corporate entities. However, it is possible to have an incorporated group working with consensus and non-hierarchical structures.

An effective organisational form for a small action group is a network. This can work within or alongside existing groups and establish itself as a political, media and social entity without the time-consuming and distracting issues of setting up constitutions and voting systems, organising annual general meetings and appointing office bearers. Involvement in a network need not imply 'membership' as such. Networks can operate in a more personal and flexible manner. Usually the network is activist-based and decisions are arrived at among 'active' members. If there is no structure within which to have a power struggle, no voting procedure to be 'stacked' and no elected office bearers to compete with each other, there is no forum for numbers games, administrative obstruction and process addiction.

Such a network must share a common ethos and aim. There must be some agreement on the ways in which differing points of view can be accommodated. Differences of opinion within the group are resolved through human processes, rather than by resorting to structure. By avoiding an 'organisation' meetings can exist solely to deal with issues. The aim is to arrive at the most appropriate action; time and energy will not be wasted on organisational housekeeping.

Instead of office bearers, members of the network occupy their positions within the group solely on the basis of skills, involvement and support from other members. It is implicit that such a network operates on a personal basis.

This type of organisation is participatory in nature and it is intended that 'top down' decision making and the 'tyranny of the majority' be replaced by full participation in decisions.

An unincorporated action has no corporate ego to defend. Rather, it is the reputation and actions of public officials which are on the line.

Regardless of their accusations and methods of intimidation, keep the issues in focus and don't allow yourself to be bullied into self defence. As a general rule, ignore attempts to personalise the campaign. Of course, there are those who have developed the personal attack into an art form. It is fraught with danger but is not to be ruled out altogether. A case in point was the attack on Alan Bond by local anti-development fighter Fast Bucks over a controversial development north of Byron Bay. It is now history that Alan Bond's business style justified the personal attacks. However, it is not a route for the faint-hearted.

Green power is enhanced by the fact that the vested interest usually has the most to lose. In cases where there is a potential for litigation, less vulnerable individuals – those without significant assets – can represent the conservation case in court. Companies and governments are not averse to a court attack on an individual or group simply to silence opposition. This type of legal attack, known as 'strategic litigation against public participation suits' (SLAPPS), has become common in the United States.

Suits like these have been seen in Australia, including two notable cases in the Byron Bay region. In 1992 Club Med threatened to sue the Byron Environment Centre over a leaflet the Centre had produced and distributed. Ballina Council took the president of the Clean Seas Coalition, 72-year-old Bill Ringland, to court for defamation over a press statement against the upgrading of the Lennox Head sewage outfall. Bill won the case through legal support and the efforts of the community, which felt that the litigation was a cowardly act by big government. This position was upheld in an historic decision by the Supreme Court of New South Wales, which brought into question the right of an elected body to sue a citizen, in this case a ratepayer, for defamation.

DEFINE PROBLEMS AND SET GOALS

Be clear on group activities and issues and define individual and group commitments from the outset. Simple goals are invaluable throughout a campaign. A written copy detailing the group's goals and objectives is invaluable for new recruits, supporters, the media and other interested parties. A loose timeframe and an action plan also keep the campaign on track.

GATHER INFORMATION

This is a vital and time-consuming component of the campaign. First, know who or what your campaign is opposing. Research information and, if need be, involve qualified, authoritative people to evaluate the issue. Information is power; in a campaign where you are often the underdog, the possession of correct information is crucial, especially if public comments or accusations are to be made.

Seek information on the local government's stance on the issue and the opponent. Legislation regulating the proposed activity should be investigated, as should detailed information on the opposition, be it a company or a government department. Often it can be difficult to obtain certain information; find out your rights under the Freedom of Information legislation. It may be necessary to be assertive. Similarly, company, title and lease searches through the Land Titles Office and Australian Securities Commission can turn up invaluable information.

Regarding the opposite flow of information, that is, from you to the police, tell them only as much as you need them to know. Nominate liaison people who will consult back to the group. Such consultation can prevent a rash response to an authority in unexpected or intimidating circumstances. The internal politics of group decision making can also be used as a defence and an opportunity to gain breathing space.

SPREAD THE WORD

The public must be made aware of the issue. Only then will you get additional recruits, increase public support (or at least controversy) and be able to pressure the opponent into answering in public. The media is an obvious channel for spreading the word. It is important to make contact with sympathetic professionals who can ably transmit the issue to the population, as their support can be utilised for more effective campaigning. Background information and position papers can involve the media more deeply in the issue.

Effective media releases are essential. At first the media will treat your information as 'opinion', especially when it is consistently contradicted by vested interests. Releases should aim to be informative. If they are consistently factual they will be taken seriously by discerning journalists.

Make predictions; when these come true it increases the group's credibility and pre-empts the other side's response.

Access to the media varies greatly depending on the locality. A country issue can be fed to local media with ensuing debate reflected and deflected in letters to the editor and talkback programmes. The city media has the opportunity to select from voluminous input and is often more cynical. Election times are horrendous, as media releases from electoral hopefuls pile up in the incoming fax basket. A catchy logo that stands out in black and white can be invaluable. If the interest of the media is tickled, it tends to chase the story. It is disempowering to attempt to persuade a disinterested media representative on a critical issue of survival. 'What frog is that?'

Public meetings can unearth a wealth of unforeseen circumstances and generate information and debate throughout the community. People like to be included. Advertising the public meeting provides an opportunity to access the media and gives an edge to a story in danger of falling flat. Post meeting offers another opportunity to broadcast attendance numbers and advertise community reaction. At meetings it is helpful to pass resolutions which can be forwarded as a concrete result in the media to assist debate or fuel controversy. Exploit all political opportunities, or create them. All relevant politicians (if such beings exist) should be forced to state their position and act on it. After all, today's protest may be next election's issue!

Networking with other environmental groups is useful – another opportunity to spread the word. Advice, ideas and support are generally forthcoming; nothing is worse than labouring away reinventing the wheel. The theme of working for the planet repeats itself endlessly. Information and strategies have been collated over many years, and those who have the information are generally happy to share it. If one has a toxics problem, for instance, critical and technical information is one call away on BIOMAR, one call away on the Internet. These systems are now highly sophisticated and offer support locally, nationally and internationally.

Ultimately, there is nothing quite like the one-to-one approach. Doorknocking and leafleting can be of great assistance in a local campaign. Although it is not altogether a safe pastime (depending upon the place and the issue), it will get the message across like no other method. In traditional society, markets were the meeting places for the trade and exchange of information and ideas. Markets have flowered in recent times and just as of old they provide an efficient conduit for getting a message across. A stall or a wandering freelancer with an information flier in hand can contact large numbers of people with little effort. Another target is public transport – for example, stations where people wait with time to read. In addition to the information, instructions of who to write to, postal addresses and a list of salient points will enhance effectiveness.

A word on petitions: these are usually the first thing a newly formed group undertakes, with keen supporters of a cause making it their full-time occupation to get signatures. Some campaigns which use this method are successful. However, to most, a petition signed is a job done; the signer, with ten seconds' effort, has done his or her bit to save the planet.

Encouraging people to write short letters is more effective for, unlike petitions, letters must be answered. Politicians judge the number of letters they receive on the issue as an indication of community support. It is recorded that in 1982 Premier Neville Wran walked into a Cabinet meeting, ready to face hostility against rainforest conservation. Armed with a huge box of letters, he slammed them onto the table – with devastating effect on his opponents.

Letters should be written to the media, all levels of government and the companies involved. They can request information, reveal the opposition, challenge statements or simply overwhelm by volume.

Government bodies are required to call for public input on development issues. This submission process can appear daunting. Everyone can make a submission on issues important to them, and sometimes anecdotal evidence is telling. If a person or group has the expertise they can write a scientific submission, or one couched in jargon, to great effect. It is important to obtain a submission outline and application form from the body conducting the process. Have something definite to say and state it clearly and simply. Suggested headings include: Summary, Purpose, Background, Conclusions, Recommendations.

THE POWER OF SONG

Ours is a revolution fired by the awesome power of music, art and drama. We use our emotional connection with the plight of the earth as a highly effective tool. The songs we sing can stem violence and move people to risk their lives; they communicate feelings across the world. Songs are the mortar in building a successful movement for social change.

Throughout this book, examples have been given of songs and their effectiveness, the way in which they colour our aural world and convey the political positions of those who sing them.

One special case was 'Tonka Toys', by Frog Smith (last verse added by Gerry Bradley). When we turned loggers back at Nightcap, next to their chainsaws we found a yellow Tonka bulldozer. Frog created a song which lightened the atmosphere and let them know how we felt. A product of the radical action of Nightcap, it travelled with us to the Franklin Blockade.

One day on the river and in front of Hydro Electric Commission executives, we sang that song with gusto. They were so offended that they complained to the Wilderness Society. We received a stern command from downriver: the song was not to be sung at the blockade.

TONKA TOYS

© Michael "Frog" Smith 1982

Chorus 1 : We wanna cut . . .

Verse 3 (same tune as v2) I've got a lunch box, you've got a thermos, and he's got a yellow hat.
After lunch we'll clear-fell the forest, and that'll be the end of that, mate!

Chorus 2 : We're all playin' with our Tonka toys. Just like little Australian boys.
Making lots of loverly noise. Playin' with our Tonka toys.

Chorus tune : We were so tough. We were so proud, but we got stopped by a noisy crowd.
The magistrate said we're not allowed to play with our Tonka toys (Ah, that's not fair!)

Transcribed : Bruce McNicol

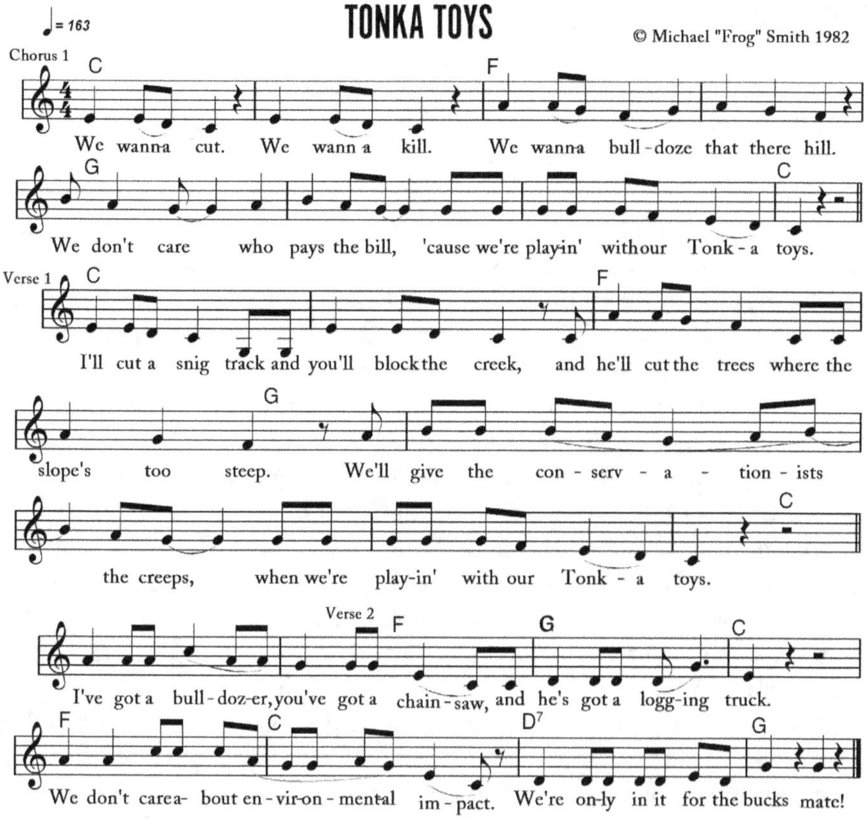

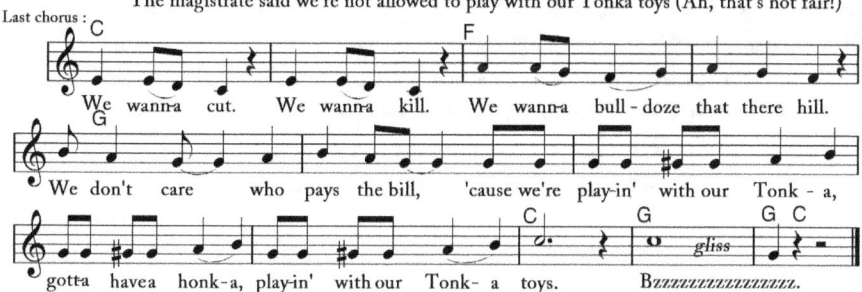

FOLLOW ISSUES THROUGH

Never concede defeat. Don't accept silence by way of a response, or 'fob offs'. Keep track of when letters are sent and follow them up. Stay on the backs of your opponents. Maintain accurate records throughout the campaign. Keep duplicates of letters sent and a book of press clippings.

Make records of phone calls and important conversations. Do not assume that public officials will tell the truth. Refer any complaints about public officials to the Ombudsman's office. Alert progressive parties and independents to any inaccuracies or inconsistencies as an effective way of heightening interest in issues and gaining media attention. Keep an ongoing 'complaint file'. Draw together links between seemingly unconnected events. Keep one eye on detail and the other on the bigger picture.

Events can unfold in weird and wonderful ways, and the impact of actions can sometimes exceed expectations. In the heart of an anti-nuclear warships campaign, my picture was taken as I rode the bow of a ship. This photograph won the National Press Club Award – a fillip for the anti – nuclear movement, we thought, until we discovered that the awards were sponsored by the tobacco giant Rothmans. The spectre of my picture plastered across the country promoting cigarettes loomed larger than the warship itself (at least in my mind). Two seemingly unrelated passions in my protesting life were drawn together. With my case ably represented by the barrister Mr Clive Evatt, Rothmans was taken to court and we won an out-of-court settlement. The ensuing media coverage extended to the anti – tobacco and anti-nuclear causes. The story did not end there. The disclaimer which it had been agreed would be printed under the photo in question was so minute as to be of interest only to students of the microscopic hieroglyph. This prompted a visit to the Royal Easter Show. While this venue catered primarily for children, it also contained the highest concentration of tobacco advertising in the southern hemisphere. I couldn't help myself; at the Rothmans exhibition I tore my picture off the wall. A policeman grabbed me.

"You can't do that," he said. "It's not your picture."

"It is!" I replied. This dialogue continued like a broken record until I tore up the picture. Rothmans executives were contacted but declined to press charges. I retired with the pieces in my pocket.

PUBLIC INTEREST VERSUS VESTED INTEREST

Public action groups represent the public interest, as opposed to vested interest groups which represent industry and those with direct financial interests. It is important to remind people that you stand to gain nothing financially from pursuing your campaign. Don't allow your group and opponents to be lumped together as pressure groups.

Most publicity generated by an action group is good publicity.

Opponents will already be benefiting from the status quo. It is simply a case of exposing their dealings to public scrutiny.

WRAP-UP

A wrap-up session is important to conclude a campaign. Files of press clippings and photos must be gathered together and stored. Loose ends must be tied up, particularly outstanding bills. Support sources are often forgotten after the event, particularly printers who work long hours for campaign deadlines. Everyone needs to be congratulated, regardless of the outcome, and a party finale is mandatory.

It must be remembered, if all else fails, that direct action can be a fun-filled and worthwhile experience.

GROUND RULES IN THE FIELD

So, out of the office and onto the front line. The name of the game is effectiveness. But what to take? What to wear? Fantasies vary from guerrilla warfare attire to high forest fashion. The assorted interpretations of the necessities of life are fascinating indeed.

The amount of gear that can be carried into an action is a function of its location, one's finances and mode of transport. Camps that are destined to last for an extended period of time will exist around the communal kitchen. Some people will be prepared food-wise, but often the needs of the longest stayers, those integral to the success of the action, will have to be carried by the camp as a whole. At Errinundra, the most valued implement was a gigantic cooking pot. It achieved mystical proportions in its ability to feed the multitudes and became the centre of controversy during heated debates between herbivores and carnivores. A well-run kitchen gives the camp a heart where meetings can occur and where people (with full bellies) can work out strategies by the warm glow of ovens and kitchen fires. The most essential and demanding job is keeping the kitchen functioning.

On a personal level there is often a need to create a base for oneself, which means a tent or fly as home space, and a second fly (which must be green) for outings into hostile territory. The majority of people who came and stayed in the forest for the long term in campaigns like the Franklin and Chaelundi had only rudimentary equipment and as a consequence were grounded at the campfire. The need for functional gear is important, and a number of basic items can be got at little expense. Much of what may be said here does not apply to those with sufficient finances to kit themselves out with top-class gear.

Garbage bags are the first essential. In Tasmania, the garbage bag proved itself useful in protecting that sacred sleeping bag (one's castle in wet and cold conditions) from saturation on route or even at 'home'. It was not unusual to return from an expedition and crawl into bed to find the highest section of the tent surrounded by a moat of water. The rain on such nights would be so heavy that only the best quality tent remained leak-free. This was where the humble garbage bag again came in handy. After emptying the sleeping bag out of its garbage bag (highly likely to be the only dry possession), one looked for the highest, hopefully driest, section of the tent. The next step is to enter the warmth and dryness, with feet pointing towards the wet end of the tent, then slide the feet end into that life-saving garbage bag for a night of heavenly dryness, or at least a sporting attempt at it.

Footwear ranges at all campaigns from barefoot to high-tech boots, with all manner of preferences in between. Northern New South Wales feral folk at the Franklin campaign were regarded as insane to be walking in the

Tasmanian Wilderness barefoot. One woman, Annie, had never done it any other way. With callused feet she could outwalk all but a few athletes in the Wilderness. While Wilderness Society operatives bemoaned our unpresentable appearance, Annie (barefooted) and I trekked the entire upriver area dealing with all terrain while we mapped it for future action.

Malaysian jungle boots were my preference. Lightweight for running, they had added ankle support and were cheap. However, they took water immediately and feet froze if you stopped moving around, hence the hyperactivity of anyone in such footwear. Back at camp, gumboots were Wilderness lounge slippers.

To state the obvious, one needs a compass in conditions such as those which existed in the Tasmanian south-west. Annie and I, imbued with an ongoing disrespect for organisational details, arrived at the upriver camp and excitedly trotted off up the hill 'to see the Wilderness'. We wandered in the spectacular new environment and arrived at a magnificent grove of moss-covered trees. We were so taken by the spot that we named it the Enchanted Forest.

We scurried through the bush to get back before dark. I scaled a giant paperbark tree to look out over an expanse of Wilderness as far as the eye could see, with no hint of human activity. We were utterly lost. Subject to a Wilderness experience on our first afternoon, we decided downhill was the only way, hoping the gullies would eventually lead us back to the Gordon River and base camp. We set off in the late afternoon, only to find ourselves an hour later back in the same 'Enchanted Forest'.

We took a moment to absorb the gravity of the situation (our first night out) in terms of our credibility as seasoned eco-warriors. Our mission had been to reconnoiter the terrain. Instead, we had gained first-hand experience at being abysmally lost. We struck out down the creek bed.

Another hour and the light of day began to fade. Resting on a rocky outcrop high above the creek, we decided not to continue in the dark.

Then moonlight extended its silvery hand down one side of the valley as a full moon rose into view. In light brighter than dusk we pushed on, traversing the steep terrain until the moon set over the other side of the narrow valley. As the light again faded we gathered bracken fern to make a bush bed where we slept till morning. When we awoke we struggled to our feet and tried to shake off the depressing feeling that we were no closer to safety.

Just as we started moving a coo-ee sounded. We replied and dashed around the corner to find ourselves at the point where the creek joined the Gordon River only one hundred metres from our base camp. From that point onwards I religiously carried my compass with me.

One grey day I took a group of highly experienced bushwalking friends into prohibited territory. Deep in the forest I asked them the direction to base camp. Each of my four companions pointed in a different direction. Which brings me to another concern: beware of the person, usually male, who professes that he never gets lost.

My claim to fame was that I was the guide who always got lost. A case in point was an expedition with a group including Pat Rose, a grandmother from the Sydney Wilderness Society. I was to lead them far into prohibited territory and find a place for them to sleep the night in striking distance of the helicopter landing pads which they intended to occupy the following morning. We cut across country in search of an old piner's track (a smooth groove in the forest, a relic of the days when the giant Huon pines were hauled out by horses or bullocks). As darkness closed in there was no sign of the track which was vital to the success of our mission.

I was forced to declare my geographical embarrassment. "It appears that you are going to have a magnificent Wilderness experience," I said. "Feel the forest dominating. There's no certainty we'll be able to get to our destination or even find our way back to base for that matter." They stared at me; I didn't dare ask what they were thinking. I took a bearing on the expected direction of the track, put my compass in my mouth and headed off thrashing at the bush to' make progress. While trying to give an impression of competence, I felt somewhat insecure in my leadership role. Finally I climbed over a huge old log and crashed down an embankment to discover the much-sought-after track. "Compasses," I thought. "Where would we be without them?"

Of no less significance than a compass is a torch. It's hard to imagine anyone going to a forest camp without one. This invaluable little (the smaller the better) article may seem like an obvious inclusion for anyone embarking on a greenie adventure, yet invariably people turn up torchless.

Is it my extremist personality which demands a penlight? Try holding a dolphin torch in your mouth while struggling on your own on a foul, wet night mounting a fly over a fallen log somewhere in forbidden territory. Discarded AA batteries from a portable radio can keep you in light a month into the campaign when orders to town invariably don't turn up for several days (due to distance, floods or police blockades; or sometimes due to the fact that couriers are having a binge in the nearest port of comfort and warmth, unable to face a return to the cold and wet Wilderness and consuming the camp's supply of chocolate while fretting for their long-suffering comrades). A waterproof penlight is recommended.

Best of all is a caving torch which, attached to a headband, allows both hands to be free.

Sitting and suffering in the Wilderness in the pouring rain, one would wonder why but a water container is essential. So are matches, either the ones that go soggy or the green waterproof ones that are impossible to light before they too go soggy. Try a lighter. Camouflage clothing, a hat and knife completes the serious basic survival kit. Finally, where would greenies be without dental floss? I kid you not; this is an essential in long campaigns. When the police closed the blockade camp on the Franklin River and people rushed the awaiting boat to escape, I stood on the dock asking all who passed for dental floss (my toothbrush was in a bad way too, I might add). The things that become important in one's life as civilisation recedes!

In defence of my penchant for floss, I must say I have a smile worth maintaining. There are, however, other less obvious reasons. Dental floss is a thread second to none for making repairs on shoes, packs and tent flies.

Made from non-perishing nylon and being extremely strong, it is excellent for binding, and if one purchases with ultimate precision, green, mint – flavoured floss is the prime choice for camouflage of both breath and repairs.

Success of any aspect of being involved in an action lies in acknowledging the importance of differing roles and skills. Goals beyond our individual dreams can be achieved with cooperation, respect for the diversity of the job at hand and unity of vision. Another outcome of involvement and commitment to a cause is the association and bonding with like-minded individuals. If done with a sense of celebration, anything is possible. To quote the famous activist Emma Goldman, "I don't want your revolution if I can't dance."

www.ingramcontent.com/pod-product-compliance
Lightning Source LLC
Chambersburg PA
CBHW051938290426
44110CB00015B/2026